Latin American Business: Equity Distortion in Regional Resource Allocation in Brazil

Latin American Business: Equity Distortion in Regional Resource Allocation in Brazil has been co-published simultaneously as *Latin American Business Review*, Volume 7, Numbers 3/4 2006.

Monographic Separates from *Latin American Business Review*™

For additional information on these and other Haworth Press titles, including descriptions, tables of contents, reviews, and prices, use the QuickSearch catalog at http://www.HaworthPress.com.

Latin American Business: Equity Distortion in Regional Resource Allocation in Brazil, edited by Werner Baer and Geoffrey Hewings (Vol. 7, No. 3/4, 2006). *An insightful collection of case studies and essays that examines Brazil's use of fiscal incentives to attract investors to help remedy disparities in the country's regional distribution of income.*

Foreign Direct Investment in Latin America: Its Changing Nature at the Turn of the Century, edited by Werner Baer and William R. Miles (Vol. 2, No. 1/2, 2001). *Examines the changing nature of foreign investments in Latin America; analyzes the role of international capital in Latin American environmental issues.*

Latin American Business: Equity Distortion in Regional Resource Allocation in Brazil

Werner Baer
Geoffrey Hewings
Editors

Latin American Business: Equity Distortion in Regional Resource Allocation in Brazil has been co-published simultaneously as *Latin American Business Review*, Volume 7, Numbers 3/4 2006.

Routledge
Taylor & Francis Group

LONDON AND NEW YORK

Latin American Business: Equity Distortion in Regional Resource Allocation in Brazil has been co-published simultaneously as *Latin American Business Review*™, Volume 7, Numbers 3/4 2006.

First published 2006 by The Haworth Press, Inc.

2 Park Square, Milton Park, Abingdon, Oxfordshire OX14 4RN
605 Third Avenue, New York, NY 10017

Routledge is an imprint of the Taylor & Francis Group, an informa business

First issued in hardback 2020

Library of Congress Cataloging-in-Publication Data

Latin American business : equity distortion in regional resource allocation in Brazil / Werner Baer, Geoffrey Hewings, editor[s].
     p. cm. – (Monographic separates from Latin American business review)
     "Co-published simultaneously as Latin American business review, volume 7, numbers 3/4 2006."
     Includes bibliographical references and index.
     ISBN-13: 978-0-7890-3535-6 (hard cover : alk. paper)
     ISBN-10: 0-7890-3535-9 (hard cover : alk. paper)
     ISBN-13: 978-0-7890-3536-3 (soft cover : alk. paper)
     ISBN-10: 0-7890-3536-7 (soft cover : alk. paper)
     1. Industrial promotion–Brazil–States. 2. Brazil–Economic conditions–1985—Regional disparities. 3. Tax incentives-Brazil-States. 4. Automobile industry and trade-Brazil. 5. Resource allocation–Brazil–Regional disparities. I. Baer, Werner, 931- II. Hewings, Geoffrey. III. Latin American business review (Binghamton, N.Y.)
HC190.I53L38 2007
338.4'76292220981–dc22

2006029705

ISBN 978-0-7890-3535-6 (hbk)

This section provides you with a list of major indexing & abstracting services and other tools for bibliographic access. That is to say, each service began covering this periodical during the the year noted in the right column. Most Websites which are listed below have indicated that they will either post, disseminate, compile, archive, cite or alert their own Website users with research-based content from this work. (This list is as current as the copyright date of this publication.)

Abstracting, Website/Indexing Coverage . . . . Year When Coverage Began

- *(IBR) International Bibliography of Book Reviews on the Humanities and Social Sciences (Thomson)* <http://www.saur.de> 2006

- *(IBZ) International Bibliography of Periodical Literature on the Humanities and Social Sciences (Thomson)* <http://www.saur.de> 1998

- **Academic Search Premier (EBSCO)*** <http://www.epnet.com/academic/acasearchprem.asp> 2006

- **Business Source Complete (EBSCO)*** 2006

- **Business Source Premier (EBSCO)*** <http://www.epnet.com/academic/bussourceprem.asp> 2006

- **International Bibliography of the Social Sciences (IBSS)*** <http://www.ibss.ac.uk> 1999

- **MasterFILE Premier (EBSCO)*** <http://www.epnet.com/government/mfpremier.asp> 2006

- *Cabell's Directory of Publishing Opportunities in Management > (Bibliographic Access)* <http://www.cabells.com> 2006

- *EBSCOhost Electronic Journals Service (EJS)* <http:/ejournals.ebsco.com> 2001

(continued)

(continued)

Bibliographic Access

- *MediaFinder <http://www.mediafinder.com/>*

- *Ulrich's Periodicals Directory: International Periodicals Information Since 1932 > <http://www.Bowkerlink.com>*

Special Bibliographic Notes related to special journal issues (separates) and indexing/abstracting:

- indexing/abstracting services in this list will also cover material in any "separate" that is co-published simultaneously with Haworth's special thematic journal issue or DocuSerial. Indexing/abstracting usually covers material at the article/chapter level.
- monographic co-editions are intended for either non-subscribers or libraries which intend to purchase a second copy for their circulating collections.
- monographic co-editions are reported to all jobbers/wholesalers/approval plans. The source journal is listed as the "series" to assist the prevention of duplicate purchasing in the same manner utilized for books-in-series.
- to facilitate user/access services all indexing/abstracting services are encouraged to utilize the co-indexing entry note indicated at the bottom of the first page of each article/chapter/contribution.
- this is intended to assist a library user of any reference tool (whether print, electronic, online, or CD-ROM) to locate the monographic version if the library has purchased this version but not a subscription to the source journal.
- individual articles/chapters in any Haworth publication are also available through The Haworth Document Delivery Service (HDDS).

As part of Haworth's continuing committment to better serve our library patrons, we are proud to be working with the following electronic services:

AGGREGATOR SERVICES

EBSCOhost

Ingenta

J-Gate

Minerva

OCLC FirstSearch

Oxmill

SwetsWise

FirstSearch

Oxmill Publishing

SwetsWise

LINK RESOLVER SERVICES

1Cate (Openly Informatics)

CrossRef

Gold Rush (Coalliance)

LinkOut (PubMed)

LINKplus (Atypon)

LinkSolver (Ovid)

LinkSource with A-to-Z (EBSCO)

Resource Linker (Ulrich)

SerialsSolutions (ProQuest)

SFX (Ex Libris)

Sirsi Resolver (SirsiDynix)

Tour (TDnet)

Vlink (Extensity, *formerly Geac*)

WebBridge (Innovative Interfaces)

LinkOut.
LINKING TO A WORLD OF RESOURCES

Gold Rush

atypon

O·V·I·D LinkSolver

ULRICH'S
RESOURCE LINKER

S·F·X

SerialsSolutions

TOUR

((extensity))

WebBridge

Acknowledgment

We wish to thank the Hewlett Foundation, whose generous grant to the University of Illinois to promote collaborative research between scholars from Brazil and from the University of Illinois made it possible to produce the essays contained in this collection. We also wish to thank Leonard Abbey and Timothy Mulrooney for their help in preparing this collection for publication.

Latin American Business: Equity Distortion in Regional Resource Allocation in Brazil

CONTENTS

ABOUT THE EDITORS

Werner Baer is Professor of Economics, University of Illinois. He received his PhD at Harvard University. He has written and edited many books on Latin America, and is currently working on the 6th edition of his book *The Brazilian Economy: Growth and Development*. He has also taught at Harvard, Yale, and Vanderbilt Universities, and was guest professor at the Fundação Getulio Vargas, University of São Paulo, and the Catholic University in Rio de Janeiro.

Geoffrey Hewings is Director of the Regional Economics Applications Laboratory and Professor of Geography & Regional Science, of Economics and of Urban and Regional Planning at the University of Illinois in Urbana-Champaign. He received his PhD from the University of Washington. He recently co-edited (with Patricio Aroca) *Structure and Structural Change in Chile* (Palgrave-Macmillan, 2006) and (with Joaquim J. M. Guilhoto) *Structure and Structural Change in Brazil* (Ashgate, 2001).

Contributors

Edmund Amann–University of Manchester (UK)

Werner Baer–University of Illinois

Suzana Quinet de A. Bastos–Federal University of Juiz de Fora, Minas Gerais

Luiz Ricardo Cavalcante–Federal University of Bahia

Kerlyng Cecchini–Technology Institute of Paraná (Teepar)

Chokri Dridi–University of Alberta, Canada, and University of Illinois (REAL)

Joaquim Guilhoto–University of São Paulo

Eduardo Haddad–University of São Paulo

Geoffrey Hewings–University of Illinois

Marcos Costa Holanda–Federal University of Ceará and General Director of Economic Institute of Ceará (IPECE)

Ricardo Luis Lopes–State University of Maringá, Paraná

André Matos Magalhães–Federal University of Pernambuco

Fernando Perobelli–Federal University of Juiz de Fora

Francis Carlo Petterini–Economic Research Institute of Ceará (IPECE)

Edgard Pimentel–University of São Paulo and University of Illinois

Alexandre Porsse–Economics and Statistics Foundation of Rio Grande do Sul

Eduardo Pontual Ribeiro–Federal University of Rio Grande do Sul and Fluminense Federal University

Liedje Siqueira–Federal University of Paraiba

Simone Uderman–State University of Bahia

Introduction

Werner Baer
Geoffrey Hewings

Can market forces be counted on to diminish remedy disparities in the regional distribution of income within one country? This question has been debated for generations both in advanced industrial countries and in developing countries. Those who believe that market forces will gradually eliminate regional differences in income argue that poor regions, where capital is scarce and labor is abundant, will benefit from an inflow of investments due to the high returns on capital (because of its scarcity) and the low cost of labor (because of its abundance). In reality, this has rarely happened. Thus, before introducing these Brazilian case studies of countering market forces in order to attain greater regional equity, let us briefly examine the experience of the United States, which should place them in a broader context.

THE IMPACT OF REGIONAL POLICIES
IN THE UNITED STATES

For seventy years after the conclusion of the Civil War in 1865, the American South was a backward region. This period was one of the

Werner Baer is Lemann Professor of Economics, University of Illinois. Received his PhD at Harvard University.

Geoffrey Hewings is Director of the Regional Economics Applications Laboratory and Professor of Geography & Regional Science, of Economics and of Urban and Regional Planning at the University of Illinois in Urbana-Champaign. Received his Ph.D. from the University of Washington.

[Haworth co-indexing entry note]: "Introduction." Baer, Werner, and Geoffrey Hewings. Co-published simultaneously in *Latin American Business Review* (International Business Press, an imprint of The Haworth Press, Inc.) Vol. 7, No. 3/4, 2006, pp. 1-9; and: *Latin American Business: Equity Distortion in Regional Resource Allocation in Brazil* (ed: Werner Baer, and Geoffrey Hewings) International Business Press, an imprint of The Haworth Press, Inc., 2006, pp. 1-9. Single or multiple copies of this article are available for a fee from The Haworth Document Delivery Service [1-800-HAWORTH, 9:00 a.m. - 5:00 p.m. (EST). E-mail address: docdelivery@haworthpress.com].

Available online at http://labr.haworthpress.com
doi:10.1300/J140v07n03_01

most freewheeling eras of *laissez-faire* the world has ever seen. The northern part of the United States moved rapidly during this period from an agricultural economy to one based on the manufacturing industry. While the North was first to industrialize, the South was rich in natural resources and had–in no small part thanks to emancipation after the war–a large pool of cheap labor. Southern officials in fact promoted the region to low-wage, labor intensive industries in the 1880s. While some firms, such as those involved in textiles, did come south, large scale industrial development did not materialize (Cobb, 1982).

This constitutes a quandary for neoclassical theory. First, neoclassical growth models, which take technological change and other factors such as savings rates as exogenous, predict convergence in growth rates and income levels for such given exogenous factors. While there might be variables that present convergence for very different countries, it is hard to understand, within the neoclassical context, the failure for areas "within" a given country, with freely functioning markets, to converge. Also, standard wage models predict that labor will migrate from low wage areas to those where worker remuneration is higher. The movement out of a low wage area will lower labor supply, increasing wages there. Analogously, migration into a high wage area will increase labor supply, and thus lower wages there. This migration will continue, in such a model, until wages in the two regions are equal. Why, then, were there such persistent differentials in wages and incomes within the U.S. over more than seventy years?

Several explanations have been offered: the hot climate of the South, which was only remedied with air-conditioning after the 1940s; high transportation costs, which existed before the Second World War, and which inhibited industrial location in the South; ties of family, culture and information, which inhibited labor from seeking higher wages. Wright (1986) argues that since the North industrialized first, the South lacked a first mover advantage in manufacturing. This was decisive since in many of the higher wage manufacturing sectors there were significant economies of scale and learning by causing effects that would favor the first to capture an industry. In addition, the lack of manufacturing fed on itself as the absence of industry meant that no indigenous community of engineers or technicians developed.

As a result of these hindrances to development, the South found itself the most vulnerable region when the Depression hit. All of the pathologies of underdevelopment would no longer be hidden as they festered and brought national attention to the region. The New Deal, rather than labor or capital flows automatically taking place through the market mechanism, would break the region out of its segmented economic cocoon.

While there was a strong tradition of relying on market forces, and many state constitutions forbade local governments from enticing new plants with subsidies, many officials in the Great Depression of the 1930s actively sought to market their states to business. This marketing had two components, the first being the provision of subsidies by state and local governments, and the second the promotion of a business-friendly labor force, which in practice came to mean low wages and little union power.[1]

The Tennessee Valley Authority (TVA) represented a massive transfer of resources from the federal government to the southern region. It was created to promote cheap electricity and to create more navigable waterways. However, five years after its beginning it had produced only modest change (Schulman, 1991).

After World War II, many southern senators and representatives had gained substantial political power in the U.S. Congress through the acquisition of seniority. They used this power to direct an increasing proportion of federal expenditures–especially defense expenditures–to the southern states. Thus, by 1975 the South had received $11.5 billion more in funds than it had paid back in taxes to the federal government, while the Midwest and mid-Atlantic states had received $30.8 billion less than they had paid (Cobb, 1982). While transfer payments accounted for some of this difference, a major factor was defense spending. The South accounted for only 7 percent of total defense expenditures in 1950, but this figure rose to 15 percent by 1960 and nearly 25 percent by 1970 (Schulman, 1991).

Powerful politicians such as Lyndon Johnson and Albert Thomas were instrumental in getting the National Aeronautics and Space Administration to locate its headquarters in Houston, although there was no logistical rationale for this.[2]

Some select areas of the South managed to develop and attract research parks and high technology employment. The first successful example was the Research Triangle Park in North Carolina, which was the result of deliberate government action to attract employment that paid higher wages. This strategy was imitated by other states such as Georgia and Virginia. However, while this phenomenon had positive implications for select areas, southern employment was still skewed toward low wages and low tech activities.

In the latter years of the 20th century, the quest for greater regional equity shifted towards the competition among states to induce foreign investments.

FISCAL COMPETITION AMONG STATES IN THE U.S.

During the last two decades of the 20th century, regional development was influenced by the decision of foreign car producers to locate their assembly plants in the U.S. Most producers were from Japan, but gradually German and Korean firms also decided to locate production facilities in the U.S. The reasons for their moves were varied: among them were the appreciation of their currency vis-à-vis the U.S. dollar and the frequent protectionist rumblings in the U.S. This resulted in fierce competition among various states to attract these firms by offering various types of attractions to both the assemblers and to component producers. Although U.S. southern states were eager competitors, many states in other regions stepped into the ring. Let us briefly examine the actions of Alabama and Illinois in attracting Mercedes and Mitsubishi, respectively.

Alabama. To induce Mercedes to establish its plant in Tuscaloosa County, the following benefits were offered: county officials agreed to buy the plant site and turn it over to Mercedes for $100; the state offered a package of tax concessions that allowed Mercedes to pay for construction of its plant with money that it would have spent on state income taxes; it also agreed to build a $35 million training center at the company's plant and pledged to pay employee's salaries while they were in training at a cost of $45 million; finally, the state gave Mercedes a 20-year exemption from state income taxes, and when the company decided to double the size of its Vance plant, it received another $115 million in incentives. The incentive package also involved the following: $77.5 million to improve water, sewer, gas and electrical services; $92.2 million to improve and develop the factory site, and $60 million to train Mercedes employees, suppliers and workers in related industries.

Among the many criticisms of the Mercedes project, the following stand out: (1) some question whether the state gave Mercedes more money than it was likely to recoup in benefits, and the 20-year tax exemption sacrificed revenues that could have helped upgrade schools and other social programs; (2) at least some of the jobs brought in since Mercedes arrived would probably have come to the state anyway; (3) The money the state spent on Mercedes and a handful of other auto companies might have been better spent on attracting companies in a variety of industries; (4) a report from the Midwest Center for Labor Research concluded that even under the best of circumstances, Alabama's state and local governments would not be able to recoup up-front expenses for a minimum of 7 years.[3]

Those who defend Alabama's incentive program argue that: (1) the incentives helped the state to reduce its traditional reliance on the shrinking textile and apparel industries; (2) Mercedes promised to create 1,500 jobs, but actually expanded that number to 4,000; (3) Mercedes assembly workers are paid about $25 an hour and thus earn more than twice the state's average hourly wage, and they receive a full range of health and retirement benefits; (4) eight of its suppliers have established themselves in the state to meet the company's requirements of just-in-time delivery, creating 1,600 jobs; (5) an Auburn University study found that the Mercedes plant and its suppliers created nearly 10,000 jobs in the state, paying a total of $354 million a year and Mercedes spends more than $1 billion a year on parts, supplies and services from Alabama companies; (6) Mercedes spends $1 million a year in sales taxes and local property taxes used for education; (7) Mercedes employees and companies that do business with Mercedes generate another $14 million a year in state income and sales taxes as a result of the company's presence.[4]

Illinois. The attraction of the Mitsubishi plant[5] to Illinois also garnered significant opposition. Chapman et al. estimate that the total incentive package was worth $274 million. Illinois competed against four other states. The issue of the opportunity cost of these incentives was raised within the state itself, however. Many opponents felt that the funds would have been better directed to upgrading infrastructure, schools or even assisting existing firms to expand production or to re-tool to enhance their competitiveness. The general location itself was controversial, as Bloomington-Normal is located on the western-most edge of the automobile core in the Midwest. Analysts pointed to this as a problem in the sense that it would be unlikely that many suppliers would relocate close to the plant. After significant downturns in the automobile industry, many suppliers diversified away from dependence on one major company, and thus locating near the Mitsubishi plant afforded few competitive advantages.

Bloomington-Normal is home to several major insurance companies, and the loss of over 2,500 manufacturing jobs in the 1970s and 1980s made the attraction of the Mitsubishi plant an important development goal for two reasons. First, it would help diversify the economy, and second, the jobs at the plant would be highly paid and thus provide significant additions to income in the region's economy. Furthermore, unemployment rates in the surrounding counties had been elevated with the erosion of manufacturing jobs, especially in nearby Peoria.

The incentive package for the firm included a commitment by the state to upgrade the physical infrastructure, adding ramps to a freeway and providing assistance to the local community to expand the sewer system. However, a significant portion of the commitment involved funds for education and worker training. The state also created legislation that provided fiscal incentives for any firm creating over 2,000 jobs and locating in an enterprise zone. These incentives included investment tax credits that could be carried over for five years. In sum, the total incentive package included $84 million for direct job training grants and infrastructure, and almost $190 million in federal, state, and local tax abatements. Miyauchi (1987) noted that Illinois' package would have placed it second behind the one offered by Kentucky to lure Toyota ($125 million) and ahead of Mazda's support from Michigan ($52 million).

THE BRAZILIAN CASE OF FISCAL COMPETITION

This volume examines various aspects of Brazil's experience with the use of fiscal incentives to attract outside investors. Brazil's economy has long been characterized by a substantial regional concentration of its GDP in the Center-South of the country, especially in the state of São Paulo.[6] Since the late 1950s, various attempts have been made by the federal government to redistribute income to the less fortunate regions of the country, especially the Northeast, through specially targeted federal expenditures, special credits and federal tax exemption schemes. Unfortunately, these efforts have not resulted in any substantial redistribution of income and investment.[7]

Since the 1990s, there has been a change in the attempts to redistribute income and investment regionally as individual Brazilian states have tried to take the initiative. Through tax and other incentive schemes, the poorer states of the Northeast and the more prosperous states like Minas Gerais, Paraná, and Rio Grande do Sul have tried to lure both domestic and foreign firms to locate within their borders. A number of these states have targeted the automobile sector, as both already-established multinationals and newcomers had plans to build new plants. Others have simply attempted to attract firms in a number of sectors such as textiles and shoe production to transfer their activities from their previous location. As a result of these trends, there has been a substantial controversy as to whether these fiscal wars have been legitimate attempts at regional economic development or whether they have resulted in a distortion in the allocation of resources. These collected essays should help to throw some light on this question.

Since a large part of the fiscal wars in Brazil have dealt with the attraction of automobile plants, it was only appropriate to include five studies of that sector–three case studies and two studies of the structural regional changes in that industry.

Cavalcante and Uderman analyze the benefits and costs to the state of Bahia in attracting a Ford plant. They find that the total incentive package given to Ford amounted to 75% of the investment, and the largest part of the incentives was due to tax breaks. Although many jobs were created by the assembler and suppliers, they conclude that the main benefits that the Ford project generated were the structural changes in Bahia's economy as a result of backward and forward linkages.

Perobelli et al. concentrate on the Mercedes-Benz project in Juiz de Fora, Minas Gerais. Through an input-output analysis they measure the impact of the project on other productive sectors in the Juiz de Fora area, in the state of Minas Gerais and in the rest of Brazil. They find that in the construction phase there was only a small impact on the local economy and on the state, while the net impact of production was evenly divided between the Juiz de Fora area and the rest of Brazil, with relatively little impact on the rest of the state.

Ricardo Luis Lopes analyzes the case of Renault in Paraná. It was one of three assembly plants which the state was able to attract. He presents this case study within the context of Paraná's economic history, and then describes the process of the plant's installation and its attraction of supplying firms. Once established, the plant functioned substantially below capacity due to a stagnant domestic market. Lopes notes that since Renault only has one plant in the country, it does not have the flexibility of switching to new products, which is the case of competitors with more than one plant.

Amann et al. analyze the Brazilian automobile industry within the context of the trade liberalization process of the 1990s, which resulted in the growth of regional production facilities. After describing this regional dispersion process, they analyze its impact through the use of an interregional input-output model. They find that despite the dispersion of the plants, a large percentage of the value added and employment generated went to the state of São Paulo. However, the degree of the latter varied. The share of São Paulo was much smaller for the southern states than for other states which attracted assembly plants.

The analysis of Cecchini et al. complements the previous paper. It uses input-output models to identify economic clusters. One of the main goals of attracting automobile plants is the hope that they will generate significant backward linkages on the region's economy through the purchases of supplies. Adopting a cluster analytical approach facilitates the identification of such clusters and the degree to which they "move" geographically within the creation of new assembly plants. The main results of the clusters analysis stress the importance of automotive economic activities located in São Paulo and in the South, but also the diversification of the productive process in the Brazilian economy, which has seen it become somewhat less dependent on the automotive sector for growth.

The articles dealing with the states of Pernambuco and Ceará do not deal with the auto industry since they did not attract plants. However, they did have fiscal incentive programs to promote outside investment in their states. Magalhães and Siqueira give an evaluation of the state of Pernambuco's fiscal incentives program. They find that for a long time the state's officials were reluctant to use fiscal incentives because of the feared tax loss that this would imply. However, by the 1990s the state began to be more active in seeking investments and developed various fiscal incentive programs. Projects were promoted in many different sectors, such as beverages, textiles, food products, non-metallic minerals, plastics, etc., and most consisted of either new plants or plant expansion. The authors consider the program successful, when considering that the state did not incur losses of the ICMS tax and did not provide funds to companies. But this frugal nature of the state with respect to new firms locating within it will make it difficult to attract large projects.

Holanda and Petterini examine the tax incentive policies of the state of Ceará. They find that the incentive program of the state helped to increase capital formation, and that incentives can average up to 80% of the tax due. They emphasize that the incentive program occurred because of the lack of adequate policies of the central government for the development of poorer regions.

In the final essay, Porsse et al. use a general equilibrium approach to evaluate the impact of a regional tax incentive program to attract investments. Their analysis concentrates on the state of Rio Grande do Sul. They find that the effects on employment and household welfare of consumers were positive. They also find that the absence of a large capital goods sector in the state caused sharp increases in production factor prices. Also, at the aggregate level, the benefits of the incentive policy tended to favor investors and consumers, while the costs were absorbed by export agents. Finally, they find that the incentive program had a positive effect on indirect tax revenues due to the increase in the tax base.

On a whole, these essays contribute a vast amount of hard facts in the continuing debate over the impact of fiscal wars in Brazil.

NOTES

1. The first state to launch a major official effort in the direction of attracting industry during the Depression was Mississippi with its "Balance Agriculture with Industry" Act (BAWI) in 1936. This provided for issuing bonds, to be serviced at government expense, in order to build plants which would be provided free to industry (Cobb, 1982).

2. All this space and defense activity had spillover effects on the local economies beyond the immediate job benefits of the installation itself. The activity required technically trained professionals, so local universities were given large grants to conduct the necessary research and development. Private technology companies would often open up branches near space and military installations to do contract work and this, of course, brought further externalities.

3. http://faculty.maxwell.syr.edu/jyinger/Classes/PPA735/Cases/Taxincen.htm

4. http://www.polsci.wvu.edu/ipa/PS220/Brooks.html

5. The plant began as a joint venture between Mitsubishi and Chrysler in 1988 and became solely owned by Mitsubishi in 1991.

6. For details, see Baer (2001), ch. 14.

7. Ibid.

REFERENCES

Baer, W. (2001). "The Brazilian Economy: Growth and Development." 5th edition. Westport: Praeger.

Chapman, M., Elhance, A. P., and Wenum, J. D. (1995). "Mitsubishi Motors in Illinois." Westport, CT: Quorum Books.

Cobb, J. C. (1982). "The Selling of the South." Baton Rouge: Louisiana State University Press.

Miyauchi, T. (1987). "The Man Who Lured Toyota to Kentucky." *Economic Eye*, March pp. 23-26.

Schulman, B. J. (1991). "From Cotton Belt to Sunbelt: Federal Policy, Economic Development, and the Transformation of the South, 1938-1980." New York: Oxford University Press.

Wright, G. (1986). "Old South, New South: Revolutions in the Southern Economy since the Civil War." New York: Basic Books.

doi:10.1300/J140v07n03_01

The Cost of a Structural Change:
A Large Automobile Plant
in the State of Bahia

Luiz Ricardo Cavalcante
Simone Uderman

SUMMARY. The aim of this paper is to evaluate the costs and benefits associated with establishing a large automobile plant in the Brazilian state of Bahia, in one of the poorest macro-regions of the country. It is argued that behind Ford's decision to establish a plant far from the economic center of the country are not only the large incentives package offered at the Federal and State levels, but also the 1999 Southern Com-

---

Luiz Ricardo Cavalcante is affiliated with the Federal University of Bahia, Brazil. Simone Uderman is affiliated with the University of the State of Bahia, Brazil.

The authors would like to express their acknowledgments to The National Council for Scientific and Technological Development (CNPq), the Development Agency of the State of Bahia (Desenbahia), the Planning Secretariat of the State of Bahia (Seplan), the University of the State of Bahia (Uneb), and the State of Bahia Research Foundation (Fapesb) for providing support for this research, and to the University of Illinois at Urbana Champaign (UIUC)/Regional Economics Applications Laboratory (REAL) for its hospitality. The authors are especially grateful to Prof. Werner Baer and Prof. Geoffrey Hewings for their assistance, comments and suggestions. Glauter Rocha, Rogério Princhak, Prof. Francisco Teixeira and Prof. André Magalhães also made helpful comments and suggestions. Of course, the authors are entirely responsible for any remaining errors.

[Haworth co-indexing entry note]: "The Cost of a Structural Change: A Large Automobile Plant in the State of Bahia." Cavalcante, Luiz Ricardo, and Simone Uderman. Co-published simultaneously in *Latin American Business Review* (International Business Press, an imprint of The Haworth Press, Inc.) Vol. 7, No. 3/4, 2006, pp. 11-48; and: *Latin American Business: Equity Distortion in Regional Resource Allocation in Brazil* (ed: Werner Baer, and Geoffrey Hewings) International Business Press, an imprint of The Haworth Press, Inc., 2006, pp. 11-48. Single or multiple copies of this article are available for a fee from The Haworth Document Delivery Service [1-800-HAWORTH, 9:00 a.m. - 5:00 p.m. (EST). E-mail address: docdelivery@haworthpress.com].

Available online at http://labr.haworthpress.com
doi:10.1300/J140v07n03_02

mon Market (Mercosur) crisis and the company's own global strategies. The incentives package given to Ford at the state level is estimated at about R$ 2,642 billion, or 75% of the total investment. Although high in absolute terms, when the total incentives are divided by the investment, they appear to be similar to the incentives given by other Brazilian states to automobile assemblers during the 1990s. It is shown that the largest part of the incentives resulted from tax breaks, which represented more than three quarters of their total value. Despite the large absolute number of jobs created by the assembler and first tier suppliers, it is argued that the main benefit associated with the project is a likely structural change in the state's economy as a result of the backward and forward linkages to be created. The strength of these linkages, however, depends upon the success of the project itself, but the state government actually has little control over this issue.

RESUMEN. El objeto de este estudio es evaluar los costos y beneficios asociados al establecimiento de una gran fábrica automotriz en el estado brasileño de Bahía, en una de las regiones macroeconómicas más pobres del país. Se suele decir que, por detrás de la decisión de la empresa Ford de establecer su planta lejos del centro económico del país, no se esconde apenas el atractivo paquete de incentivos fiscales ofrecidos en los distintos niveles federal y estatal, sino también la crisis de 1999 sufrida por el MERCOSUR–Mercado Común del Cono Sur, y las propias estrategias globales de la empresa. El paquete de incentivos otorgado a Ford en esos niveles gubernamentales ronda los 2.642 mil millones, o 75% de la inversión total. Los incentivos otorgados, a pesar de ser altos en términos absolutos, no difieren mucho de los otorgados por otros estados brasileños a los ensambladores automotrices durante los años 1990, al dividir el total de los incentivos por la inversión. El estudio muestra que la porción más grande de los incentivos provenía de ventajas fiscales, que representaban más de la tercera parte de su valor total. Sin embargo, a pesar del gran número absoluto de empleos creados por la montadora y por los proveedores de primera línea, queda en discusión si el mayor beneficio asociado con el proyecto es un probable cambio estructural en la economía del estado, como resultado de los vínculos progresivos y regresivos que tendrán que crearse. Por otra parte, la fuerza de dichos vínculos depende del éxito que logre el propio proyecto, auque el gobierno del estado tenga en realidad poco control sobre esta cuestión.

RESUMO. Este estudo tem por objetivo avaliar os custos e benefícios associados à criação de uma montadora de automóveis grande no estado brasileiro da Bahia, em uma das macrorregiões mais pobres do país. Argumenta-se que por trás de decisão da Ford de criar uma montadora longe do centro econômico do país estão não apenas o grande pacote de incentivos oferecidos nos níveis federal e estadual, mas também a crise de 1999 do Mercado Comum do Sul (Mercosul) e as próprias estratégias globais da empresa. O pacote de incentivos oferecido à Ford no nível estadual está estimado em cerca de R$ 2.642 bilhões, ou 75% do investimento total. Embora alto em termos absolutos, quando os incentivos totais são divididos pelo investimento, parecem semelhantes aos incentivos oferecidos por outros estados brasileiros às montadoras de automóveis durante a década de 1990. Mostra-se que a maior parte dos incentivos resultou de brechas fiscais, que representaram mais de três quartos de seu valor total. Apesar do grande número absoluto de empregos criados pela montadora e pelos fornecedores de primeiro nível, argumenta-se que o benefício principal associado ao projeto é uma provável mudança estrutural na economia do estado como resultado dos vínculos progressivos e regressivos a serem criados. A força desses vínculos, porém, depende do sucesso do próprio projeto, mas o governo do estado na verdade tem pouco controle sobre esta questão. doi:10.1300/J140v07n03_02 *[Article copies available for a fee from The Haworth Document Delivery Service: 1-800-HAWORTH. E-mail address: <docdelivery@haworthpress.com> Website: <http://www.HaworthPress.com> © 2006 by The Haworth Press, Inc. All rights reserved.]*

KEYWORDS. Fiscal war, fiscal incentives, territorial competition, automobile industry, regional development, Bahia (Brazil), Ford Motor Company

1. INTRODUCTION

In June 1999, Ford Motor Company announced that the state of Bahia would be the site for a US$ 1.9 billion automobile plant.[1] It was to be the largest single automobile plant built so far in the country, and because of the strong competition among Brazilian states for new investments, much attention was given to the project. The plant was the first large scale automobile factory outside the southern and southeastern regions of Brazil, an area in which about three quarters of Brazil's GDP is concentrated.[2] In contrast, the state chosen by Ford Motor Company is located in one of the poorest macro-regions of the country, around 1,250 miles from São Paulo, Brazil's economic center. Ford Motor Company announced its decision a few months after having given up on installing a plant in the southernmost state of Rio Grande do Sul, strategically located between São Paulo and Buenos Aires, and after severe competition among Brazilian states for the investment.

Both federal and state incentives were given to Ford Motor Company in order to attract the plant to Bahia. This incentives package was an object of many debates and became a symbol of the territorial competition among Brazilian states in the 1990s for new investments. Opponents of the incentives package argued that it not only broke with economic rationality, but it also created unnecessary fiscal costs for the federal and state governments (Rodríguez-Pose and Arbix, 2001). On the other hand, some authors suggest that the attraction of new investments can generate positive spillovers and increase local welfare (Greenstone and Moretti, 2003). As a consequence of this last viewpoint, incentives might be a useful tool to promote economic growth and correct market failures that cause territorial inequalities.

In any case, tax incentives historically had been a major policy instrument to attract private investments and promote regional distribution of income in Brazil (Baer, 2001, pp. 341-2), a country widely known for its strong territorial inequalities. Furthermore, over the past years state and local governments have assumed a greater responsibility for economic development in several countries (Greenstone and Moretti, 2003). This has been particularly true for Brazil since the promulgation of the new Constitution in 1988, which endowed states with greater flexibility to deal with fiscal policy and investment attraction.

Considering all these features, a case study on the installation of a large automobile plant in a less-developed Brazilian region during a period marked by strong territorial competition for new investments could enlighten the discussion about location decisions of firms and the externalities likely to result from their operation. Despite the close attention paid both to Ford Motor Company's investment and to the associated incentives package, the costs and benefits of the project at the state level have not yet been evaluated. This work tries to meet this challenge, addressing two main interrelated issues: the factors behind Ford Motor Company's location decision and the impacts of the project on the state's economy. The approach adopted is chiefly qualitative, as many aspects associated with these issues are subjective. Nevertheless, the present value of the incentives package given to the company has been estimated and the main benefits associated with the project have been widely discussed. An effort towards a measurement as concrete as possible of the costs and benefits of such a large investment from the state's point of view certainly not only has academic purposes, but it can also help policy makers to understand and improve their actions in promoting economic development.

2. THE AUTOMOBILE INDUSTRY STRUCTURAL CHANGES

It is widely recognized that the automobile industry underwent significant structural changes beginning in the 1980s as a result of both the microelectronic revolution and changes in global regulation patterns. In fact, innovative management and production techniques, higher international trade volumes, new labor regulation models and increasing levels of productivity by Japanese producers brought about deep changes in the automobile industry throughout that period. In spite of the diversity of trajectories followed and industrial models established, companies all over the world were influenced by the lean production patterns described by Womack, Jones and Ross (1990). In a broad sense, the switch from mass to lean production was characterized by the following changes:

- Single purpose machines were progressively replaced by integrated, flexible and automated machines that benefited from advances in the microelectronic industry. These capital goods not only became less expensive in the 1980s, but were also required to allow the manufacture of a larger mix of products in order to face the developed countries' saturated markets (product differentiation strategy).
- Labor requirements switched from semi-unskilled to multi-skilled workers who were able to operate more complex and flexible machines. As a consequence of the increased productivity, a significant reduction in the total number of jobs in the assembly sector could be noticed. Although this cutback was sometimes compensated by a growth in the components and service sectors, the precarious nature of the new posts that were created, the low levels of remuneration and the lack of collective bargaining may have led to

an overall decrease in worker's real wages (Freyssenet and Lung, 2000, p. 79).

• The traditional vertical relationship between assemblers and suppliers was replaced by a large number of different arrangements including quasi-independent suppliers who were progressively involved with the development of parts and components. In the 1990s, some of these schemes evolved into experiments such as the creation of modular supply[3] and the formation of industrial condominiums,[4] the current vanguard of innovation in assembler-supplier relations.

• Low stocks and just in time supply requirements contrasted with the patterns established up until that time, impacting on the traditional relationship between assemblers and suppliers.

In addition to physical proximity between assemblers and suppliers, these new arrangements require interactions that imply the transfer of some activities to suppliers and an increase in the service content associated with manufacturing work. Although modular supplying increases the importance of transportation costs and production synchronization, not all components suppliers must necessarily be positioned close to the assembler. Some parts, which differ insignificantly between vehicles, can for that very reason be produced at a centralized place, especially if they benefit from economies of scale. In this case, just in time delivery can be managed from decentralized warehouses (Humphrey and Salerno, 2000, p. 161).

3. THE AUTOMOBILE INDUSTRY IN BRAZIL

3.1. A Brief View of the 1990s

After a period of high inflation and low growth in the 1980s and early 1990s, when the pace of investments in the automobile industry could be considered low, a large amount of Foreign Direct Investment (FDI) from assembly companies flowed into Brazil. As a result, between 1995 and 2001, total investments in the country's automobile industry reached US$ 14 billion (Anfavea, 2003). These investments supported the restructuring of existing plants, as well as the building of new ones, using modern and advanced technologies. Domestic vehicle production rose from slightly above 900 thousand units in 1990 to about 1,800 thousand in the early 2000s,[5] while total employment during the same interval fell from more than 117 thousand to roughly 82 thousand, on account of resultant increased productivity. In fact, in 2003 a single worker produced on average about three times the production attributed to one employee in 1990, as shown in Table 1.

A number of factors contributed to this scenario of visible growth of investments and productivity indexes. First, the solid expansion of vehicle sales in emerging countries along with good perspectives for the future led to a "scramble for position" among car manufacturers (Humphrey and Salerno, 2000, p. 153). In the early 1990s, when its population was approaching 150 million, Brazil seemed to offer a huge market with a very low level of car ownership in comparison with markets in the United States, Canada, Europe, Japan, and even some Latin American countries such as Argentina, Chile and Mexico. Brazil's level of car ownership became especially attractive to FDI in the automobile sector after the monetary stabilization that occurred in 1994, when the Real Plan was launched. Indeed, following more than a decade of inconstant and low GDP growth rates, and after the failure of sundry mone-

TABLE 1. Automobile Industry: Vehicle Production and Employment in Brazil

| Year | Vehicle Production | | | | Employment | Vehicle/ Employee |
	Cars	Light Commercials	Heavy Commercials	Total		
1990	663,084	184,754	66,628	914,466	117,396	7.8
1991	705,303	182,609	72,307	960,219	109,428	8.8
1992	815,959	201,591	56,311	1,073,861	105,664	10.2
1993	1,100,278	224,387	66,770	1,391,435	106,738	13.0
1994	1,248,773	251,044	81,572	1,581,389	107,134	14.8
1995	1,297,467	239,399	92,142	1,629,008	104,614	15.6
1996	1,458,576	279,697	66,055	1,804,328	101,857	17.7
1997	1,677,858	306,545	85,300	2,069,703	104,941	19.7
1998	1,254,016	247,044	85,231	1,586,291	83,049	19.1
1999	1,109,509	176,994	70,211	1,356,714	85,100	15.9
2000	1,361,721	235,161	94,358	1,691,240	89,134	19.0
2001	1,501,586	214,936	100,594	1,817,116	84,834	21.4
2002	1,520,285	179,861	91,384	1,791,530	81,737	21.9
2003	1,504,998	216,112	105,928	1,827,038	79,153	23.1

Source: Anfavea (2003; 2005).

tary stabilization plans, Brazil's GDP growth prospects became very optimistic, as the inflation rate seemed to be under control.

Other factors that companies took into account were low production costs and opportunities for testing new approaches to production and work offered by emerging markets. In fact, the relative weakness of trade unions, lower remuneration levels and, in a certain way, the straightforward processes of introducing new manufacturing styles played an important role in attracting FDI to countries like Brazil (Humphrey, Lecler and Salerno, 2000, p. 1).

Trade liberalization was an additional aspect that contributed to fostering investments in Brazil in the 1990s, not only because it allowed firms to set up their international supply and sales arrangements in a more efficient way, but also because it created an FDI-friendly environment. The reduction of external tariffs on assembled passenger cars by 20% by 1994, along with the revival of domestic demand (Humphrey and Oeter, 2000, p. 56), led to successive trade deficits involving vehicles and components (Table 2), and in 1995 the Brazilian government decided to raise import duties by up to 70%. These taxes functioned as an additional incentive for automobile FDI, because they could fall by 35% for companies assembling in the country. Moreover, these companies could also benefit from a reduction in tariffs on imported components. As a result, even after the trade liberalization wave the car manufacturing sector in Brazil remained highly regulated and protected. Not surprisingly, Brazil became one of the favorite investment targets in the world, and, according to Baer (2001, p. 257), 32.4% of the investment intentions of multinationals in the country's manufacturing sector were aimed at the automobile industry.

The regional integration process resulting from the creation of Mercosur also encouraged a visible rush of FDI. The removal of import duties on transactions among Brazil, Argentina, Paraguay and Uruguay was launched in 1991 by the Asuncion Treaty, and, in 1995, a common external tariff applying to 85% of total trade was instituted. Investments in the automobile sector could then benefit from larger markets (Baer, 2001, pp. 212, 255 and 260) and from complementary supply procedures, and Brazilian production rose to a competitive scale. However, as pointed out by Baer, Cavalcanti and Silva (2002, p. 271), although "trade integration in Mercosur has undeniably increased since the Asuncion Treaty," the lack of macroeconomic policy coordination among the participants of the block, especially with regard to exchange rates, brought about a number of trade protection measures and produced a tense atmosphere, especially between the two main partners,

TABLE 2. Brazilian Automotive Trade, 1989-2004 (US$ Million)

	Exports			Imports			Trade Balance	
	Total	Mercosur	%	Total	Mercosur	%	Total	Mercosur
1989	1,506	79	5.2%	6	-	0.0%	1,500	79
1990	929	76	8.2%	34	0	0.2%	895	76
1991	871	227	26.1%	198	36	18.4%	673	191
1992	1,631	699	42.9%	339	105	30.8%	1,292	595
1993	1,432	614	42.9%	879	233	26.5%	553	381
1994	1,414	600	42.5%	1,841	306	16.6%	(427)	295
1995	1,075	434	40.4%	3,898	586	15.0%	(2,823)	(152)
1996	1,249	717	57.5%	2,109	1,032	48.9%	(860)	(315)
1997	2,494	1,296	52.0%	3,397	1,970	58.0%	(903)	(674)
1998	2,831	1,382	48.8%	3,812	2,386	62.6%	(980)	(1,004)
1999	1,893	703	37.2%	1,790	1,083	60.5%	103	(380)
2000	2,590	780	30.1%	1,893	1,156	61.1%	697	(376)
2001	2,588	465	18.0%	2,015	1,297	64.4%	573	(832)
2002	2,569	187	7.3%	1,104	643	58.2%	1,465	(456)
2003	3,448	665	19.3%	867	418	48.2%	2,581	247
2004	4,636	1,446	31.2%	891	464	52.1%	3,746	981

Source: Ministério do Desenvolvimento, Indústria e Comércio Exterior (MDIC)/Secretaria de Comércio Exterior (SECEX)/Sistema de Análise das Informações de Comércio Exterior (ALICE)

Brazil and Argentina. After the devaluation of the Brazilian currency at the beginning of 1999, disagreements turned into a real problematical issue, imposing a very disadvantageous position on the Argentinean motor industry. This situation led some authors to affirm along with Humphrey and Oeter (2000, p. 59) that "a free market in automotive products within Mercosur is still some distance away."[6] To clarify this assertion, which is crucial for comprehending some hypotheses proposed in this paper, and before discussing the location patterns of the automobile industry in Brazil, it seems proper to take a look at the evolution of the Brazilian automotive trade over the past several years, focusing also on the share of Mercosur in these commercial flows (Table 2).

Between 1991 and 1993, when the Brazilian currency was undervalued and the Argentinean Peso was already pegged to the US Dollar, both total and Mercosur trade balances were favorable to Brazil. In the period between 1994 and 1998, conversely, the Brazilian Real significantly appreciated against the US Dollar and, consequently, against the Argentinean Peso. Not surprisingly, Brazil had successive trade deficits throughout this period, both in total and in Mercosur trade balances. The devaluation of the Brazilian currency in 1999 once again changed the sign of the total trade balance as a consequence of an impressive fall in total imports (over 50% between 1998 and 1999). However, the Mercosur trade balance remained unfavorable to Brazil until 2002 because of the significant decrease in Brazilian exports to Mercosur caused by protectionist measures implemented by the other countries, and especially because of the severe recession that struck Argentina during that period.

In fact, the instability of the trade balance between Brazil and the other partners that comprise Mercosur–especially Argentina–led these countries to adopt several protectionist measures to counterbalance the effects of overvalued currencies in some instances. Many of these countries also occasionally adopted additional measures to deal with this kind of problem. Particularly concerned about the automobile industry, Brazil and Argentina, for instance, issued their "Automotive Regimes" to encourage FDI and promote exports during the 1990s. In 1991, Argentina created its own program, triggering, as pointed out by Zauli (2000, p. 79), a bias in FDI attracted to Mercosur. In 1995, it was Brazil's turn to launch its so-called "New Automotive Regime," containing a package of fiscal incentives offered by the federal government. Among the tax incentives offered, a 50% reduction on import duties on cars produced was granted to companies assembling in Brazil.[7]

Furthermore, at the federal level additional incentives were offered in 1997 to firms interested in installing plants in the northern, northeastern and mid-western regions of the country in order to attend to pressures from the poorest states.[8] As would be expected, several disagreements with other countries or economic blocks–such as the US, the European Union and Japan–occurred, and some adjustments had to be introduced into the original Brazilian Automotive Regime. The regional incentives provided by the "Special Automotive Regime" had also been questioned by Argentina. In spite of these controversies, the results of the efforts made to attract productive capital to the Brazilian automobile sector were significant: as stated previously, between 1995 and 2001, investments in this industry are estimated to have been US$ 14 billion and, as detailed in Table 3, during this period almost all major world car producers announced the building of automobile plants in the country.[9]

TABLE 3. New Automobile Plants in Brazil 1995-1999

Company	Invest. (US$ million)	Planned Capacity (1,000 vehicles)	Jobs	Announcement	Start Up	City	State
Volkswagen (1)	250	50	1500	n.a.	Nov-96	Resende	RJ
Honda	100	30	450	Apr-96	Oct-97	Sumaré	SP
MMC Automotores (2)	35	8	500	Jul-1996	Jun-98	Catalão	GO
DaimlerChrysler (3)	315	12	400	Mar-97	Jul-98	Campo Largo	PR
Toyota	150	15	350	Aug-96	Sep-98	Indiatuba	SP
Land Rover/BMW	148	5	800	Dec-97	Oct-98	São Bernardo do Campo	SP
Renault	1000	120	2000	Mar-96	Dec-98	São José dos Pinhais	PR
Volkswagen/Audi	750	160	1000	Dec-96	Jan-99	São José dos Pinhais	PR
Mercedes-Benz (DaimlerChrysler)	820	70	2000	Apr-96	Apr-99	Juiz de Fora	MG
Iveco/Fiat	120	12	n.a.	Apr-97	Nov-00	Sete Lagoas	MG
Peugeot Citroën	600	100	1000	Jul-97	Feb-01	Porto Real	RJ
General Motors (5)	600	120	2000	Dec-96	Jul-01	Gravataí	RS
Ford	1900	250	5000	Jun-99	Oct-01	Camaçari	BA

Note 1: Trucks and buses
Note 2: Mitsubishi licensed; light commercials.
Note 3: Announced suspension of operations in Jan 2001.
Note 4: Light commercials, trucks and buses.
Note 5: Incentives renegotiated in May 1999.
Source: Prepared by the authors from data available in "O Estado de São Paulo," several editions, Anfavea (2003), Rodríguez-Pose and Arbix (2001), and Santos and Pinhão (1999).

3.2. Location Patterns

During the first migration of the automobile industry to Brazil between 1956 and 1970, productive units clustered basically around São Paulo.[10] Even though in the 1970s Fiat installed a plant in Minas Gerais, while a few smaller plants located outside São Paulo, the automobile industry remained highly spatially concentrated until the latter 1980s. During the 1990s, however, the expansion of this industry was not as geographically concentrated as it used to be, as illustrated in Table 3. As pointed out by Rodríguez-Pose and Arbix (2001, pp. 142 ff.), several factors contributed to the dispersion process:

- Wage differentials within Brazil were quite significant, and the educational gap across the country had been reduced in recent years;
- The development of the highway infrastructure, combined with the need of larger markets, as well as a technological evolution in car manufacturing, increased companies' flexibility to choose the location of their factories;
- In addition to the vigor and the organization of trade unions, the level of congestion and pollution, along with several administrative problems, was much higher in São Paulo than in other regions.

The opportunities created by these factors and the opening up of the Brazilian economy led to a process of territorial competition among Brazilian states, not surprisingly strengthened by the Automotive Regimes (despite their federal nature) and the boom of FDI in the automobile sector. Besides massive tax incentives (10 or more years in all cases), the major weapons used in the fiscal wars (or tax competitions) were the donation of land, the provision of the necessary infrastructure for site preparation (highway infrastructure and utilities, rail links, port terminals, etc.), the provision of loans by the state at fixed rates below the Brazilian credit market, a series of financial and legislative guarantees, and sundry other additional benefits, which ranged from providing public transportation for workers to a variety of environmental measures (Rodríguez-Pose and Arbix, 2001, p. 145).

Furthermore, behind the territorial competition for the announced investments there is one crucial fact that cannot be missed: the role of state intervention clearly changed from the 1980s onward. In effect, the strengthening and enlargement of neo-liberal ideology, along with the financial-fiscal crisis, eliminated the ability of the central government to make direct investments and to implement a regional policy, as it had done in the past.[11] This contributed to competition by states for new investments. Although Rodríguez-Pose and Arbix (2001, p. 150) argued that the Brazilian federation was not well prepared to handle this kind of competition after so many years of policies subordinated to federal governmental directives, especially during the authoritarian period, the fact remains that the bidding war was obviously triggered by the absence of central coordination and by the lack of a centralized policy that could ensure conditions for the less developed states to improve their economic situation.[12]

Regardless of this explanation, the unquestionable result was that many Brazilian states competed for the new plants. From a geographical point of view, as can be seen in Table 3 and also in Figure 1, the effect was a kind of concentrated distraction. It meant that São Paulo remained the core, but a higher geographical dispersion could be observed, compared to the distribution pattern that developed during the first development of the industry. This new configuration in the automobile sector seems quite similar to the polygon proposed by Diniz (1993), who argued that the Brazilian economy would grow in the 1990s, outlining, territorially speaking, a polygonal area including Belo Horizonte (MG), Uberlândia (MG), Londrina (PR), Porto Alegre (PR) and Florianópolis (SC). This location pattern is also consistent with Ó hUallacháin and Wasserman's (1999) arguments about Brazil's automobile component parts industry's spatial configuration. It is noteworthy that the only point out of this area is Ford's plant in Camaçari,[13] not coincidentally, the last one to be built.[14]

As can be observed in Figure 1, until the end of the 1990s Mercosur played an important role in the location decision made by firms. As pointed out by Humphrey and Oeter (2000, p. 57), it seems that, "by the late 1990s, a genuine regional automotive production system was developing in Mercosur, based on a division of labor in vehicle and components production between Brazil and Argentina." Actually, not only from a market point of view, but also considering the sourcing of major components, Mercosur seemed to be performing well at that time. Another piece of strong evidence that Mercosur was behind the location decision made by the assemblers is the fact that it was explicitly mentioned as a target for many companies investing in Brazil, as Santos and Pinhão state (1999, p. 188).

Most of these investments were announced when the trade flow involving Brazil and the other countries of Mercosur was very high (see Table 2). By that time, the location pattern, as a rule, seemed to pursue the following rationale: newcomers in Brazil built their plants around São Paulo (Honda,

FIGURE 1. Location Patterns of the Automobile Industry in Brazil

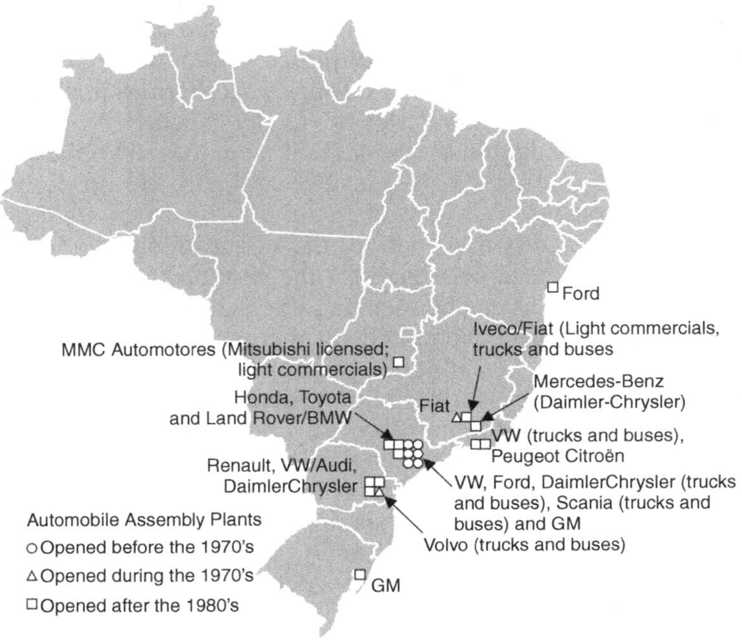

MMC Automotores (Mitsubishi licensed; light commercials)

Honda, Toyota and Land Rover/BMW

Renault, VW/Audi, DaimlerChrysler

Ford

Iveco/Fiat (Light commercials, trucks and buses

Mercedes-Benz (Daimler-Chrysler)

Fiat

VW (trucks and buses), Peugeot Citroën

VW, Ford, DaimlerChrysler (trucks and buses), Scania (trucks and buses) and GM

Volvo (trucks and buses)

GM

Automobile Assembly Plants
o Opened before the 1970's
△ Opened during the 1970's
□ Opened after the 1980's

Source: Prepared by the authors from data available in "O Estado de São Paulo," various editions, Anfavea (2003), Rodríguez-Pose and Arbix (2001), and Santos and Pinhão (1999).

Renault, Peugeot, Chrysler), while firms already based in the country (GM and Ford, as originally intended) announced the southern area as their focus (Alban, Souza e Ferro, 2000, p. 20). After the Mercosur crisis, triggered by the Brazilian Real devaluation of 1999 and aggravated by the Argentinean recession, expectations changed a great deal, affecting the companies' forecasts and strategies. Indeed, besides the previous tensions involving taxes, quotes and subsidies, the uneven exchange rates in Brazil and Argentina made the regional automotive market no longer reliable. From this moment on, Mercosur did not seem to play the same role in the location decision made by assemblers.

4. THE FORD PROJECT IN BAHIA

After a crisis that almost led the company to discontinue its operations in Brazil,[15] in 1997 Ford Motor Company announced a US$ 1.0

billion investment in an automobile plant in Rio Grande do Sul, Brazil's southernmost state and strategically located between São Paulo and Buenos Aires. Because of its geographical position, this state could be considered the gravity center of Mercosur, and Ford Motor Company at the time seemed to follow the strategy adopted by GM, which a few months before had announced an investment in the same state. As usual, an agreement between the company and the state government was signed, and an incentives package involving tax breaks, loans, infrastructure and other advantages was offered.

In 1998, when the site's groundwork had already begun and the state government had transferred part of the loan to the company, there were gubernatorial elections in all Brazilian states, and the Workers Party candidate—then in the opposition—was elected in Rio Grande do Sul. In January 1999, the newly elected governor decided to renegotiate the incentives package offered to both GM and Ford by the previous administration. Although the renegotiation succeeded with GM, Ford stopped building its plant in April 1999, as no agreement between the company and the state government had been reached. In May 1999, according to the company's chairman in Brazil at the time, all Brazilian states (excluding Rio Grande do Sul and three small northern states) submitted proposals to attract the firm ("O Estado de São Paulo," May 5, 1999). Amongst the strongest candidates were the remaining southern states (Paraná and Santa Catarina), three states in the southeast region (São Paulo, Rio de Janeiro and Espírito Santo), and two northeastern states (Pernambuco and Bahia).[16] Not surprisingly, this competition became an icon of the fiscal war among Brazilian federation members, and several discussions took place in the media focusing on concerns associated with the investment incentives offered.

In June 1999, within a skeptical atmosphere, Ford announced that Bahia had been selected as the site for a new investment that was to be the biggest ever made in a single new plant in Brazil during the 1990s:[17] it was estimated at R$ 3.515 billion[18] and the total income, when operating at full capacity, would possibly reach R$ 6.0 billion (see section 5). Although these numbers have to be used with care for many reasons, even a very imprecise calculation could show that the total investment represented 8.4% of the state's GDP in 1999, and the estimated amount of income could reach more than 10% of this aggregate value.[19] Five thousand direct jobs—referring to the assembly plant and the first tier suppliers—and 50,000 indirect jobs—estimated using a rough 10:1 relationship between direct and indirect jobs—were announced by both the company and the state government, and arrangements were made for 17 first tier suppliers to follow the assembler to Bahia. It was also announced at the time that 60% of the value added would be produced in the state, and 95% would be created in the country as a whole after some years of operation.

The incentives package was considered by the press as the main (and sometimes the only) factor behind Ford's decision to establish a plant in Bahia ("O Estado de São Paulo," various editions). This hypothesis, however, does not explain why the same decision had not been made back in 1997, when the company had announced the investment in Rio Grande do Sul. At that time, Bahia did not even figure among the candidates to host Ford's plant, despite the local government's efforts to attract other automobile industries.[20] On the other hand, the factors that attracted Ford to Rio Grande do Sul in 1997 no longer seemed to prevail in 1999; otherwise, the company would have chosen another state in the southern macro-region of Brazil after the failure of its renegotiation with the government of Rio Grande do Sul. In fact, when the announced characteristics of the projects in Rio Grande do Sul and Bahia are compared (Table 4), it can be seen that not only the location but the project itself had changed.

Table 4 makes it clear that while the first project was visibly developed to meet the Mercosur market, the second one was more likely to be a world-scale project, for which Mercosur was just a part of the target market. The incentives package and the institutional problems between Ford and the Rio Grande do Sul government are thus not sufficient to explain why Ford gave up on investing in the southern region of Brazil and decided to build a plant in Bahia. As pointed out by Alban, Souza and Ferro (2000), and reinforced by some arguments mentioned above, the 1999 Real devaluation made the Mercosur strategy–as it had been conceived beforehand–no longer interesting to Ford, the last company to begin the construction of an automobile plant in Brazil.[21]

TABLE 4. Announced Characteristics: Ford Project in Rio Grande do Sul and Bahia

	Ford Project in Rio Grande do Sul	Ford Project in Bahia
Investment	1.0 billion	1.9 billion
Capacity	150,000 vehicles/year	250,000 vehicles/year
Direct Jobs	1,500	5,000

Source: Prepared by the authors from data available in "O Estado de São Paulo," various editions.

Of course, the preexisting conditions of the state played an important role in the location decision, as there are several key location requirements for a 250,000-vehicle world-scale plant besides the tax incentives, such as infrastructure (especially access to an efficient port), labor skills and wage costs. Between the 1950s and the 1980s, Bahia developed an industrial structure based on intermediary goods, which was supplementary to the economic structure of the southeastern regions of the country and highly concentrated in petrochemical and metallurgical products that represented around 75% of the gross value added to the local manufacturing sector.[22] This background is important, as it created a positive environment for new investments, which could take advantage of the available infrastructure and the potential connections with other producers, thereby benefiting from agglomeration economies. On the other hand, attracting final goods production became one of the main objectives of the state's industrial strategy. In effect, it is largely recognized that the extreme concentration in intermediate goods not only has negative impact on employment levels (as these sectors are more capital intensive, particularly when facing international competition, which happened after the opening up of the Brazilian economy), but also exposes the state's economy as a whole to the typical fluctuations of commodities markets, which explains the aggressive policies adopted.[23]

Another central consequence of the economic development path in Bahia was an excessive concentration around Salvador's metropolitan region, which represents approximately 50% of the state's economic activity and almost 25% of its population. In spite of its harmful effects on the state's territorial development, this feature contributed towards creating around the city of Salvador, the state's capital, a satisfactory infrastructure supply when compared to the resources available in other areas that had access to the incentives offered by the Special Automotive Regime, especially when the harbor system is considered. Finally, the geographic position of Bahia between the other northeastern states and the major industrial production and consumption area of Brazil, as well as its location closer to the North American and Europeans markets, represented a favorable point.

An additional issue is the lower cost of labor in the Northeast. According to research carried out by the Inter Union Institute, Dieese, the wages paid in Camaçari represented only 30.4% of the average wage in the Greater ABC, while in Gravataí, Rio Grande do Sul, where GM installed its plant, this proportion was 41.1% ("O Estado de São Paulo," July 24, 2003). Because of this discrepancy, workers in Camaçari went on strike in March 2003, demanding a 25% increase in salary and others benefits. Immediately, the company counter-offered with increments that varied from 8% to 10%, depending on the employee's wage level ("O Estado de São Paulo," March 21, 2003).[24]

Some questions remain as to whether savings on labor in Bahia could offset the cost of transporting supplies and a large share of the final products to the traditional automotive districts in Brazil, located 1,250 miles away. Ford bet that it would be worthwhile if supported by the development of a network to collect materials from tier one and tier two suppliers and the assurance of just in time delivery. According to Ford's head of business strategy in 2002, the plant built in Camaçari would be Ford's lowest-cost factory in the world, and it would quickly turn into a key regional asset for the company, particularly for exports (Brown, 2002).

Without doubt, Ford Motor Company had pondered all these different aspects before it made the decision to start the so-called Amazon Project in Bahia, which seemed to be totally adjusted to the Ford 2000 plan launched in 1994. This restructuring proposal–an effort to reduce cost and increase efficiency–meant to focus on globalizing corporate organizations and to take advantage of the economies of scale in purchasing and manufacturing by consolidating international automobile operations and launching a reengineering process of several basic procedures. According to Studer-Noguez (2002, p. 118), "the underlying aim [of this program] was to transform the company's organization from one based on regional profit centers to a global car-manufacturing business organized by product line." Some market analysts claim that the Amazon Project would be a model for Ford's future manufacturing organization, increasing outsourced supply of entire sub-systems for the first time.[25]

To sum up, the differences between the plant installed in Bahia and the one originally to be installed in Rio Grande do Sul suggest that what really happened was not a simple project relocation (as a result of territorial competition among Brazilian states), but rather a shift in the company's business plans. Thus, the main factors behind Ford's decision to establish a plant far from the economic center of the country and from Mercosur seem to have been not only the large incentives package offered at the federal and state levels, but also the 1999 Mercosur crisis and the global strategies of the company itself.

5. THE INCENTIVES PACKAGE[26]

During the 1960s and 70s, fiscal incentives played a highly important role in the development of Bahia. The nature of these previous incentives was, however, quite diverse, because they were mostly given through a national agency (Sudene), which had been created to foster the economic development of the northeastern region as a whole. Furthermore, the main instruments employed were the incentives involving federal income taxes, either reducing their amount or using them to provide funding for new investments.[27] As most of these incentives were given by the federal government, their effects on the states' fiscal positions were actually reduced. Moreover, territorial competition was really kept under control because of the coordination role played by Sudene and the lack of states and municipalities' autonomy resulting from the earlier Constitution.

As pointed out in Section 3, after the fiscal crisis of the 1980s and the significant changes in both the political situation and the economic environment, a territorial competition among Brazilian states began, generally based upon incentives provided by the sub-national governments themselves. Since by that time each state had created specific programs and policies, comparisons between the incentives packages turn out to be not an easy task. The aim of this section is to establish a calculation method for determining the incentives package given to Ford Motor Company in Bahia, in order to estimate its monetary value so that it can be compared to the incentives given to other automobile plants and, to some extent, to the expected benefits the project might create in the state.

Estimating the fiscal sacrifice associated with the incentives package, however, imposes some methodological problems. First, not all contract conditions and clauses are made public, according to the argument that negotiations must be kept secret. The agreement between GM and Rio Grande do Sul's government, for instance, was made public only after a judicial inquiry triggered by Workers Party state representatives. In Bahia, even after the publication of State Law 7.537, which established the main conditions of the incentives package negotiated with Ford Motor Company, credit contracts and other instruments were protected against disclosure. Second, the estimate required some parameters to be forecast, like the real cost of capital or the company's income level during the incentives period. Some authors have tried to estimate the present value of the incentives with respect to other automobile plants. Alves (2001), for example, projected the "fiscal sacrifice" for three projects in Brazil, based upon some simplifications and certain assumptions about the unknown parameters.

Centering the attention on Bahia, the incentives package offered to Ford Motor Company can be divided into three parts:[28]

- *Fiscal incentives* (F_c), i.e., the incentives associated with tax breaks or the financing of taxes due by the company. As Brazilian states cannot simply reduce their VAT taxes (because it would require unanimity on the National Fiscal Policy Council, where all states are represented), these incentives assume the form of working capital financing. In practice, however, the company pays the VAT and the state returns the payments in the form of working capital credit, creating a sort of triangular transaction. In spite of the naive argument that these *fiscal incentives* cost the state nothing (since it would be sacrificing taxes that would not otherwise exist), the point is that several budgetary duties are directly associated with state tax collection. Since the state actually collects the taxes, these obligations must be enforced. This means that *fiscal incentives* do in fact generate a cost for the state (and, as will be shown, they represent the main cost).[29]
- *Financial incentives* (F_n), i.e., credit programs at lower interest rates, either directly financed or "equalized" by the state.[30] In both cases, these incentives create a cost opportunity, as the interest rates charged to the company are smaller than market interest rates.
- *Budget incentives* (B), i.e., infrastructure provisions, land and building subsidies, job training sponsored by the state and any other incentives that directly affect the state's budget.

5.1. Calculation Method

The present *IP* value of the incentives package is given by the sum of the present value of its three parts, as shown in Equation 1:

$$IP = F_C + F_N + B \qquad (1)$$

Where F_c, F_N, and B are the present value of the three parts that comprise the incentives package. To simplify the calculations, it was assumed that plant construction began in 2000 (actually it was in mid-1999) and the startup was in 2002 (in fact, it was towards the end of 2001). The values for F_C, F_N, and B have been calculated at their present value in 2000.

5.1.1. Fiscal Incentives

Present value F_c of the *fiscal incentives* is given by:

$$F_C = \sum_{i=0}^{14} \frac{F_{C,i}}{(1+r_s)^i} \qquad (2)$$

Where $i = 0$ stands for the year 2000, and so on; r_s is the real cost of capital to the state, and $F_{C,i}$ is the fiscal incentive given in year i. The sum entails the period between 2000 and 2014 (a total fifteen-year fruition incentive).[31]

According to State Law n. 7.537, the *fiscal incentives* given to Ford Motor Company can be divided into two parts:

- During the six first years (2000 through 2005), up to 12% of total income is to be financed under special conditions. If the payments are made ahead of schedule, a 98% discount is offered. In practice, it was assumed that all payments would be made ahead of schedule, which means that only 2% of the VAT due would actually be paid during this period.
- During the following nine years (2006 through 2014), the VAT due is to be financed at 0% interest. There is to be a ten-year grace period and a twelve-year amortization period.

Thus, during the first period (2000 through 2005), for each year i *fiscal incentives* $F_{C,i}$ are estimated as indicated by the following equation:

$$F_{C,i} = 0.98 T_{D,i} \qquad (3)$$

The taxes due in year i $T_{D,i}$ are given by the sum of the taxes due on vehicle sales in the domestic market ($T_{DI,i}$), the taxes due on vehicle exports ($T_{DX,i}$), and the taxes due on imported vehicles sold in the domestic market ($T_{D,M,i}$), as shown in the following equation:

$$T_{D,i} = T_{DI,i} + T_{DX,i} + T_{DM,i} \qquad (4)$$

The taxes due on vehicles sales in the domestic market ($T_{DI,i}$) are given by:

$$T_{DI,i} = \left(N_{I,i} P_{I,i}\right)\left[t_v - (1 - L_i) t_C\right] \qquad (5)$$

Where $N_{I,i}$ is the number of vehicles sold on the internal market in year i, $P_{I,i}$ is the average price of vehicles on the internal market, L_i is the percentage of value added locally, t_V is the value added tax on the vehicles sold, and t_C is the average value added tax on the components produced elsewhere.

The taxes due on vehicles exports ($T_{DX,i}$) are, as a consequence of Brazilian export promotion policies, given by this equation:[32]

$$T_{DX,i} = -\left(N_{X,i}P_{X,i}\right)\left(1-L_i\right)t_C \tag{6}$$

Where $N_{X,i}$ is the number of vehicles exported in year i, and $P_{X,i}$ is the average price of exported vehicles.

Finally, the taxes due on imported vehicles sold on the domestic market ($T_{DM,i}$) are given by:

$$T_{DM,i} = M_{BA,i}t_V \tag{7}$$

Where $M_{BA,i}$ is the total amount of income resulting from the sales of vehicles imported by Ford Motor Company into the state of Bahia in year i.

During the second period (2006 through 2014) *fiscal incentives* $F_{C,i}$ are given by:

$$F_{C,i} = T_{D,i} - T_{P,i} \tag{8}$$

Where $T_{D,i}$ is the tax due in year i and $T_{P,i}$ is the present value of the mortgages financed at 0% interest with a ten-year grace period and a twelve-year amortization period.

Assuming that 0% interest will be charged to the company during the grace period, $T_{P,i}$ is given as:

$$T_{P,i} = \frac{T_{P,i+10}}{\left(1+r_s\right)^{10}} \tag{9}$$

Where $T_{P,i+10}$ is the present value in year $i + 10$ of the twelve annual mortgages paid in years $i + 11$ to $i + 22$. Considering that 0% interest will also be charged to the company during the amortization period, $T_{P,i+10}$ is given by the equation below:

$$T_{P,i+10} = \left(\frac{T_{D,i}}{12}\right)\left[\frac{1-(1+r_s)^{-12}}{r_s}\right] \tag{10}$$

Where $T_{D,i}/12$ is the annual mortgage, since 0% interest is charged to the company. Now, placing equations 9 and 10 into equation 8, an equation to define $F_{C,i}$ during the second period is obtained:

$$F_{C,i} = T_{D,i} - \frac{\dfrac{T_{D,i}}{12}\left[\dfrac{1-(1+r_s)^{-12}}{r_s}\right]}{(1+r_s)^{10}} \tag{11}$$

5.1.2. Financial Incentives

A credit for fixed investments and their associated installation expenditures was given to Ford Motor Company by the state. According to State Law no. 7.537, an annual nominal interest rate R_C of 6% is to be charged to the company. The total credit has a five-year grace period (interest is charged during grace period) and a ten-year amortization period. The present value F_N of the **financial incentives** is then given as:

$$F_N = C - \sum_{i=6}^{15}\frac{PMT_i}{(1+r_s)^i} \tag{12}$$

Where C is the total amount of credit given by the state (assumed to be concentrated in 2000, i.e., at $i = 0$) and PMT_i is the annual amortization paid by the company after the grace period, i.e., between 2006 and 2015. PMT_i is given by the following equation:

$$PMT_i = \frac{FV_5}{\left[\dfrac{1-(1+r_C)^{-10}}{r_C}\right]} \tag{13}$$

Where FV_5 is the future value of the debt at $i = 5$, as shown in this equation:

$$FV_5 = C(1+r_C)^5 \tag{14}$$

In order to perform the calculations in real terms (instead of nominal terms), the real interest rate r_c, as defined by the Fisher effect,[33] was used:

$$r_C = \frac{1+R_C}{1+h} - 1 \tag{15}$$

Where h is the expected inflation rate.

Now placing equations 13 and 14 into equation 12, the present value F_N of the *financial incentives* is thus given as:

$$F_N = C - \sum_{i=6}^{15} \frac{\dfrac{C(1+r_C)^5}{\left[\dfrac{1-(1+r_C)^{-10}}{r_C}\right]}}{(1+r_s)^i} \tag{16}$$

5.1.3. Budget Incentives

The present value B of the *budget incentives* is given by the sum of the M investments made by the state in infrastructure and other items provided to support Ford Motor Company's installation in Bahia during the years between 2000 and 2015 ($i = 0$ to 15). Although infrastructure is the main item in this part, job training, along with land and building subsidies, among other investments, should be considered. As some of these investments may have externalities, i.e., may be used by other economic activities in the state, a use factor u_j was multiplied by each investment j. In practice, u_j belongs to the interval between 0 and 1. If u_j is equal to zero, the company does not benefit from the investment at all; on the other hand, if $u_j = 1$, the incentives are entirely appropriated by the company. For each investment, the present value is calculated, so that B is given by:

$$B = \sum_{i=0}^{15} \sum_{j=1}^{M} \frac{u_j b_{i,j}}{(1+r_s)} \tag{17}$$

5.2. An Estimation of the Value of the Incentives Package

As shown in the preceding section, several parameters have to be estimated or forecast in order to calculate the present value of the incentives package. Considering an investment of R\$ 3.515 billion,[34] the total incentives were calculated in two different scenarios. The first one is based upon the following assumptions:

- The real cost of capital to the state r_s had been fixed at 10% per year.
- The number of vehicles produced $N_i = N_{l,i} + N_{x,i}$ in 2002 was assumed to be 100 thousand and the volume of production was considered to grow at 50 thousand units per year so that in 2005 the plant would be operating at full capacity.[35]
- It was assumed that 20% of the vehicles produced in 2002 were exported. From 2003 onward, the value assumed was 25%.
- The average prices of vehicles $P_{l,i}$ and $P_{x,i}$ were assumed to be R\$ 24.2 thousand in 2000 values.[36]
- The percentage of value added locally was set at 60% for all years. This is a more conservative approach, since the higher the value added, the higher the incentives.
- The total amount of income resulting from the sales of vehicles imported by Ford Motor Company into the state of Bahia in 2000, 2001 and 2002 was R\$ 819 million, R\$ 1,133 million and R\$ 673 million, respectively.[37] From 2003 onward, an average of these values was considered.
- The total amount of credit given by the state was R\$ 1.081 billion. This number was estimated using data from the Finance Secretariat of the State of Bahia and from the executive group created within the government staff to support the project's installation.[38]
- Inflation rate h was set at 5% per year.
- Based upon data from the Planning Secretariat of the State of Bahia and the Ford Executive Group, an investment of R\$ 170 million in infrastructure was considered in 2000 (excluding the harbor structure). A conservative use factor of 100% was assumed for this investment.
- To the R\$ 30 million investment in the port scheduled for 2003, a use factor of 100% was set, as the port was to be used exclusively by the company.
- Other *budget incentives* (as the investment in labor qualification) were not considered because there was no estimate for them, they would have had little influence on the results, and they were truly small when compared with the *fiscal and financial incentives*. Besides, the conservative 100% use factor assigned to the R\$ 170 million infrastructure investments would overcome these other investments.

A second scenario considering an inflation rate equal to zero was also constructed. In this scenario, neither vehicle exports nor imports were considered. As a result, it was assumed that the total production was sold on the domestic market. Though quite unrealistic, these hypotheses are the same accepted by Alves (2001), who makes her results and the ones obtained here directly comparable to each other. The outcomes for both scenarios are reported in Table 5.

Under the assumptions made in the first scenario, the present value of the incentives package in 2000 reaches R$ 2,642 million, or 75% of the total investment. The largest part of the assistance is due to *fiscal incentives* (69%), followed by financial support (24%). Since *budget incentives* represent only 7% of the whole package, the influence of some omitted items (such as land cost or investment in qualified labor) should not have a significant impact on the results, as presumed previously. In the second scenario, the *budget incentives* are the same as in the first one. The *fiscal incentives*, however, are slightly higher (as a consequence of the assumption of no international trade). On the other hand, as a result of the zero inflation rate assumed, the *financial incentives* are much lower than the ones observed in the first scenario. Consequently, the total incentives reach a lower value than the one obtained in the first scenario (R$ 2,402 million, or 68% of the total investment).

One must realize that the incentives package is strongly affected by the success of the project itself, since the *fiscal incentives* are proportional to the volume of production. This means that in case of a breakdown, when total income declines, *fiscal incentives* decline as well. As a result, if the project had not succeeded (since the government would have removed the incentives related to the vehicles imported), the hidden costs for the state at the beginning of 2000 would have reached R$ 819 million or R$ 524 million, considering the first and the second scenarios, respectively.[39]

TABLE 5. Present Value of the Incentive Package (R$ million)

	Scenario 1		Scenario 2	
Fiscal Incentives	1,823	69%	1,878	78%
Financial Incentives	626	24%	331	14%
Budget Incentives	193	7%	193	8%
Total Incentives	2,642	100%	2,402	100%
Incentives/Investment		75%		68%

Source: Prepared by the authors.

5.3. The Incentives Package: A Comparison

As shown in the previous section, and based on the assumptions made, the present value of the total incentives offered to Ford Motor Company is estimated at R$ 2,642 million, or 75% of the total investment. When considering a zero inflation rate during the period, the value of the incentives package falls to R$ 2,402 million, or 68% of the total investment. In spite of their imprecise nature, these numbers can be roughly compared with some other similar calculations reported in the literature. Alves (2001) estimated the value of the incentives package for three automobile plants installed in Brazil in the 1990s (Mercedes-Benz, GM and Renault), and the calculation method employed in this paper is fully compatible with the one used in that study. Chapman, Elhance, and, Wenum (1995) also worked with this subject, reporting the total incentives given to Mitsubishi in order to attract a plant to Illinois. Even though following a different calculation method, the number obtained by these authors may provide an additional reference to be compared with the results achieved for Ford's plant in Camaçari. Table 6 reports the incentives package given to the aforementioned companies, as well as the results found in the second scenario formerly described.

As can be seen, the total incentives given to Ford Motor Company in Bahia are by far the largest in absolute terms. They are more than three times the incentives given both to Mercedes-Benz and GM, and even much higher than the incentives given to Mitsubishi in Illinois[40] and to Renault in Paraná (in this last case, however, one must take into account that the *fiscal incentives* are clearly underestimated, because they do not include the benefits given to suppliers, considered in all other situations). The extent of the incentives helps in understanding why smaller states could not compete for the project, since the total incentives might reach very high proportions of their respective budgets. Even in the case of Bahia, the incentives are still significant for the state budget and might affect the public investment capacity in future years.

Considering the whole assistance package vis-à-vis total investment, the incentives given to Ford Motor Company are not especially high in contrast when compared with the other cases in Brazil. In fact, the relative incentives granted to this firm (equivalent to 68% of the investment) were lower than those given both to GM (127%) and to Mercedes-Benz (82%).[41] This conclusion was quite unforeseeable, because in spite of lower labor costs in Bahia, externalities and agglomeration economies in this state are lower than in the other two states, and the site chosen by

TABLE 6. Incentive Package: A Comparison (R$ Million; US$ Million to Mitsubishi)

	Ford (BA) (1)	Mercedes-Benz (MG)	GM (RS)	Renault (PR)	Mitsubishi (IL)
Fiscal Incentives	1,878	556	520	188 (Note 4)	160 (5)
Financial Incentives	331	85	98	0	24
Budget Incentives	193	51 (2)	141	165	60
Total Incentives	2,402	691	760 (3)	353 (4)	244
Investment	3,515	845	600	1,000	680
Total Incentives/ Investment	68%	82%	127%	35%	36%
Share of Fiscal Incentives in Total Incentives	78%	80%	69%	53%	66%
Source	Prepared by the authors	Alves (2001, pp. 58-66).	Alves (2001, p. 14 and pp. 67-75).	Alves (2001, pp. 75-79).	Chapman, Elhance, and, Wenum (1995, pp. 19, 26-7).

Note 1: Results refer to simulation using similar conditions as used by Alves (2001) to make the results comparable.
Note 2: Refers only to land cost; does not include infrastructure.
Note 3: Incentives calculated using the conditions before the renegotiation between GM and Rio Grande do Sul's government. According to RS government staff, the total incentives could be R$ 103 million lower (Alves, p. 77-78).
Note 4: Fiscal incentives do not include the ones given to suppliers. Total incentives could be much higher (Alves, 2001, p. 79).
Note 5: US$ 29.7 million in federal incentives are not considered in this table.

Ford is also distant both from the major domestic market and the Mercosur countries. All these circumstances together would suggest that the relative incentives in Bahia might be higher than those offered in southern or southeastern states (such as Rio Grande do Sul and Minas Gerais). The results, however, could be explained by three complementary hypotheses:

- Negotiations do not involve just material incentives but also certain intangible factors such as political stability and a reliable partnership.
- Coordination failures and imperfect understanding, along with the discontinuous nature of the opportunities of attracting large automobile plants, make it hard for state governments to know how far they should go in the negotiation process.[42]

- This particular project, designed to produce on a larger scale and export not only to Mercosur but also to northern countries (like Mexico, which represented three quarters of Ford exports from Bahia in 2002 and 2003, and around 68% of the automobile exports from the state in 2004) was not jeopardized by the competitive disadvantages of Bahia, which, on the contrary, presented compensations connected with its strategic geographic position and its harbor system.[43]

Another conclusion that can be drawn from Table 6 is that, as would be expected, the *fiscal incentives* are the most important, representing more the 65% in all cases–except for Renault, since its *fiscal incentives* are underestimated. This fact is especially important as not only the benefits that the project might create are strongly associated with its success, but so also are the effects it might generate for the state's accounts. In other words, it means that if the project fails, there would be no benefits to the state, but the total cost (strictly from the state's point of view) would also be reduced.

6. ECONOMIC BENEFITS

Estimating the economic impacts of such a large investment is certainly not an easy task, because several issues have to be taken into consideration simultaneously. In addition, some effects may be asymmetrically distributed over time, making their estimate even harder. Finally, it may be quite difficult to distinguish real and false expectations and to predict authentic results, for many things are uncertain and highly dependent of other related and doubtful issues. Despite these caveats, some previous studies analyzed and estimated the impacts of automobile industry investments in Brazil. Most of them were particularly concerned with the relationship between investment, economic growth rates and employment, as per Haddad and Hewings (1999), and Alban, Souza and Ferro (2000).

Although many impacts are to be felt in the future, it is already possible to measure some outcomes of the factory's operation. According to data issued by Ford itself in August 2004, i.e., when the plant began to operate at full capacity, the assembly plant, together with the 33 first tier suppliers already installed in the state, employed 7,039 workers (more than 40% above the 5,000 jobs mentioned when the project was announced). However, direct employment should not be considered the main benefit of the project. Because of the increasing capital intensity of the automobile industry, the total investment and, as a consequence, the total incentives per direct job are definitely very high. A rough calculation indicates that the cost to the state of each job created is around R$ 375 thousand.[44] Of course, there are less expensive ways of creating direct jobs, such as the support given to widely-recognized, labor-intensive small and medium enterprises, especially in some specific sectors.[45] It could be argued as well that the amount spent by the state could be allocated directly to social assistance. Although a similar argument could have also been evoked in the seventies, when Fiat was installed in Minas Gerais, today, after the structural changes that have taken place in the local economy and the subsequent development path of the state, this line of reasoning would hardly be defendable.

In effect, the main benefit the project can bring to Bahia is not direct job creation, but a genuine structural change that connects the local offer of intermediary supplies to the final goods production industry, establishing solid backward and forward linkages among different segments of the production chain located in the state. This would be a worthwhile step forward, which could trigger a vigorous growth cycle and place the local economy in an advanced stage of development.[46] This is the reason why the estimates based upon the preexisting input-output relationships cannot capture all the benefits the project might generate for the state. Because these forecasts take into consideration an exogenously defined input-output matrix or other equivalent representation of the productive structure in order to reach their results, they are not able to capture changes in the input-output matrix itself. Of course, it does not hinder the possibility of testing the impacts of the project based upon ad hoc alterations in the economic structure in order to evaluate the sensitivity of some variables (such as employment and income) to these changes. This seems to be an important subject for future research.

Nevertheless, some changes in the economic structure of Bahia can, to some extent, already be noticed as the official statistics begin to include the project data. Between 1999 and 2004, while Brazilian GDP grew 13.1%, the cumulative GDP growth rate in Bahia was 19.5%. This performance can partly be credited to the vehicle manufacture growth rates in 2003 and 2004, which raised the share of the sector in the total manufacture production in Bahia from 6.5% in 2003, to 13.3% in 2004.[47] Based on these data, it is possible to estimate the share of the car manufacturing sector in Bahia GDP in 2003 at almost 2.1%. In 2004, although the numbers were not yet officially available, this share is likely to be greater than 4.6%. Moreover, automobile exports by now represent about 16% of total Bahian export values, contributing significantly to the increase of the state's share of durable goods exports in the total exports of the country.

Together with these direct effects on GDP and exports, the project also increased Bahia's attractiveness to other important firms, which have already announced their interest to operate in the state. This is the case for two big tires producers (*Continental do Brasil* and *Bridgestone/Firestone*), along with other smaller automotive supply manufacturers. Together, these announced investments represent something near R\$ 3.0 billion from 2002 onward. Some technological spillover may be expected as well, because Ford Motor Company has already set up its Product Creation Center (housing 300 engineers), and an advanced technological center (Integrated Center of Manufacturing and Technology–Cimatec) was inaugurated in 2002 in a partnership involving the Industry Association of the State of Bahia (FIEB), the state government and other partners. Finally, qualitative institutional and cultural changes involving organization structures and business environment are likely to occur, along with changes in the labor market. These are not really consolidated trends, but still indicate a potential movement that should be investigated and followed with attention.

7. CONCLUSIONS

This paper has addressed two main interrelated issues: the reasons behind Ford Motor Company's location decision to install a plant in Bahia, and the impacts of the project on the state's economy. Based upon a discussion about the automobile industry and its main location factors in the 1990s, it has been argued that behind Ford's decision to establish a plant far from the economic center of Brazil are not only the incentives package offered to the company, but also the 1999 Mercosur crisis and the global strategies of the automobile corporation itself. After the devaluation of the Brazilian currency in January 1999, perspectives concerning the performance of the Southern Common Market seriously deteriorated, and might have spurred Ford Motor Company's decision to give up on installing a plant in the Brazil's southernmost state. The fact that the plant installed in Bahia is two times bigger than the one originally announced to be installed in Rio Grande do Sul suggests that what really happened was not a project relocation (as a result of territorial competition among Brazilian states), but rather a shift in the company's business plans. While the plant that was meant to be installed in Rio Grande do Sul seemed to have been designed for the Mercosur market, the larger scale one established in Bahia seems not only to have been planned for the internal and Mercosur markets, but also to take advantage of exports to northern countries such as Mexico.

This does not mean that the incentives offered to Ford Motor Company to install the plant in Bahia did not play an important role in its location decision, nor that the present value of these incentives is not extremely significant in monetary terms. After having segmented the incentives into three main parts (*fiscal, financial* and *budget incentives*), and having made several assumptions about the future behavior of the variables associated with them, the present value of the incentives in the year of reference was estimated at R\$ 2,642 million, or 75% of the total investment. It was shown that the largest part of the incentives was due to fiscal support, which represented more than three quarters of the total value. This calculation indicates that the total costs the project creates for the state are strongly affected by the success of the project itself, since the *fiscal incentives* are proportional to the volume of production.

Although extremely high in absolute terms, in relative terms (i.e., considering the total incentives divided by the investment), however, the incentives given to Ford Motor Company, calculated using the same assumptions employed to estimate their value for three other automobile projects in Brazil during the 1990s, are not especially substantial. This reinforces the argument that the incentives were not the only factor behind Ford Motor Company's decision to install its plant in Camaçari. Moreover, there seems to be no clear reason why the incentives (in relative terms) are higher in Rio Grande do Sul than in Bahia. This suggests the existence of coordination failures, indicating that state governments involved in territorial competition do not have enough information to set the maximum incentives they are about to offer.

As a final point, the economic impacts are supposed to go beyond short run growth rates and employment. As was shown, short run impacts on employment levels are in fact quite reduced when compared with the cost of the incentives. It was argued, however, that the main benefit the project might create for the state is a genuine structural change that connects the local offer of intermediary supplies to the final goods production industry, establishing backward and forward linkages between different segments of the production chain in the state, as was observed in Minas Gerais' experience with Fiat.[48] Of course, the economic impacts of the project are directly associated with the success of the plant, and also with the events that may affect Ford Motor Company's performance all over the world. Up to this time, the project is succeeding, and the cars produced in Camaçari have been well accepted by the market. Nonetheless, Bahia's economic trajectory is naturally exposed to the risks and uncertainties associated with this specific project, and the factors behind its success or failure go far beyond the state's control.

To sum up, in an environment characterized by the absence of a national policy of regional development, and by coordination failures that have exacerbated the territorial competition among states, incentives seem to be the cost to be paid to promote structural change. As pointed out by Baer (2001, p. 363), "left to the forces of the market, the allocation of resources will probably favor the Southeast and South of Brazil."

NOTES

1. This amount was equivalent to R$ 3.515 billion at the time the investment was made, according to official information.

2. Data about Brazilian states' GDP can be found on the web page of the Brazilian Institute of Geography and Statistics (http://www.ibge.gov.br).

3. The modularization concept is strongly related to the idea of communalizing platforms and standardizing designs at the global level (Humphrey and Salerno, 2000, p. 149). The automobile assembler, in this case, is supposed to work with the same first-tier suppliers at several locations around the world, setting up strategies referred to as follow design (which means the use of the same design as much as possible across different markets) and follow sourcing (which means the use of one single supplier for a specific part or system across all markets where it is needed).

4. As defined by Humphrey and Salerno (2000, p. 158), an industrial condominium is formed when the assembler sets the facilities of the main suppliers around its factory. The assembler in such an arrangement defines which part or modules will be produced, chooses the supplier, and stipulates that suppliers must construct dedicated plants. As they operate on the same site and build up mutual dependency relationships involving a kind of hierarchical network, the assembler plans all the supplier facilities as part of its plant development strategy.

5. This includes cars, light commercial and heavy commercial vehicles. Most of this growth is due to car production.

6. It is interesting to point out that the same authors admitted that a "considerable and effective integration of auto industries of Argentina and Brazil was achieved by 1998" (Humphrey and Oeter, 2000, p. 2), which strongly indicates that some important changes occurred.

7. A detailed description of the "New Automotive Regime" can be found in Negri (1999).

8. Compared to the "New Automotive Regime," the so-called "Special Automotive Regime" enlarged federal tax incentives, especially those related to imports.

9. Although investments, planned capacities and job creation are usually based upon ex-ante announced data, and jobs may also in some cases include direct suppliers,

the list can provide a basis for understanding the location patterns observed in the automobile industry in Brazil in the 1990s.

10. For a detailed description of the automobile investment attraction policies adopted in Brazil during this period, see Shapiro (1994).

11. The regional policies conducted by the federal government were based upon institutions that sustained differential conditions to support the poorest regions' development, and upon the use of large fiscal instruments, surrounded by significant direct investments.

12. The promulgation of the new Constitution in 1988, which increased the states' autonomy, also contributed to the fiscal competition in focus.

13. Camaçari is the municipality where Ford built its plant. The city is in the metropolitan region of Salvador, the capital of the state of Bahia.

14. Also MMC Automotores, a Mitsubishi licensed plant, was built outside the mentioned polygonal area. It is, however, a small investment to produce light commercial vehicles. Moreover, the investment was located in Catalão, a city in Goiás close to the Uberlândia (MG) region.

15. The share of Ford in the automobile industry's revenue in Brazil fell from 20% in 1980 to 7% in 1996 (McKinsey Global Institute, 1998, pp. 11-12).

16. "O Estado de São Paulo," June 16, 1999.

17. The Special Automotive Regime, no longer valid in 1999, was revived due to successful political pressure applied by the representatives of this state.

18. The announced investment included first tier suppliers' investments; and the values have been converted to Brazilian currency based upon the 1999 average US Dollar rate.

19. In 1999, the state's GDP was around R$ 42 billion (http://www.ibge.gov.br/home/estatistica/economia/contasregionais/2001/tab02.pdf).

20. In the second half of the 1990s, the state government tried unsuccessfully to attract other automobile plants to Bahia (Asia Motors, Hyundai and Skoda).

21. It is important to remember that, at the same time, pressures for the creation of ALCA had increased.

22. These data refer to the period prior to the beginning of Ford's operations in the state. Data about the composition of Bahia's GDP can be found on the web page of the official statistic institute of the state (http://www.sei.ba.gov.br).

23. The political dividends associated with the attraction of a large project to the state have to be also considered a good reason for the assertive policies implemented.

24. Currently, the productivity level estimated for Ford's plant in Bahia is around 31.6 cars/employee/year. This level is higher than the Brazilian index average (23.1 vehicles/employee/year) shown in Table 1.

25. Over the course of the 1990s, most carmakers progressively outsourced their supplies, but union opposition always prevented them from contracting out final assembly, especially to the US. In Bahia, Ford would try some different methods, which could be extended to other new plants in emerging markets, depending on their success (Ford to farm out key jobs in final assembly, 1999).

26. Between the first and the last versions of this paper, the agreement between the state of Bahia and Ford Motor Company was reviewed. The changes, however, seem to have a relatively small and negative effect on the present value of the incentives package. As a result, the estimates presented henceforth can be considered conservative.

27. This is essentially what came to be called in Brazil the 34/18 System and, later on, the Finor System.

28. A discussion of these instruments and their fiscal implications can be found in Varsano (1997).

29. According to the Brazilian Constitution, from the total VAT collected by the states, 25% must be directed to the municipalities, 18.75% to a fund for education (actually, 25% of the remaining 75%) and 5.25% (actually, 7% of the remaining 75%) to a fund for health. Although the constitutional obligations do not add up to 100%, it was conservatively assumed here that all fiscal incentives generate costs to the state.

30. This means that the state government pays for the differences between the market interest rates and the lower interest rates settled upon in the agreement.

31. Although production began only in 2001, imports through the state began in 2000. According to State Law no. 7.537, these imports also benefit from the *fiscal incentives*, as they refer to the total income.

32. The negative sign is because no debts are due on exports, but there remain fiscal credits on raw materials acquired. As a result, the more the company exports, the fewer *fiscal incentives* are given by the state, as the taxes are, in any case, not due on export operations.

33. The Fischer effect deals with the fact that the differences between the real and the nominal interest rates should consider the accumulated inflation rate in the period.

34. This is the value mentioned by the agreement signed by Ford Motor Company and the state government. As the announced investment was US$ 1.9 billion (including the first-tiers suppliers' investments), a 1.85 R$: 1.00 US$ exchange rate was used to convert the values. This is approximately the average exchange rate in 2000, when the bulk of the investments were supposed to have taken place.

35. These numbers are roughly consistent not only with the ones actually observed in 2002, 2003 and 2004, but also with the projected production announced by the company for 2005.

36. To estimate $P_{l,i}$ and $P_{M,i}$, two kinds of vehicles were considered: a lower price car (Fiesta, whose average price in 2000 was around R$ 17,000), and a medium price car (Ecosport, whose price ranged, in 2003, between R$ 31,100 and 47,590; the average price of this car in 2000 was considered to be R$ 35,000). Although originally the Fiesta should represent 80% of total vehicle production, the production mix observed in October 2003 was considered. In this case, the Fiesta represents only 60% of total vehicle production. This mix of production was considered for both $P_{l,i}$ and $P_{M,i}$ to avoid underestimating the incentives package.

37. Based upon the values of the incentives effectively observed in past years (the source for these data was the Development Agency of the State of Bahia–Desenbahia).

38. This group was called the "Ford Executive Group" and lasted until 2003.

39. If the incentives on vehicle imports in 2000 and 2001 (i.e., before plant start up) were also considered, the present values of the hidden costs in 2000 would have reached R$ 1,036 million in the first scenario.

40. Even considering that this amount was given in 1986, it is certainly smaller than the incentives given to Ford Motor Company in Bahia. Taking into consideration both the inflation rates and the exchange rates in the period between 1986 and 2000, it is estimated that the incentives given to Mitsubishi did not reach 30% of the incentives given to Ford.

41. Again, the underestimated values reported for Renault (35%) do not permit any comparison with this case. Not surprisingly, the incentives given to Mitsubishi in Illinois (36%) are the smallest (excluding Renault data).

42. This is essentially the point of view of Braybrooke and Lindblom (1970), who argue: "decisions marked by large change and quite imperfect understanding are not rare, even if they are not the typical instrument of policy-making. Nor are such decisions made only in error or by foolish decision-makers. On the contrary, some decisions are sometimes inescapable, forced on decision-makers by circumstances. In addition, such decisions are sometimes deliberately taken by decision-makers because the potential rewards seem attractive enough to outweigh the perils posed by imperfect understanding."

43. In 2002, more than 35% of Ford's exports (in units) from Brazil were already shipped from Bahia.

44. If the indirect jobs were considered, this cost would be much lower, but even then there is no evidence that this would be the least expensive way of creating jobs in the short run.

45. Teixeira and Vasconcelos (1999) are also sceptical about the impacts of automobile assemblers on direct employment.

46. As mentioned before, attracting final goods production has become, at least since the beginning of the 1990s, one of the major purposes of the state's industrial development strategy.

47. The authors would like to thank Gustavo Pessoti (SEI), who provided recent information about the car manufacturing sector not yet available on the web page of the official statistics institute of the state of Bahia (http://www.sei.ba.gov.br).

48. For information about Fiat in Minas Gerais, see Lemos et al. (2000) and Montero (2001).

REFERENCES

Alban, M., Souza, C., and Ferro, J. R. (2000) "O Projeto Amazon e seus Impactos na RMS." Salvador: Seplantec. *Mimeo.*

Alves, M. A. da S. (2001). "Guerra Fiscal e Finanças Federativas no Brasil: O Caso do Setor Automotivo." *Master's Thesis.* Campinas: Universidade Estadual de Campinas/ Instituto de Economia.

Anfavea. "Anuário Estatístico da Indústria Automobilística Brasileira 2002." Accessed on Oct. 7, 2003. Available at: <http://www.anfavea.com.br.>

Anfavea. "Anuário Estatístico da Indústria Automobilística Brasileira 2004." Accessed on Mar. 11, 2005. Available at: <http://www.anfavea.com.br.>

Baer, W. (2001). "The Brazilian Economy: Growth and Development." 5th edition. Westport: Praeger.

Baer, W., Cavalcanti, T., and Silva, P. (2002). "Economic Integration without Policy Coordination: The Case of Mercosur." *Emerging Markets Review*, Vol. 3, pp. 269-291.

Bahia. "Lei N. 7.537 de 28 de outubro de 1999." Accessed on Oct. 6, 2003. Available at: <http://www.bahia.ba.gov.br.>

Braybrooke, D., and Lindblom, C. E. (1970). "A Strategy of Decision: Policy Evaluation as a Social Process." New York: The Free Press.

Brown, T. (2002). "Ford may Ship Brazil-Built Vehicles to US. *Reuters*, Jul. 2. Accessed on Sept.10, 2003. Available at <http://www.labournet.net/world/0202/fordus1.html.>

Chapman, M. L., Elhance, A. P., and Wenum, J. D. (1995). "Mitsubishi Motors in Illinois: Global Strategies, Local Impacts." Westport, Conn.: Quorum Books.

Consórcio Intecsa–Inarsa–Concremat–JW–Boursheid (2003). "Estudo Prospectivo do Impacto Sócio-Econômico da Implantação da Montadora Ford em Camaçari e seus Reflexos em Municípios da Região Metropolitana de Salvador." *Mimeo.*

Diniz, C. C. (1993). "Desenvolvimento Poligonal no Brasil: Nem Desconcentração, nem Contínua Polarização." *Nova Economia.* Belo Horizonte: FACE/UFMG, Vol. 3, No. 1, pp. 35-64.

Ford to Farm Out Key Jobs in Final Assembly: Carmaker's Chief Executive Sees Move as the Model for Future Manufacturing. (1999). *Financial Times*, Aug. 4.

Freyssenet, M., and Lung, Y. (2000). "Between Globalisation and Regionalisation: What is the Future of the Motor Industry?" In John Humphrey et al. (Eds.), *Global Strategies and Local Realities: The Auto Industry in Emerging Markets.* pp. 72-94. New York: St. Martin's Press.

Greenstone, M., and Moretti, E. (2003). "Bidding for Industrial Plants: Does Winning a 'Million Dollar Plant' Increase Welfare?" *Working Paper 9844*, National Bureau of Economic Research.

Haddad, E. A., and Hewings, G. J. D. (1999). "The Short-Run Regional Effects of New Investments and Technological Upgrade in the Brazilian Automobile Industry: An Interregional Computable General Equilibrium Analysis." *Oxford Development Studies*, Vol. 27, No. 3, pp. 359-383.

Humphrey, J., Lecler, Y., and Salerno, M. S. (2000). "Introduction." In John Humphrey et al. (Eds.), *Global Strategies and Local Realities: The Auto Industry in Emerging Markets.* pp. 1-15. New York: St. Martin's Press.

Humphrey, J., and Oeter, A. (2000). "Motor Industry Policies in Emerging Markets: Globalisation and Promotion of Domestic Industry." In John Humphrey et al. (Eds.), *Global Strategies and Local Realities: The Auto Industry in Emerging Markets.* pp. 42-71. New York: St. Martin's Press.

Humphrey, J., and Salerno, M. S. (2000). "Globalisation and Assembler-Supplier Relations: Brazil and India." John Humphrey et al. (Eds.), *Global Strategies and Local Realities: The Auto Industry in Emerging Markets.* pp. 149-175. New York: St. Martin's Press.

Klier, T. H. (1998). "Geographic Concentration in U.S. Manufacturing: Evidence from the U.S. Supplier Industry." *Working Paper.* December. Federal Reserve Bank of Chicago.

Lemos, M. B. et al. (2000). "O Arranjo Produtivo da Rede Fiat de Fornecedores: Arranjos e Sistemas Produtivos Locais e as Novas Políticas de Desenvolvimento Industrial e Tecnológico. Estudos Empíricos." Nota Técnica 15, Relatório Final. Rio de Janeiro: Instituto de Economia da Universidade Federal Rio de Janeiro.

Mckinsey Global Institute (1998). "Productivity: The Key to an Accelerated Development Path for Brazil." With the assistance of M. Abreu, E. Bacha and J. Scheinkman and contributions from A. C. Pinheiro. São Paulo, Washington: McKinley Brazil Office.

Montero, A. P. (2001). "Making and Remaking 'Good Government' in Brazil: Subnational Industrial Policy in Minas Gerais." *Journal of Interamerican Studies*, Vol. 43, No. 2, pp. 49-80.

Negri, J. A. de. (1999). "O Custo do Bem-Estar do Regime Automotivo Brasileiro." *Pesquisa e Planejamento Econômico*, Vol. 29, No. 2, pp. 215-242.

O Estado de São Paulo, various issues.

Ó hUallacháin, B., and Wasserman, D. (1999). "Vertical Integration in a Lean Supply Chain: Brazilian Automobile Component Parts." *Economic Geography*, Vol. 75, No. 1, pp. 21-42.

Rodríguez-Pose, A., and Arbix, G. (2001). "Strategies of Waste: Bidding Wars in the Brazilian Automotive Sector." *International Journal of Urban and Regional Research*, March, Vol. 25, No. 1, pp. 134-154.

Rubenstein, J. M. (1986). "Changing Distribution of the American Automobile Industry." *Geographical Review*, July, Vol. 76, No. 3, pp. 288-300.

Santos, A. M. M., and Pinhão, C. M. A. (1999). "Pólos Automotivos Brasileiros." *BNDES Setorial*, September, No. 10, pp. 173-200. Rio de Janeiro: BNDES.

Shapiro, H. (1994). "Engines of Growth: The State and Transnational Auto Companies in Brazil." New York: Cambridge University Press.

Studer-Noguez, I. (2002). "Ford and the Global Strategies of Multinationals: The North American Auto Industry." New York: Routledge.

Teixeira, F. L. C., and Vasconcelos, N. (1999). "Mudanças Estruturais e Inovações Organizacionais na Indústria Automotiva." *Conjuntura e Planejamento,* November, No. 66. pp. 17-24.

Varsano, R. (1997). "A Guerra Fiscal do ICMS: Quem Ganha e Quem Perde." *Planejamento e Políticas Públicas*, July, No. 15, pp. 3-18.

Womack, J. P., Jones, D. T., and Ross, D. (1990). "The Machine that Changed the World." New York: Basic Books.

Zauli, E. M. (2000). "Políticas Públicas e Targeting Setorial: Efeitos da Nova Política Industrial sobre o Setor Automotivo Brasileiro." *Revista de Economia Política*, July-September, Vol. 20, No. 3, pp. 76-94.

doi:10.1300/J140v07n03_02

Fiscal Incentives
and Regional Development Projects:
Mercedes-Benz in Juiz de Fora (MG)–
Brazil 1996/1999

Fernando Salgueiro Perobelli
Eduardo Amaral Haddad
Suzana Quinet de A Bastos
Edgard Pimentel

SUMMARY. The principal aim of this paper is to analyze the Mercedes-Benz project in the municipality of Juiz de Fora (Minas Gerais state). This will be accomplished in two ways. First we will analyze the use of fiscal incentives, at both the state and municipal level, which were used in the negotiation with Mercedes-Benz Corporation. Second, through an input-output exercise we will measure the impact of the Mercedes-Benz unit upon the other productive sectors located in Juiz de Fora, the rest of Minas Gerais state and the rest of Brazil. It is important to emphasize that we will measure these impacts in two steps: (a) the construction of the production unit: we will use the fiscal incentives (e.g.,

---

Fernando Salgueiro Perobelli is affiliated with the Federal University of Juiz de Fora, Minas Gerais, Brazil. Eduardo Amaral Haddad is affiliated with the University of São Paulo, São Paulo, Brazil. Suzana Quinet de A Bastos is affiliated with the Federal University of Juiz de Fora, Minas Gerais, Brazil. Edgard Pimentel is Research Assistant, FEA/USP, Brazil.

[Haworth co-indexing entry note]: "Fiscal Incentives and Regional Development Projects: Mercedes-Benz in Juiz de Fora (MG)–Brazil 1996/1999." Perobelli, Fernando Salgueiro et al. Co-published simultaneously in *Latin American Business Review* (International Business Press, an imprint of The Haworth Press, Inc.) Vol. 7, No. 3/4, 2006, pp. 49-75; and: *Latin American Business: Equity Distortion in Regional Resource Allocation in Brazil* (ed: Werner Baer, and Geoffrey Hewings) International Business Press, an imprint of The Haworth Press, Inc., 2006, pp. 49-75. Single or multiple copies of this article are available for a fee from The Haworth Document Delivery Service [1-800-HAWORTH, 9:00 a.m. - 5:00 p.m. (EST). E-mail address: docdelivery@haworthpress.com].

budget benefits) offered to Mercedes-Benz (1996), and (b) the forecast production for the first year of operation: we will use the forecast of Class A production–40,000 units for 1999–to implement the shock.

RESUMEN. El principal propósito de este estudio consiste en analizar el proyecto de Mercedes-Benz en la municipalidad de Juiz de Fora (Estado de Minas Gerais), que se ejecutará desde dos enfoques. Primero, analizaremos el uso de los incentivos fiscales, tanto al nivel del estado como de la municipalidad, que se utilizaron durante la negociación con la corporación Mercedes-Benz. Segundo, a través de un ejercicio de entrada-salida, mediremos el impacto que la unidad de Mercedes-Benz tendrá sobre otros sectores productivos que operan en Juiz de Fora, y el resto del Estado de Minas Gerais y Brasil como un todo. Consideramos importante hacer hincapié que realizaremos dichas mediciones en dos etapas: (a) la construcción de la unidad de producción: cuando utilizaremos los incentivos fiscales (Ej.: beneficios presupuestarios) ofrecidos a Mercedes-Benz (1996), (b) producción estimada para el primer año de funcionamiento: cuando utilizaremos las proyecciones elaboradas para una producción Clase A–40.000 unidades para 1999 para calcular el impacto del cambio.

RESUMO. Este estudo tem por objetivo principal analisar o projeto da Mercedes-Benz no município de Juiz de Fora (Minas Gerais). Isto será implementado de duas maneiras. Primeiro analisaremos os incentivos fiscais, nos níveis estadual e municipal, que foram usados na negociação com a Mercedes-Benz Corporation. Segundo, através de um exercício de entrada-saída, mediremos o impacto da unidade da Mercedes-Benz sobre os demais setores produtivos localizados em Juiz de Fora, o resto do estado de Minas Gerais e o resto do Brasil. É importante enfatizar que mediremos esses impactos em duas etapas: (a) a construção da unidade de produção: usaremos os incentivos fiscais (por exemplo, benefícios orçamentários) oferecidos à Mercedes-Benz (1996); (b) produção prevista para o primeiro ano de operação: usaremos a previsão de produção de Classe A–40.000 unidades para 1999–para implementar a mudança. doi:10.1300/J140v07n03_03

KEYWORDS. Input-output, Mercedes-Benz case and fiscal incentives

1. INTRODUCTION

The principal aim of this paper is to analyze the Mercedes-Benz project in the municipality of Juiz de Fora (MG). This will be accomplished in two ways. First we will analyze the use of fiscal incentives, both at the state and municipality level, which were used in the negotiation with Mercedes-Benz Corporation. Second, through an input-output exercise we will measure the impact of the Mercedes-Benz unit upon the other productive sectors located in Juiz de Fora, the rest of Minas Gerais state and the rest of Brazil. It is important to emphasize that we will measure these impacts in two steps: (a) the construction of the production unit: we will use the fiscal incentives (e.g., budget benefits) offered to Mercedes-Benz (1996); (b) a forecast of production for the first year of operation: we will use the forecast of Class A production–40,000 units for 1999 to implement the shock.

The paper is presented as follows: after the introduction, the second part presents a brief history of the fiscal incentives used by the state of Minas Gerais to promote regional development; the third part presents an analysis of the recent period of Minas Gerais's fiscal incentives and of the Juiz de Fora fiscal incentives; the fourth part contains an analysis of the Mercedes-Benz project, and the fifth part presents some conclusions.

2. FISCAL INCENTIVES IN THE STATE OF MINAS GERAIS

2.1. First Period (1969-1985)

The use of fiscal instruments to attract investments at the state level is not a recent phenomenon. In Minas Gerais, the policy of fiscal and financial incentives began in 1969. Law 5261 made the state sales tax "ICM" the principal instrument for promoting the industrialization process. The main objective of this law was to use 40% of the sales tax (ICM) generated in the following manner: (a) 25.6% was to be used as compensation for the investments made in the state for firms that had their process approved; (b) 4% was to go to the Minas Gerais state development bank; and (c) 2.4% was to go to the João Pinheiro Foundation in order to finance institutional research. The firms that were able to benefit from the law were those that had opened a new industrial plant in the state and those that upgraded their output without decreasing the existing levels of production (Oliveira and Duarte Filho, 1997).

It is important to emphasize that in 1973 Law 6196 was implemented in order to maximize the impact of the state's fiscal incentives policy. The projects that took advantage of this law were those that were given high priority. Such priority was evaluated according to the following criteria: the value of the projected investment, the importance of the investment to the de-concentration of economic activities in the state, the integration of the productive structure, the use of raw materials and regional inputs and, finally, the employment created in specific areas.[1]

The restrictions imposed by the federal government for using the state sales tax *"ICM"* as an incentive instrument to promote industrialization (Law 24/75) induced the Minas Gerais state government to adopt new fiscal incentives programs. Among these programs we can highlight the Fund for Industrialization (FAI), which was established by Law 6875/76. The FAI was a fund that had the state's budget as its principal source of financial support. New plants and improvement in existing industrial plants are supported by the fund.

In 1983 the state created the Social and Economic Development Fund (FUNDES), whose purpose was to integrate all of the state's financial programs. The sources of financial support for this fund were: (a) a budget endowment; (b) resources from credit operations, both internal and external; (c) a fixed share from taxes levied by the Union that were to be transferred to the state; (d) yields from temporary investments and from state financial resources; and (e) interest and other resources from funding and from investment income bonds.

In August 1985 the state government created the "GT-Incentives" for companies that settled in the state, enabling them to possibly increase the time period they needed to pay the state sales tax (ICM), and it also offered some tax alleviation to companies that bought raw materials within the state.

2.2. Second Period (1989-1993)[2]

The second period of fiscal incentives policy in Minas Gerais was initiated in 1989 with the implementation of the Pro-Industry program. This period was characterized by a lack of concern about the spatial and sectoral problems incurred during the process of development. In other words, the sole aim was to promote the state's industrial growth. The principal instrument that the Pro-Industry program used for promoting development was to increase the term of payment of the state sales tax (ICMS) by companies that opened a unit or increased their productive capacity in the state.

In 1993, with the introduction of law 34.504, the PROIM (Program of Industrial Modernization) was created. Its objectives were: (a) the development and modernization of priority sectors and (b) the funding of high-tech companies and key sectors.

3. RECENT REGIONAL DEVELOPMENT STRATEGIES

3.1. State Strategies

The strategies for promoting industrial development, and which were implemented after 1994 by the state of Minas Gerais, had the Integrated Development Plan for Minas Gerais (PMDI) as their principal instrument. The objective of this plan was the transformation of the Minas Gerais economy through: (a) structural programs, (b) public policies and (c) priority sectoral programs. The plan was based on the adoption of public policies both in the social area (health, education, etc.) and in the development of infrastructure (for industry and trade, science and technology, and urban and regional development). Thus, the plan's aim was to enhance the region's endogenous capacity and also to promote investments in a specific sub-region (e.g., Mercedes-Benz) (PMDI, 1994).

In other words, the PMDI was a plan that brought together all social agents (e.g., government, non-governmental organizations) in order to maintain the growth process of the most developed regions and also to improve the development process of the poorest ones. (Perobelli et al., 1997).

The expected result was an increase in the state GDP and, as a consequence, an improvement in the state per-capita income. In spatial terms, the plan had as an objective the promotion of industrial development towards the periphery, in other words, the promotion of a de-concentration in the Belo Horizonte metropolitan area (PMDI, 1994).

3.1.1. Fiscal Instruments

To guarantee that the new state development strategy was implemented, the fiscal instruments underwent some changes. Among these changes, the most import was Law 11.393 (Industry Incentive Fund–FIND). This fund entailed all the legislation of the Pro-Industry program and the PROIM (Induction of Industrial Modernization Program). The main modifications in those programs were:

- *Pro-Industry–Industry Diversification and Integration Program*

  a. funding working capital from 50% to 70% of state sales tax "ICMS" paid monthly, with an exemption of 12 to 36 months and a term of 5 to 10 years;
  b. implementing an inflation adjustment: IGP-M (Brazilian inflation index) with a reduction of 50% to 82%, depending on the region:
     *50%-Metropolitan area of Belo Horizonte, southern region and the Mineiran Triangle;
     *60%-*Zona da Mata, central region, Alto Parnaíba and the Midwest*;
     *70%-Northwest, *North and Vale do Rio Doce*;
     *82%-*bacias dos rios Jequitinhonha, São Mateus and Mucuri*;

- *PROIM–Industrial Modernization Program*

  a. Funding of fixed investments of up to 50% of the total investment forecast for the project, with a grace period of 36 months and an amortization of 60 months after the end of the grace period.

In 1996, with the increase in competition among Brazilian states for new investments, Minas Gerais introduced modifications to FIND. Among these modifications we can highlight the creation of the Strategic Industries Development Fund. (FUNDIEST).

- *The Strategic Industries Development Fund (FUNDIEST)*

This fund was created by Law 12.228/1996. Its objective was to give financial support for the development of specific sectors in the state. Among the programs that formed the fund we can highlight: (1) a program for funding support for the opening of strategic industries (Pro-Industry). This program can be characterized by: (a) the inclusion of sectors that would receive benefits: automobile and electronics, and (b) the funding of working capital up to 70% of the state sales tax "*ICMS*" debt, with an exemption of 36 to 120 months, and with a 10 year payment term (in 120 payments). These funds were to be made available to enterprises that made fixed investments of a minimum of R$150 million and created 500 direct jobs; (2) a program for agricultural industries (Pro-Agriculture); and (3) a program to improve the commercialization of strategic industries.[3]

3.2. Municipality Strategies

In recent years, the city of Juiz de Fora has had the General Plan of the Municipality as a principal instrument for its development. This plan was intended to stimulate the economic development of Juiz de Fora by increasing the city's income and employment. The plan contained three steps: (a) the diagnosis phase (potential development sectors and bottleneck areas that could have a negative impact on the development process), (b) the placing of the development of the municipality into a broader perspective and (c) the construction of development scenarios (Bastos, 2000).

3.2.1. Fiscal Instruments

The set of policy instruments used to stimulate the development of the municipality can be divided as follows:

- *Municipal Fund for the Development of Strategic Industries (FMDI)*. This fund was set up by Municipal Law 8.914/1996. It provides working capital for the development of economic activities that improve income and employment in the municipality, and it also aims to improve inter-sectoral interactions.
- *Law 7.771*. This law entails an exemption from municipal taxes: Municipal Property Taxes (IPTU), Municipal Service Taxes (ISS) and Municipal Transfer of Property Taxes (ITBI) spread over 10 years for firms that establish a plant in an industrial district. For those firms that open units outside the districts, the municipality will decide on tax exemptions on a case-by-case basis.
- *Law 8.717*. This law created the Municipal Development Fund. The principal source of this fund is the FAT (Transfer from Federal Government). This fund is for the improvement of micro and small companies in the municipality, and the resources will be used to buy equipment and provide working capital. The benefits will be for the industry, trade, service, technology-intensive sectors and agriculture. The limit for funding is R$ 50,000 and it must be repaid in 36 months at an interest rate of 8%.

4. THE MERCEDES-BENZ CASE

4.1. Contractual Aspects

The contract for the opening of the plant (Mercedes-Benz, 1996, pp. 2, 37-38) affirms that: *"Mercedes has the following obligations: (1) to* *make a fixed investment of a minimum of R$ 400 million; (b) to create direct employment, giving preference to local workers (. . .) reaching 1,500 direct jobs." The contract also obligates Mercedes-Benz:*

> (. . .) to make all efforts to buy inputs and business services, including the use of architectural firms and contractors, located in Minas Gerais. Sellers of inputs and business services will be chosen by Mercedes after an evaluation of the following factors: product and service quality and technology; the economic and financing situation of the input seller, product or service price. However, quality and technology will always have a greater weight over other factors; (. . .) to find input sellers that have incentives for a unit in Minas Gerais, preferably in Juiz de Fora, or in the surrounding area. (Mercedes-Benz, 1996, pp. 3-37–trans. ours)

Figure 1 presents the principal aspects of the contract signed by Mercedes-Benz, the Minas Gerais government and the local government.

4.2. Fiscal Benefits

The fiscal benefits of the Mercedes-Benz project can be divided into budget benefits (credit offered to the company before operations) and tax benefits (based on the state sales tax–ICMS). Figure 2 shows the incentives offered to the company.

4.3. Aspects of the Mercedes Unit

4.3.1.Suppliers Localization

In this section we will make an analysis of the spatial distribution of the suppliers of the Mercedes unit in Juiz de Fora (MG). The aim of this section is to verify, in a simple way, what the impact of opening the Mercedes-Benz in Juiz de Fora was in the short-run. The spatial distribution of the sellers will be analyzed between 1996 (construction of the production unit) and 1999[4] (the first year of production of Class A models).

The relation among the initial sellers and the unit located in Juiz de Fora can be classified in three ways: (a) *Follow Sourcing*;[5] (b) *Joint-Venture*;[6] and (c) *New*. The sellers are located mainly in the states of Minas Gerais and São Paulo, as shown in Table 1. The *just-in-time* method of production of the Mercedes unit makes use of three regional points in Brazil.[7]

FIGURE 1. Contract Signed by Mercedes-Benz, Minas Gerais Government and Municipality of Juiz de Fora

Donation	• **Land** • Area with 2.8 million m², with estimated value of R$ 50.51 million
Infrastructure	Urbanization of *Paraibuna* River Sanitary systems and drainage Road Access Parking Test track Electricity connections, water, natural gas and other facilities
Capital participation by state/municipal government	No information
Credit granted	FIND/PROIM–R$ 112.16 million for fixed and working capital • Adjusted for inflation • Interest rate 3.5% per year. • R$ 25 million with exemption of 12 months • R$ 80 million with exemption of 36 months **FUNDIEST/PRO-Industry**–R$ 16 million for fixed capital • Two payments: 03/1999 (60%) and 03/2000 (40%) • Without interest or adjustment for inflation • Exemption of 120 months • **FUNDIEST/Pro-structure** Value: number of vehicles imported and tradable by the company • Term: 10 years • Exemption: 10 years • Without interest or adjustment for inflation
Deferment of state sales tax (ICMS) payments	**FUNDIEST/PROE-Industry and FMDI** • Funding for working capital • State–7.75% on monthly revenues over 10 years • Municipality: 1.35% on monthly revenues up to the fourth year and 0.67% from the fifth through the tenth year. • Without interest or adjustment for inflation • Exemption of 120 months
Taxes exemptions granted	**Taxes** (IPTU, ISS, e ITBI) **municipal taxes.** • Term: 10 years
State government guarantees for credit facilities provided	**State:** R$ 101.9 mil. in CEMIG (a power utility) shares • Adjusted for inflation **Municipality:** R$ 3.1 mil. bond • Adjusted for inflation

Source: Bastos (2000)
Obs: Monetary values refer to 1996

These points work as a linkage between the sellers and the unit located in Juiz de Fora. The Brazilian cities where the consolidation centers are located are: São Bernardo do Campo (SP), which includes the sellers from the city of São Bernardo do Campo and those from the states of Paraná and Rio Grande do Sul; Betim (MG), which includes the sellers from Minas Gerais and the city of Campinas (SP); and Juiz de Fora (MG), which entails the sellers located at the Mercedes unit itself (Neves, Oliveira e Brandão, 2002).

FIGURE 2. Value of Incentives Offered to Mercedes-Benz (R$ 1000)

Budget Benefits	
Property	50,500.00
Infrastructure[1]	0.00
Credit for fixed and working capital	60,636.71
Credit for fixed capital	7,117.81
Credit for trade	16,757.79
Sub-Total	135,012.31
Tax Benefits	
Credit for fixed and working capital (discount)	555,535.44
Sub-Total	555,535.44
Overall Total	690,547.74

[1]The infrastructure indicated in Figure 1 was not included, because it was not a credit for the company, but was rather a cost that the state and local government was responsible for.
Source: Alves (2000)

TABLE 1. Class A–Distribution of Sellers

Locale	Items		Auto-parts		Sellers	
	Absolute Value	(%)	Absolute Value	(%)	Absolute Value	(%)
MG (except JF)	325	15.52	72	6.32	28	9.09
Juiz de Fora	172	8.21			10	3.25
São Paulo	610	29.13			70	22.73
Paraná	17	0.81			2	0.65
Rio Grande do Sul	9	0.43			3	0.97
Nacional (except JF)	961	45.89	737	64.71	103	33.44
Imported			330	28.97	92	29.87
Total	2094	100.00	1139	100.00	308	100.00

Source: Prepared by authors based in Mercedes-Benz publications.

At the beginning of its operations Mercedes had 94 Brazilian sellers. Among them, 10 were installed on a property alongside the Mercedes unit in Juiz de Fora. Table 2 presents the distribution of sellers by city. The cities with the highest concentration of sellers are: Juiz de Fora (10), the place where the Mercedes unit is located; São Paulo (12); São Bernardo do Campo (11), where one of the consolidation centers is located and a region with intense activity for the automobile sector; Lavras (05); Betim (04); and Campinas (04).

Table 2 enables us to affirm that there is a concentration of sellers in the metropolitan area of São Paulo, but there are some units in the interior (Campinas, Americana, Piracicaba, etc.), and there are also some in Minas Gerais (mainly in the metropolitan area of Belo Horizonte and the southern part of the state: Lavras, Santa Rita do Sapucaí, Varginha and Três Corações).

4.3.2. Production and Employment During the First Years of Operation

This section presents data about production and employment in order to characterize the first years of the Mercedes-Benz unit's operations in Juiz de Fora (MG).

Table 3 shows that production of the Juiz de Fora unit was below what had been forecast. The project forecast a production of 40,000 units for 1999 and 70,000 units for 2000.[8] However, effective production did not even reach 16,000 units during both years considered. In order to make up for excess capacity, the Juiz de Fora unit began to produce the Class C model (a model for export) in 2001. The forecast was 10,000 units per year. In 2003 the lack of production capacity was around 80%. This worsened at the beginning of 2004 with the end of

TABLE 2. Distribution of Mercedes-Benz Sellers by Municipality (1999)

City	No. of sellers
Juiz de Fora	10
São Paulo	12
São Bernardo do Campo	11
Lavras	05
Betim	04
Campinas	04
Caçapava	03
Porto Alegre	02
Buenos Aires	02
Jundiaí	02
Americana	02
Valinhos	02
Ibirité, Monte-Mor, Arujá, Guarulhos, Juatuba, São José dos Campos, Guararema, Araraquara, Hortolândia, Três Corações, Santa Rita do Sapucaí, Mauá, Rio Grande da Serra, Varginha, Barueri, Ribeirão Pires, Piracicaba, Itapecerica da Serra, Monte Alto, Cotia, Sete Lagoas, Osasco, Limeira and São Caetano do Sul	01

Source: Martins et al. (1998)

the production of the Class C model. The model Smart Formore (DaimlerChrysler), announced for 2006, was the principal project for the Juiz de Fora unit. However, in March 2005 the Smart Project was cancelled and the company awaited communication from Germany (Mercedes-Benz . . . , 2005).

Table 4 enables us to verify that the majority of employees were from Juiz de Fora, as was required by the contract signed by Mercedes-Benz and the state and local governments. However, Mercedes did not respect the minimum amount of 1,500 jobs stated in the contract as a counterpart to the budget and fiscal benefits offered by the state of Minas Gerais and by the local government. The decline in employment was due to the decrease in production.

4.4. An Analysis of the Impact of the Mercedes-Benz Unit in Juiz de Fora (MG)

4.4.1. Methodology and Database

The input-output framework is frequently used to analyze the impact of growth of one region or country upon the sectors of the economy. Impacts can be calculated through economic multipliers. These multipliers enable us to verify, as an example, the direct and indirect impacts of a change in the final demand of a specific sector upon sales, income and employment (Miller and Blair, 1984).

In the present paper the inter-regional input-output matrix for Minas Gerais and the rest of Brazil (BDMG e FIPE, 2002) is used. The impacts on Juiz de Fora could be calculated because the technical coefficients

TABLE 3. Effective Production and Sales (Class A Model)

Year	Production (Class A)	Sales (Internal Market)	Exports
1999	14307	9831	3521
2000	15682	12006	3622
2001	9041	8661	852
2002	8168	8088	496
2003	6989	-	-
2004	5560	-	-

Obs: 1999–production began in April
The Class A Model was exported to Mexico, Venezuela and Argentina
Source: Mercedes-Benz Brazil–1999 and 2000
DaimlerChrysler Brazil–2001, 2002 and 2003.

TABLE 4. Jobs (1999/2001)

Year	Total Employment	Employment origin	
		Juiz de Fora	*Other*
1999	1558	1058 (68%)	500
2000	1350	900 (72%)	350
2001	1529	nd	nd
2002	1114	nd	nd
2003	1098	nd	nd
2004	1060	nd	nd

Source: Bastos (2004)
OBS: nd–data not available

matrix and the Leontief Inverse were regionalized through the locational coefficients.[9]

4.4.1.1. Basic Input-Output Model

Normally, the input-output model describes the monetary flow of goods and services through the economy. All sectors purchase goods from other sectors and use these goods to produce final goods. Mathematically, these interactions can be represented as follows (e.g., Miller and Blair, 1984; Dorfman et al., 1986; Perobelli, 2004):

$$x_{11} + x_{12} + \cdots x_{1n} + y1 = X_1$$
$$x_{21} + x_{22} + \cdots x_{2n} + y2 = X_2$$
$$\vdots$$
$$x_{n1} + x_{n2} + \cdots x_{nn} + y_n = X_n \qquad (1)$$

where,

x_{ij}–Sales from sector i to sector j, $(i, j = 1,2,\ldots,n)$
y_i–final demand for goods from sector i, $(i = 1,2\ldots,n)$
X_i–total production of sector i, $(i = 1,2\ldots,n)$

The input-output framework shows that the intersectoral flows from *i* to *j* for a specific period depend completely and exclusively on the total production of sector *j* for the same period. Thus:

$$a_{ij} = \frac{x_{ij}}{X_j} \qquad (2)$$

Therefore, the equation system (1) that shows the interdependencies among the sectors can be rewritten as follows:

$$a_{11}X_1 + a_{12}X_2 + \cdots + a_{1n}X_n + y_1 = X_1$$
$$a_{21}X_1 + a_{22}X_2 + \cdots + a_{2n}X_n + y_2 = X_2$$
$$\vdots$$
$$a_{n1}X_1 + a_{n2}X_2 + \cdots + a_{nn}X_n + y_n = X_n$$

(3)

The following matrix can represent this equation system:

$$AX + Y = X \tag{4}$$

Where,

X = nx1 sectoral production vector
Y = nx1 final demand vector
A = nxn technical coefficients matrix

In order to verify the effects of a change in the final demand of the economy of a specific region, equation (4) can be rewritten as follows:

$$X = (I - A)^{-1}Y \tag{5}$$

Where,

I = identity matrix nxn

In order to verify which are the impacts from the project of opening a Mercedes-Benz unit in Juiz de Fora (MG) upon the sectoral production of Juiz de Fora, the rest of Minas Gerais and the rest of Brazil, we must implement a decomposition at final demand (Y component) in equation 5. In other words, we must make the investment component explicit in order to implement the exercise and thus calculate the impact upon the economy. This exercise will be implemented for: STEP I–the construction of the unit in Juiz de Fora (through a shock in the investment) and STEP II–the first year of operation, considering the production values forecast in the contract for the year 1999 (through a shock in the transportation sector–forecast of an increase in the supply of this sector). Thus, equation (5) can be re-written as follows:

$$X = (I - A)^{-1} \left[\underbrace{C + I + G}_{\text{internal absorption}} + \underbrace{E}_{\text{exports}} \right] \tag{6}$$

Based on equation (6), we will implement the following simulation exercise:[10]

STEP I–Construction of the unit in Juiz de Fora (MG)

$$\Delta X = (I - A)^{-1} * \Delta Y$$
$$\Delta Y = \underbrace{C}_{\text{constant}} + \underbrace{\Delta I}_{\text{variation}} + \underbrace{G}_{\text{constant}} + \underbrace{E}_{\text{constant}} \tag{7}$$

The construction of vector ΔI will be explained in section 4.4.1.3

STEP II–Forecast for the first year of production

$$\Delta X = (I - A)^{-1} * \Delta Y$$
$$\Delta Y = \underbrace{\Delta C}_{\text{variation}} + \underbrace{I}_{\text{constant}} + \underbrace{G}_{\text{constant}} + \underbrace{\Delta E}_{\text{variation}} \tag{7A}$$

where:

ΔC and ΔE are the direction of the production

4.4.1.2. Inter-Regional Input-Output Model

A region is not self-sufficient. Thus, it is necessary to exchange production and production factors with other regions. In order to describe such transactions, Isard applied the Isard Model for the first time in 1951. This model is known as the inter-regional input-output model (Miller and Blair, 1984).

The inter-regional input-output model describes the monetary flow of goods and services through the economy, but for more than one region. The model can be represented mathematically as follows:

$$x_{11}^{LL} + x_{12}^{LL} + \cdots x_{1n}^{LL} + x_{11}^{LM} + x_{12}^{LM} + \cdots x_{1n}^{LM} + y_1 = X_1$$
$$x_{21}^{LL} + x_{22}^{LL} + \cdots x_{2n}^{LL} + x_{21}^{LM} + x_{22}^{LM} + \cdots x_{2n}^{LM} + y_1 = X_2$$
$$\vdots$$
$$x_{n1}^{LL} + x_{n2}^{LL} + \cdots x_{nn}^{LL} + x_{n1}^{LM} + x_{n2}^{LM} + \cdots x_{nn}^{LM} + y_n = X_n$$
$$x_{11}^{ML} + x_{12}^{ML} + \cdots x_{1n}^{ML} + x_{11}^{MM} + x_{12}^{MM} + \cdots x_{1n}^{MM} + y_1 = X_1$$
$$x_{21}^{ML} + x_{22}^{ML} + \cdots x_{2n}^{ML} + x_{21}^{MM} + x_{22}^{MM} + \cdots x_{2n}^{MM} + y_1 = X_2$$
$$\vdots$$
$$x_{n1}^{ML} + x_{n2}^{ML} + \cdots x_{nn}^{ML} + x_{n1}^{LM} + x_{n2}^{MM} + \cdots x_{nn}^{MM} + y_n = X_n \tag{8}$$

Where:

L = region L (e.g., Minas Gerais)
M = region M (e.g., the other Brazilian states)
x_{ij}^{LL} = Purchases of sector i from sector j in the same region (i,j = 1,2,. . . ,n)
x_{ij}^{LM} = Purchases of sector i, located in L, from sector j, located in M (i,j = 1,2,. . . ,n)
x_{ij}^{ML} = Purchases of sector I, located in M, from sector j, located in L (i,j = 1,2,. . . ,n)
x_{ij}^{MM} = Purchases of sector i from sector j within the region (i,j = 1,2,. . . ,n)
yi = Final demand for products of sector i (i = 1,2,. . . ,n)
Xi = Total production of sector i (i = 1,2,. . . ,n)

To summarize, matrix X is the union of four matrices and is represented by:

$$X = \begin{bmatrix} X^{LL} & X^{LM} \\ X^{ML} & X^{MM} \end{bmatrix} \tag{9}$$

To arrive at the equation system that shows the interdependence among different sectors in the economy in both regions, we have the inter-sectoral technical coefficients:

Region L:

$$a_{ij}^{LL} = \frac{x_{ij}^{LL}}{X_j^L}$$

$$a_{ij}^{LM} = \frac{x_{ij}^{LM}}{X_j^L}$$

Region M: (10)

$$a_{ij}^{ML} = \frac{x_{ij}^{ML}}{X_j^M}$$

$$a_{ij}^{MM} = \frac{x_{ij}^{MM}}{X_j^M}$$

Thus, the equation system that shows the interdependence among the different sectors of the two regions is known as the technical coefficient matrix and can be represented by:

$$a_{11}^{LL}X_1 + a_{12}^{LL}X_2 + \cdots + a_{1n}^{LL}X_n + a_{11}^{LM}X_1 + a_{12}^{LM}X_2 + \cdots + a_{1n}^{LM}X_n = y_1 = X_1$$
$$a_{21}^{LL}X_1 + a_{22}^{LL}X_2 + \cdots + a_{2n}^{LL}X_n + a_{21}^{LM}X_1 + a_{22}^{LM}X_2 + \cdots + a_{2n}^{LM}X_n = y_2 = X_2$$
$$\vdots$$
$$a_{n1}^{LL}X_1 + a_{n2}^{LL}X_2 + \cdots + a_{nn}^{LL}X_n + a_{n1}^{LM}X_1 + a_{n2}^{LM}X_2 + \cdots + a_{nn}^{LM}X_n = y_n = X_n$$
$$a_{11}^{ML}X_1 + a_{12}^{ML}X_2 + \cdots + a_{1n}^{ML}X_n + a_{11}^{MM}X_1 + a_{12}^{MM}X_2 + \cdots + a_{1n}^{MM}X_n = y_1 = X_1$$
$$a_{21}^{ML}X_1 + a_{22}^{ML}X_2 + \cdots + a_{2n}^{ML}X_n + a_{21}^{MM}X_1 + a_{22}^{MM}X_2 + \cdots + a_{2n}^{MM}X_n = y_2 = X_2$$
$$\vdots$$
$$a_{n1}^{ML}X_1 + a_{n2}^{ML}X_2 + \cdots + a_{nn}^{ML}X_n + a_{n1}^{MM}X_1 + a_{n2}^{MM}X_2 + \cdots + a_{nn}^{MM}X_n = y_n = X_n \quad (11)$$

As a matrix, we have:

$$AX + Y = X \quad (12)$$

Where:

$A = nxn$ technical coefficients matrix
$X = nx1$ sectoral production vector
$Y = nx1$ final demand vector

We can define the coefficients matrix of an inter-regional model with two regions by:

$$A = \begin{bmatrix} A^{LL} & A^{LM} \\ A^{ML} & A^{MM} \end{bmatrix} \quad (13)$$

The sectoral production vector is represented by:

$$X = \begin{bmatrix} X^L \\ X^M \end{bmatrix} \tag{14}$$

The final demand vector is represented by:

$$Y = \begin{bmatrix} Y^L \\ Y^M \end{bmatrix} \tag{15}$$

Equation (12) can be described as follows:

$X = (I-A)^{-1} Y$

Or

$$\left\{ \begin{bmatrix} I & 0 \\ 0 & I \end{bmatrix} - \begin{bmatrix} A^{LL} & A^{LM} \\ A^{ML} & A^{MM} \end{bmatrix} \right\} \begin{bmatrix} X^L \\ X^M \end{bmatrix} = \begin{bmatrix} Y^L \\ Y^M \end{bmatrix} \tag{16}$$

4.4.1.3. Impact Calculation

4.4.1.3.1. Production Due to a Variation in the Investment–STEP I– Construction of the Mercedes Unit in Juiz de Fora

The calculation of the impact upon production due to a variation in the investment (i.e., the construction period of the Mercedes unit in Juiz de Fora) is based on the methodology used by Chahad et al. (2004). The calculation was arrived at based on the following steps:

a. Regionalization of the direct technical coefficients matrix (A) and the Leontief inverse matrix (B). In this step, the values in the quadrant Minas Gerais x Minas Gerais of matrices A and B were regionalized through the locational quotient. This regionalization is necessary to construct matrices A and B for the Juiz de Fora municipality.

b. Construction of a pattern unit of investment

$$UPI_{ij} = \frac{X_{ij}}{\displaystyle\sum_{i=1}^{n}\sum_{j=1}^{k} Xij}$$

Where: *UPIij*–Brazilian investment pattern unit
Xij–investment of sector "i" in region "j."

$$\sum_{i=1}^{n} \sum_{j=1}^{k} Xij\text{–total investment in Brazil}$$

a. Construction of a shock vector for calculating the impact of the investments. This vector will be constructed by the pre-multiplication of the invested value in the construction by the UPI vector.

*Shock(ΔI) = Investment value * UPIij*

b. Calculation of the impact of investments

This vector will be constructed through the pre-multiplication of the shock vector (ΔI) by the Leontief inverse matrix. Thus,
Investment impact = B*ΔI

4.4.1.3.2. Production Due to a Forecast of Production–STEP II–the First Year of Operation, Considering the Production Values Forecast in the Contract for the Year 1999. The impact upon production will be measured as follows:

$$\Delta X = (I - A)^{-1} * \Delta Y \tag{17}$$

where:

ΔY–final demand vector–(production values forecast for the transportation sector)
ΔX–impact upon sectoral production (R$)
$(I-A)^{-1}$–Leontief inverse.

4.4.2. Results Analysis

In order to calculate the impact of the investments upon sectoral production in the Juiz de Fora municipality, the rest of Minas Gerais and the rest of Brazil from STEP I–construction of the Mercedes unit in Juiz de Fora (MG)–we used the value of budget benefits (see Figure 2) to construct the shock vector in the simulation exercise.

Table 5 presents the 10 sectors in Juiz de Fora, the rest of Minas Gerais (RMG) and the rest of Brazil (RBR) that had the greatest impact upon production due to the budget benefits offered to the Mercedes-Benz unit.

In Juiz de Fora, we can verify that the construction sector presents the highest impact. The sector with the second highest impact is transportation equipment. It is important to note that the absorption of the impact by the 10 sectors in Juiz de Fora is around 95%. In other words, the sectoral distribution of benefits for the sectors located in Juiz de Fora is concentrated.

For the rest of Minas Gerais, we can observe that: (a) the concentration of the sectoral distribution of benefits in the rest of Minas Gerais is smaller than in Juiz de Fora. The absorption of the first 10 sectors that had the highest impact was around 75% of the total impact, and (b) the results for nonmetallic minerals, other metals and the steel sector should be emphasized. The absorption of these sectors is around 34% of total impact.

For the rest of the Brazil, we can observe that sectoral distribution of benefits on the productive structure is less concentrated than in Juiz de Fora. The absorption of the 10 sectors with the highest impact is around 78%. Another interesting point is that the construction sector also presents the highest impact.

A very important result is the intra-sectoral one. It is important to note the impact within the transportation equipment sector. We can observe that this sector is one of the 10 most important sectors, in terms of impacts upon production in Juiz de Fora, and also in the rest of Brazil. However, the same does not occur for the rest of Minas Gerais. This can represent more linkage towards the other Brazilian states.

Another relevant point is the verification of the share of the 10 sectors with the highest absorption in the total sectoral impact. For example, it is interesting to check the contribution of transportation equipment in Juiz de Fora against the total sectoral impact (Juiz de Fora plus rest of Minas Gerais plus rest of Brazil). Table 6 presents those results.

According to Table 5, 66% of the impact of the investment in the Mercedes unit (e.g., budget benefits) during the construction phase in Juiz de Fora is absorbed by the construction sector. It is important to emphasize that from the total variation in the production of this sector, 13.65% is due to the sector located in Juiz de Fora. Another important result is the contribution of the transportation equipment sector located in Juiz de Fora to the total impact of the transportation equipment sector. In Table 6 we can observe that this contribution is around 19%. As

TABLE 5. Sectoral Distribution of the Investment (Construction)

Juiz de Fora		Rest of MG		Rest of Brazil	
Sector	(%)	Sector	(%)	Sector	(%)
Construction	66.655	Nonmetallic minerals	17.502	Construction	43.775
Transportation equipment	8.402	Agriculture	15.309	Trade	4.785
Trade	5.504	Other metal products	10.530	Machinery	4.553
Steel	4.353	Construction	8.444	Agriculture	4.546
Other metal products	2.607	Steel	6.572	Nonmetallic minerals	4.412
Business services	2.047	Machinery	4.824	Petroleum refining	3.780
Transportation	2.018	Trade	4.557	Transportation equipment	3.717
Nonmetallic minerals	1.863	Electrical equipment	4.122	Other metal products	3.656
Machinery	1.256	Petroleum refining	3.570	Electronic equipment	2.758
Financial institutions	1.087	Other chemicals	2.915	Electrical equipment	2.211

Source: Based on the simulation exercise.

TABLE 6. Spatial Distribution of the Investment During the Construction Phase for Relevant Sectors in Juiz de Fora

Sectors	Contribution		
	Juiz de Fora	Rest of MG	Rest of Brazil
Construction	13.65	0.66	85.68
Transportation equipment	19.11	0.11	80.79
Trade	10.39	3.29	86.31
Steel	19.49	11.27	69.25
Other metal products	6.27	9.70	84.03
Business services	9.07	1.56	89.37
Transportation	9.22	4.74	86.04
Nonmetallic minerals	3.67	13.21	83.12
Machinery	2.69	3.96	93.34
Financial institutions	10.59	3.93	85.47

Source: Based on the simulation exercise.

we expected, the highest contributions for all sectors are located in the rest of Brazil.

From the impact upon the productive sectors (Juiz de Fora, rest of Minas Gerais and rest of Brazil) due to a variation in the investment (construction phase), we can observe that 9.14% of this impact occurs in Juiz de Fora, 3.50% in the rest of Minas Gerais and 87.36% in the rest of Brazil.

Another point to be analyzed is the impact on production in Juiz de Fora, the rest of Minas Gerais and the rest of Brazil due to the production forecast for the first few years of the Mercedes unit's operations in Juiz de Fora. In order to implement this kind of analysis, we make use of the production forecast for the first year of operations as stated in the contract signed by the agents (Mercedes and the state and local governments). This forecast was for 40,000 units. It is important to emphasize that in order to find the revenue from the supply of these units, we took the medium price of the Class A model (R$ 40,000.00), which was the first model produced by the Mercedes unit in Juiz de Fora (MG).

Observing Table 7, we verify that in Juiz de Fora the greatest impact due to the forecast of production in the transportation equipment sector (STEP II–first year of operation) is upon the sector itself–around $72. Steel sector production in Juiz de Fora varies by 8.11% due to the positive variation in transportation sector production (value forecasted). We observe that the impacts are concentrated among the sectors. In other

TABLE 7. Sectoral Distribution of the Impact During the First Year of Operations (Forecast for Class A Production)

Juiz de Fora		Rest of MG		Rest of Brazil	
Sector	(%)	Sector	(%)	Sector	(%)
Transportation equipment	72.81	Other metal products	30.93	Steel	17.12
Steel	8.11	Machinery	17.97	Other metal products	9.13
Trade	3.65	Nonmetallic minerals	12.53	Trade	8.02
Transportation	3.19	Trade	5.48	Transportation	7.12
Other metal products	2.60	Steel	5.23	Petroleum refining	6.32
Financial institutions	2.54	Agriculture	4.96	Machinery	5.99
Machinery	1.97	Chemicals	4.26	Business services	4.93
Electric, gas and sanitary services	0.95	Transportation	4.13	Electric, gas and sanitary services	4.73
Communication	0.86	Electric, gas and sanitary services	3.75	Financial institutions	3.92
Public administration	0.83	Electrical equipment	3.52	Transportation equipment	3.81

Source: Based on the simulation exercise.

71

words, the 10 sectors presented in Table 7 are responsible for 97% of the variation in production in Juiz de Fora (MG).

In the state of Minas Gerais, the concentration in the variation in production due to the production forecast for the first year of operations of the Mercedes-Benz unit in Juiz de Fora is also high. The 10 sectors presented in Table 7 are responsible for 92% of the total variation in the state's production. It is important to note the variation in the production of other metal products, machinery and nonmetallic minerals.

The impact on the sectoral production in the rest of Brazil, given the production forecast for the Mercedes unit's first year of operations, is less concentrated than in Juiz de Fora and the rest of Minas Gerais. The impact is around 71%. The production of the other metals sector is the one that varies most–around 17%.

The spatial distribution of the impacts upon the sectoral production in Juiz de Fora, the rest of Minas Gerais and the rest of Brazil due to the production forecast for the first year of operations is distributed as follows: 74.20% of the impact on production is in Juiz de Fora, 20.25% in the rest of Brazil and 5.55% in the rest of Minas Gerais.

5. CONCLUSIONS

In this paper we have broadly analyzed the project of opening a Mercedes-Benz unit in Juiz de Fora, Minas Gerais state. Both Minas Gerais and Juiz de Fora had fiscal incentives (e.g., immunity from tax payments) as one of the main instruments for attracting industrial projects. In other words, the promotion of regional and local development is based mainly on fiscal benefits. It is also important to emphasize that this kind of policy is common in the majority of Brazilian states and was largely used in Brazil in the 1990s.

It was not the aim of this paper to validate or not to validate the use of fiscal instruments as a way of attracting new enterprises. The strategy adopted in this paper was to improve the reader's knowledge of the available instruments at both the state and local levels, and also to make an analysis of the impact of the Mercedes-Benz unit project in Juiz de Fora by analyzing the construction and the production forecast for the first year of operations. We can observe that the Mercedes-Benz unit in Juiz de Fora did not reach an effective capacity. Since the first year of operations, the unit at Juiz de Fora has been working below capacity. It had the Class A model as the first model produced, but due to the small level of production of the Class A, the Class C model (for export) began to be produced. For 2005, there was a plan to build the Smart Formore model in Juiz de Fora. Mercedes-Benz was negotiating a new contract with the state government.

In order to analyze the Mercedes-Benz unit within the context of regional and local development promotion, the results of the simulation exercises, using an input-output framework, enabled us to verify the structure of inter-sectoral and inter-regional relations. These interactions were presented during the construction period (budget benefits) and during the first year of the unit's operations (production forecast). In sectoral terms, we found that: (a) there is a concentration in the interactions for a small number of sectors in the productive structure in Juiz de Fora, and (b) there is an impact with a smaller degree of concentration upon the sectoral production in the rest of Minas Gerais and the rest of Brazil.

Another point to emphasize is that in the investment (construction) phase the structure of interactions is as follows: around 9% within Juiz de Fora, around 3% for the rest of the Minas Gerais and 88% for the rest of the Brazilian economy. The structure of linkages for the production forecast for the first year of production is: (a) total impact (taking into account the intra-sectoral impacts, which means the impact upon the transportation equipment sector of Juiz de Fora)–74.20% in Juiz de Fora, 5.55% in the rest of Minas Gerais and 10.25% in the rest of Brazil and (b) net impact (not taking into account the intra-sectoral impacts in Juiz de Fora)–43.80% in Juiz de Fora, 12.08% in the rest of Minas Gerais and 44.05% in the rest of Brazil.

NOTES

1. It is important to point out that the criterion of spatial de-concentration and productive integration was not taken into account. In other words, a project was approved if it demonstrated its viability only from the economic and financial point of view.

2. Some authors include the Integrated Development Plan for Minas Gerais (PMDI) in the second period of fiscal incentives. In this paper, the PMDI will be considered as a third period of fiscal incentives adopted by the state. It is with the implementation of this plan that regional imbalances are systematically discussed. In the previous period, these questions were present, both in Pro-Industry and in the PROIM (Induction of Industrial Modernization Program), but they were not implemented.

3. This program is for working capital companies that import and sell on the internal market products similar to those that will be produced by the company itself. This resource will be used during the construction period and the first few years of activity (Bastos, 2000).

4. The 1999 data was collected from research developed by Martins et al. (1998).

5. A *Follow Sourcing* system consists of hiring the same seller in Germany (where the Class A model is also produced) and Brazil. The seller can be located wherever it wants (in Brazil or in Germany).

6. The company association that develops and executes a project.

7. The company also has a consolidation center in *Bremerhafen*, Germany.

8. Among the facts that can explain this difference between forecast production and actual production we can highlight: (a) the exchange rate devaluation, (b) the increase in the interest rate, (c) a decrease in internal consumption and d) a decrease in exports. As a consequence, the price of the Class A model changed. The forecast value for 1996 (US$25 to US$30 thousand) in April 1999 was between R$43 thousand to R$51 thousand. (exchange rate of 1.7). Thus, the final price of the product changed from R$33 thousand to R$36 thousand.

9. See *Procedimento de regionalização por Quociente Locacional* in Miller and Blair (1984).

10. It should be emphasized that the simulation exercise will be implemented in the inter-regional input-output model, whose structure is presented in the next section.

REFERENCES

Alves, M.A. de S. (2000). "Guerra Fiscal e Finanças Federativas no Brasil: O Caso do Setor Automotivo." *Master's Thesis*. Campinas: Universidade Estadual de Campinas/ Instituto de Economia.

DaimlerChrysler (2001). Relatório de Atividades da DaimlerChrysler no Brasil.

DaimlerChrysler (2002). Relatório de Atividades da DaimlerChrysler no Brasil.

DaimlerChrysler (2003). Relatório de Atividades da DaimlerChrysler no Brasil.

Dorfman, R., Samuelson, P. A., and Solow, R. M. (1986). "Linear Programming and Economic Analysis." New York, Dover.

Bastos, S. Q. de A. (2000). "Estratégia Locacional da Indústria Automobilística: O Caso as Mercedes-Benz em Juiz de Fora." *Master's Thesis*. Rio de Janeiro: Universidade Federal do Rio de Janeiro / IPPUR.

BDMG and FIPE (2002). "Matriz Inter-Regional de Insumo-Produto Minas Gerais x Resto do Brasil." BDMG and FIPE.

Chahad, J. P. Z., Comune, E., and Haddad, E. A. (2004). "Interdependência Espacial das Exportações Brasileiras: repercussões sobre o Mercado de Trabalho." *Revista Pesquisa e Planejamento Econômico*, Vol. 34, No. 1, pp. 93-122.

Martins, H. E. de P., Perobelli, F. S., Resende, P. T. D., and Paula, G. M. (1998). "Sistemas Regionais de Inovação na Indústria Automobilística: O Caso da Mercedes-Benz em Juiz de Fora (MG)." In: *Anais do II Congresso da Sociedade de Economia Política*. pp. 956-969.

Mercedes-Benz do Brasil (1996). Contrato de Implantação da Indústria. Juiz de Fora.

Mercedes-Benz do Brasil (1999). Relatório de Atividades da Mercedes-Benz do Brasil.

Mercedes-Benz do Brasil (2000). Relatório de Atividades da Mercedes-Benz do Brasil.

Mercedes-Benz produzirá importados em Minas Gerais (2005). *Revista Auto Esporte*. Edição 478, March.

Miller, R. E., and Blair, P. D. (1984). "Input-Output Analysis: Foundations and Extensions." New Jersey: Prentice Hall.

Neves, M. A., Oliveira, A. M., and Brandão, N. A. (2002). "A Complexa Montagem de um Veículo: A Mercedes-Benz em Juiz de Fora." In M. R. Nabuco, M. A. Neves and A. M. Carvalho Neto, *A Indústria Automotiva: A Nova Geografia do Setor Produtivo.* pp. 141- 172. DP&A editora.

Oliveira, F. A., and Duarte Filho, F. C. (1997). "Aspectos da Guerra Fiscal no Brasil: A Política de Incentivos Fiscais em Minas Gerais." *Work prepared for IESP/FUNDAP for the project Aspectos da Guerra Fiscal no Brasil.* February. Mimeo.

Perobelli, F. S. (2004). "Análise Espacial das Interações Econômicas entre os Estados Brasileiros." Tese de doutorado. São Paulo: Universidade de São Paulo / IPE.

Perobelli, F. S., Oliveira, A.F., Novy, L.G.G., and Ferreira, M.V. (1997). "Avaliação do Potencial de Desenvolvimento dos Municípios de Minas Gerais na Região do em torno de Juiz de Fora (MG): Uma Aplicação de Análise Fatorial." *Research Report FEA/UFJF and FAPEMIG.*

PMDI (1995). "Plano Mineiro de Desenvolvimento Integrado." Belo Horizonte: Government of Minas Gerais, 110pp.

doi:10.1300/J140v07n03_03

The Automobile Industry in Paraná: The Case of Renault

Ricardo Luis Lopes

SUMMARY. The development process of Paraná has traditionally been closely linked to agriculture. However, given the state's proximity to São Paulo, there have always been attempts to promote industrial development. This occurred initially in the 1970s and became more intensive in the 1990s with the development of fiscal wars between the states to attract investments, especially in the automobile industry. The paper concentrates on an analysis of how the Renault assembly plant was attracted to Paraná, its impact on the state's industrial product and on employment, and on the attempt to attract component producers.

RESUMEN. Tradicionalmente, el proceso de desarrollo del estado de Paraná siempre se mantuvo estrechamente vinculado a la agricultura. Sin embargo, debido a su proximidad al estado de São Paulo, se realizaron constantes esfuerzos para promover su desarrollo industrial. El paso inicial se remonta a los años 70, que evolucionó considerablemente en los 90 con el surgimiento de guerras fiscales entre los estados instigadas para atraer inversiones, especialmente de la industria automotriz. El estudio se concentra en el análisis de cómo se atrajo la instalación de la fábrica Renault al estado de Paraná, su impacto sobre el producto industrial del estado y el empleo, y la tentativa de atraer fabricantes de componentes.

Ricardo Luis Lopes is affiliated with the State University of Maringá, Paraná, Brazil.

[Haworth co-indexing entry note]: "The Automobile Industry in Paraná: The Case of Renault." Lopes, Ricardo Luis. Co-published simultaneously in *Latin American Business Review* (International Business Press, an imprint of The Haworth Press, Inc.) Vol. 7, No. 3/4, 2006, pp. 77-96; and: *Latin American Business: Equity Distortion in Regional Resource Allocation in Brazil* (ed: Werner Baer, and Geoffrey Hewings) International Business Press, an imprint of The Haworth Press, Inc., 2006, pp. 77-96. Single or multiple copies of this article are available for a fee from The Haworth Document Delivery Service [1-800-HAWORTH, 9:00 a.m. - 5:00 p.m. (EST). E-mail address: docdelivery@haworthpress.com].

RESUMO. O processo de desenvolvimento do Paraná esteve intimamente ligado à agricultura. Mas dado sua proximidade com São Paulo, sempre se procurou dar um impulso ao desenvolvimento industrial. O primeiro passo para isto ocorreu na década de 70. No entanto, foi a partir de década de 90 que se observa uma maior evolução do desenvolvimento industrial. Parte desse processo foi conseqüência da guerra fiscal travada entre os estados brasileiros para atração de investimentos, principalmente da indústria automobilística. O objetivo desse artigo é de apresentar o processo de atração da montadora francesa Renault para o estado do Paraná, analisar os investimentos realizados e seus impactos, principalmente na geração de emprego e na tentativa de atrair fabricantes ligados ao setor de autopeças. doi:10.1300/J140v07n03_04 *[Article copies available for a fee from The Haworth Document Delivery Service: 1-800-HAWORTH. E-mail address: <docdelivery@haworthpress.com> Website: <http://www.HaworthPress. com> © 2006 by The Haworth Press, Inc. All rights reserved.]*

KEYWORDS. Paraná, investment, employment, auto industry, component producers

INTRODUCTION

The economic history of Paraná is intimately connected with agriculture. However, an industrialization process began in the second half of the twentieth century, making great forward leaps in the seventies and nineties. The latter period was characterized by substantial competition among the states for foreign investments. This was especially the case with the automobile sector, with Paraná winning the battle for Renault and Audi-Volkswagen. The objective of this paper is to present the concessions made by the state and city in order to attract Renault, in addition to the effect on job creation. The paper is divided as follows: in the first part the economic evolution of the state of Paraná will be presented, as well as the long-run incentives programs; the second part describes the automobile industry in Paraná; the third discusses the Renault agreement and the degree to which it attracted other investments and created jobs.

ECONOMIC EVOLUTION
AND THE INCENTIVES PROGRAMS IN PARANÁ

Some noteworthy economic activity began in Paraná in the nineteenth century. The gold discovery in the region of Paranaguá attracted a colonizing population. The Paranaean gold cycle did not last long, however, and it was followed by a new cycle called *tropeirismo*, which consisted of supplying the market of São Paulo with animals. The construction of the railroad system caused this activity to decline, however. Subsequently, two new activities appeared: the cultivation of *erva-mate*, followed by the lumber industry. The development of these two sectors led to the appearance of industrial activities and a capitalist mentality in the state. The lumber sector developed and attracted foreign investments that concentrated on the railroad sector. These two sectors were the major influence on the industrialization process of the lumber and food processing industries. The 1940s saw the development of the energy sector and the production of non-metallic minerals (Magalhães Filho, 1996 and Verri, 2003).

Paraná's economy flourished with the spread of coffee production, which occurred in three distinct regions of the state. *Gauchos* from the South developed modern agriculture in the western part of the state, while in the North settlers from São Paulo spread the cultivation of coffee, accompanied by a strong agro-industrial sector. The eastern part was settled by Europeans, who also began to set up firms producing metal products. These distinct regions of the state were ultimately bound together by the construction of highways and railroads.

The coffee cycle was most important for Paraná's development. It began at the end of the 19th century, replacing the decaying cultures of erva-mate and lumber. It was the coffee sector that had an impact on the development of some industries related to it. These new economic activities were influential in developing the port of Paranaguá and improving the state's road network, which linked the state to the rest of the country.

The high profits made from coffee exportation, along with the industrial policies adopted by the federal government–policies that were financed by the coffee sector–resulted mainly in the industrialization of São Paulo, while Paraná only developed activities connected to the coffee sector. To restrain the drain of resources from the Paraná coffee sector to São Paulo's growing industrial sector, the state government gradually adopted a more ample policy of industrialization within the state.

In sum, the process of Paraná's development can be divided into the following phases, according to Macedo et al. (2002): Until the end of the sixties the *Paranaen* economy was based on the production of matte, while a peripheral industrialization developed, which was based on the expansion of the coffee sector in the subsequent period. By the eighties, the state had entered an industrialization phase, which complemented that of the state of São Paulo, its neighbor and most dynamic state in the country. In this phase one observes an expansion of the metal industry and of the agro-industrial sector. At the same time, some of the traditional sectors underwent a period of modernization, including the lumber, paper, and food processing sectors. The last phase, initiated at the end of the eighties, saw the process of integrating the Paranaean economy into the dynamic nuclei of the Brazilian economy.

The Sixties and Seventies

The Economic Development Fund–FDE–was created in 1962. Its resources were initially provided by obligatory loans, and the FDE became Paraná's most important instrument for financing infrastructure projects. Currently, its resources come from energy royalties from the Paraná Development Bank (BADEP) (Vasconcelos and Castro, 1999; Lourenço, 2000; Lourenço, 2001).

Also, in 1962 the Paraná Development Company (CODEPAR) was created. Its main objective was to promote the financing–via the FDE– of the state's basic infrastructure development, especially in the energy, transportation and telecommunications sectors (Lourenço, 2000). This resulted in a spurt in the supply of energy, in the construction of highways and railroads, and the modernization of the harbor of Paranaguá. These Paranaean development policies made the implementation of modern manufacturing sectors possible, such as cement, metallurgy and oil refining, and also the modernization of traditional branches of agri-business.

The tax reform of 1966 extinguished the IVC and created the ICM. In 1975 CONFAZ–the National Council on Fiscal Policies–was established. In the same year, a complementary law (LC 24/75) restricting the concession of tax benefits was created. Individual states could only use the ICM as an incentive to attract industrial firms, subject to the approval of CONFAZ.

Also in the seventies, an industrial district was created in Curitiba (called CIC), which, according to Lourenço (2001), could be considered an embryonic attempt at diversification and upgrading of the industrial structure. This industrial park received financing from the FDE and an extension of the grace period for payments to the ICM. In addition, the CIC was provided with a well developed infrastructure for industrial installation, consisting of water, sewer system, energy and telecommunications (Vasconcelos and Castro, 1999).

Furthermore, in the seventies a modern agro-industrial complex and a metallurgical industry sprang up in the metropolitan region of Curitiba (Vasconcelos and Castro 1999). Traditional activities such as coffee and lumber lost importance in favor of newer ones such as tobacco, chemicals and machinery. Also growing in importance were sectors linked to more elaborate raw materials, mainly those connected to meat packing plants, refined oil, lumber products and non-metallic minerals. It is important to take into account that the proximity of the São Paulo market and the political and financial support of the state government had been decisive for attracting industries to the region; beyond that, of course, a good offer of basic infrastructure, institutional support mechanisms for industry and a dynamic and modern agriculture were of importance.

The share of the state's industrial production in 1980 reached 6.35% of the gross national product. Within the state the industrial sector grew by 387%, while agriculture grew only 44% and services 167%. The sectors that experienced a decline in their share of the state's production were coffee and lumber, while tobacco, chemicals and metallurgy increased their share (Ipardes, 1982).

The Eighties

The eighties were characterized by the creation of some incentive programs for investing in Paraná, among which were the Special Program of Financing to Industries (PEFI) and the Program to Stimulate Productive Investments (PROIN). The former was created in 1981, and had the granting of credit for working capital as its objective. It consisted in financing 70% of the ICMS generated by companies which engaged in fixed investments–either for expansion or for the construction of new industrial enterprises. In 1988 the PROIN was created to support the expansion and/or implementation of industrial units by financing up to 25% of the fixed investment. To be eligible, a firm would have to present a project in the range of 50,000 to 100,000 ORTN, and in case of expansion a 2% production increase would have to occur. This program was discontinued in 1998 (Alves, 2001).

The economy of Paraná grew faster than that of the country. This period was characterized by agricultural diversification, mainly the consolidation of the raising of soybeans, and also the growth of cotton. The industrial sector also displayed a notable dynamism, especially in electric and communication goods, paper and cardboard, chemicals and transportation equipment. In the 70s, its share of Paraná's GDP amounted to 11.5%, increasing to 32.1% in 1989. Paraná's energy needs were solved with the inauguration of the plants in Foz da Areia and Segredo. However, the decade witnessed a decline of investment in infrastructure and a decline in growth (Verri, 2003; Vasconcelos and Castro, 1999).

The Nineties

In the first half of the 1990s, Paraná's GDP grew at a yearly rate of 3.6%, while Brazil's GDP grew at only 2.7%. In the second half of the decade, Paraná's GDP growth was always higher than that of the country overall, with the exception of 1997 (Verri, 2003). There was notable progress in the agricultural sector, with substantial productivity increases in grains, in addition to the appearance of new products such as sugar cane, poultry and eggs. The sector became increasingly modern in its use of more capital intensive techniques, modern administrative methods, and the use of modern technologies in support services (Verri, 2003).

During the nineties as a whole, Paraná used two important incentive programs: "Parana with more Jobs" and the "Paraná Technological and Social Program" (PRODEPAR). The former was created in 1992 and offered longer grace periods for payment of the incremental ICMS (Alves, 2001).

PRODEPAR consisted of a program of tax incentives for the promotion of new industrial investments. Its mechanism consisted of allowing payments of the ICMS in installments, giving preference to the working capital of firms. The ICMS tax could be paid in two installments, the first being paid normally and the second in up to 48 months. The latter could amount to 30% to 99% of the total value to be collected (SEIT, 2003).

This decade presented two distinct characteristics. In the first half, the behavior of the economy was similar to that of the previous decade: a strong industrial sector as opposed to the agricultural sector. Industry, whose share of the state's GDP had been 18.8% in 1985, rose to 39% in 1995. On the other hand, agriculture's share declined from 18.8% to 13.5% in the same period. The fundamental situation changed in the second half of the nineties. First, there was the national stabilization program known as the Real Plan. Second, a substantial increase of foreign direct investments (FDI) occurred, a large part of these being linked to privatization. One of the major sectors to benefit from FDI was that of automobile enterprises. This was the sector that was mainly responsible for the fiscal competition among states. The various benefits and concessions that the states offered became known as the "Fiscal War among the States."

In the period 1996 through 1999, Paraná received investment pledges of $27 billion. According to Fonseca and Peris (2003), 56% of this total was destined for the metal-mechanic sector, while the remaining 44% was to go to the automobile industry.

THE AUTOMOBILE INDUSTRY IN PARANÁ

Already in the 1970s, Paraná had received investments in the automobile sector, most notably, those of Volvo (trucks and buses) and New Holland (agricultural tractors). A small park of local supplier components arose around the implantation of these firms (Santos and Pinhão, 1999).

In 1995 the government introduced a new set of policies for the automobile sector, which was similar to that of Argentina. The idea was to consolidate existing investments and to attract new ones. The government selected automobile assembly companies as one of the main instruments towards achieving industrial modernization and technological reorganization capable of achieving new access for Brazilian products to the world-wide market (Abrix, 1999).

The result was rapidly felt (Abrix, 2003). Starting in 1996, 16 major assembly plants, 150 component producing firms and 29 firms of other complementary sectors had adhered to the new automobile policies. The greatest beneficiaries were the states of Paraná, Minas Gerais, Rio Grande do Sul, Bahia and Rio de Janeiro. Paraná became host to the assembly plants of Renault, Audi-Volkswagen, Nissan, Chrysler and their suppliers. The production of vehicles in the state grew rapidly with output rising to close to 200 thousand units produced in 2003, as is shown in Table 1.

In Paraná, according to Meiners (1998), the first consultations by Volkswagen, General Motors and Mercedes Benz began in 1994. These firms desired information on the local advantages regarding the state's strategic location with respect to Mercosul, the availability of a chain of supply firms, adequate water, electric energy, road and water transportion infrastructure, telecommunications, skilled labor, and the quality of life in the Curitiba metropolitan area.

Sesso Filho et al. (2004), using input-output analysis, showed that the automobile sector in Paraná would have impacts on the production of commerce, chemicals, machinery and equipment within the state, and on metallurgy, chemicals and the automobile industry in the rest of the country. According to Lourenço (2001), the automobile complex had

TABLE 1. Production of Automobiles in Paraná, 1999-2004, in Units

Company	1999	2000	2001	2002	2003	2004
Volvo	4,176	6,272	5,854	5,512	6,147	9,153
New Holland	6,205	7,943	12,353	12,200	13,561	13,766
Renault	24,809	58,083	71,108	48,040	58,606	66,645
Audi-VW	17,055	74,066	98,333	124,886	112,833	94,222
Nissan	-	-	-	3,744	8,025	10,196
Total	52,245	146,364	187,648	194,382	199,172	193,982

Source: Anfavea, 1999-2004

already made its influence felt on the local real estate, hotel, construction and food sectors.

The development of the automobile sector in Paraná and the announcement of the installation of large assembly plants had the expected impact. Between 1995 and 2000, about US $1.7 billion was invested in the automobile tooling sector. Most of this sector–93%–was concentrated in the metropolitan region of Curitiba (Table 2). According to Rodrigues (2000), Paraná lost the opportunity at that time to promote a regionally de-concentrated industrial structure within the state.

RENAULT'S ASSEMBLY PLANT

According to Meiners (1998), Renault's decision to build an assembly plant in Brazil was motivated by its plan to consolidate its position within Mercosul, its biggest market outside Europe. The firm was a major producer in the Argentine market and was interested in winning 6% of the Brazilian market and also in raising its share in Mercosul to 10%.

The inauguration of the Brazilian plant was the result of Renault's aggressive protectionist strategy in the Latin American market, the 5th most sold brand in the region at the time. Renault inaugurated the Airton Senna plant on December 4th, 1998 in São José dos Pinhais. The estimated production for 1999 was 30,000 automobiles. By 2000 the installed capacity was 90,000 units. In addition, Renault also installed a division to produce engines, which began to operate in 2000 (Sindimetal,1998).

The negotiations with Renault can be considered as a point of inflection in the fiscal war, resulting in a substantial rise in the volume of resources the public sector made available to attract new firms to the state.

TABLE 2. Main Investments Announced in Auto Parts, Per Company, 1995-2000

Company	US$ millions	Company	US$ millions
Tritec Motors	659.0	Detroit Diesel Motors	130.0
Renault motores	120.0	Denso	50.0
Sommer Allibert	50.0	Brose	46.0
Simoldes	43.2	Robert Bosch	40.0
Thera	35.0	American Axie	35.0
KMAB-Krupp	35.0	Gonvarri	30.0
Peguform	29.0	SNR roulements	25.0
Krupp Presta	25.0	Koyo	20.0
Arvin	20.0	Plastauto	17.0
Dana	14.0	Wlaker do Brasil	14.0
Vemetek	13.5	Edscha	12.0
Sofedit	12.0	Johnson Controls	12.0
Manuli	11.0	Metagal	7.0
Rütegers	7.0	Etablissements Caillu	5.0
Lear Co.	4.5	Hella-Arteb	4.5
Brandl do Brasil	4.0	Inylbra	4.0
Auto Chassis	3.5	Ecia	3.0
S.A.S. automotiva	2.8	T.E.A.M. robótica	2.5
Delphi	2.5	Grammer	2.0
Solvay	1.0	Adwest heidmann	0.7
Continental*	80.0	Siemens*	20.0
Iracome*	15.5	TCA*	6.5
Iramec*	3.4		

Source: Macedo et al. (2002)
*Investments outside of the metropolitan region of Curitiba (7%).

With its various concessions, Paraná's government was able to defeat some competing states. One of its innovative gestures was to assume responsibility for 40% of the total investment. The only similar participation of a state was that of Minas Gerais in connection with the establishment of Fiat in the 1970s. The agreement between the state of Paraná and Renault contained the following items (Alves 2001; Abrix,1999; Santos and Pinhão 1999):

Commitments of Renault

- Install the plant and cover 60% of the capital;
- Generate 1,500 jobs in 2 years;

- Pay R$ 50 million for the deactivation of the plant prior to the 20 year expiration of the contract.

Commitments of the State of Paraná

- Land
  The state and the city donated land of 2.5 million m², plus 500 thousand m² of contiguous area was reserved at no cost for 10 years to help the expansion of the company.

- Infrastructure
  - Drainage and land preparation;
  - Construction, illumination and signaling of road access to the industrial park;
  - Illumination and signs for the road system within the industrial park;
  - Construction of an energy substation by Copel and a 25% reduction in the energy tariff;
  - Construction of a railroad connection linking the company's plant with the terminal of the RFFSA in Curitiba;
  - Construction of special facilities for the firm at the port of Paranaguá;
  - Construction of artesian wells and a complete sewer system by the state's development company in São José dos Pinhais;
  - Construction of a drinkable and industrial water supply network;
  - Construction a sewer network;
  - Construction of an electric plant for the exclusive use of the firm.

- Capital Participation
  The state committed itself to a 40% participation in the initial capital of the company, estimated at US$ 300 million, with resources from the FDE, which would be receiving income from selling stocks of COPEL and royalties from the defunct BADEP.

- Credit
  Financing commercial activity: this was to occur through the FDE, the total amount to be determined by the revenue from sales

of new cars and replacement components produced within the state and/or imported through the state's customs facilities. This financing would be released on a monthly basis for a period of 10 years.

Contributing to investment: financed by the FDE, the total of which would be established in accordance with the price of the equipment and imported or acquired tools in the state. The funds would be released in monthly installments over 10 years, without payment of interest, commissions or indexation during such 10-year period.

• Tax Exemptions
Exemptions from IPTU, ISS and taxes and special asessments for 10 years; these exemptions extended to suppliers.

• Tax Incentives
Non-obligation on a charge of the differential rates of ICMS due to the acquisition of tools and industrial goods in other states;
Deferment of the ICMS due to the acquisition of raw materials, parts and/or imported and/or acquired components in the state, used in the manufacture and maintenance of vehicles;
Use of 100% of credits from ICMS accumulated for the payment of suppliers or for the rendering of services in the state of the Paraná, including electric energy, and for the payment of the ICMS due to other entities or the Renault group installed in the state;
The tax incentives were extended to suppliers.

• Collateral
Collateral on loans would consist of: (1) machinery; (2) components and vehicles of the firm; (3) if needed, a mortgage on the property in order to guarantee the total value of the loan.

The Benefits

Due to the difficulty, exemptions from municipal taxes, from taxes on property and the transmission of goods, among others, were not included; however, these exemptions would be small when compared to the other incentives. When it comes to the infrastructure, the difficulty is found when repairs are not totally the responsibility of the company, such as highway duplication, which also benefits the population (Alves, 2001).

The total value granted to Renault, according to Alves (2001), amounted to 353 million Reals (Table 3). It must be pointed out that these values represent only the benefits offered directly to the companies. The agreement foresaw the extension of such benefits to suppliers. However, as agreements were signed with each supplier, estimating benefits became very difficult. For the initial agreement, the benefits would surpass 2 billion Reals due to the credit for commercial activities, and the credit for investments was available for a 10-year period, as well as a grace period of 10 years.

Suppliers

Renault's own installations were composed of car body assembly lines, the paint division and the final assembly unit (Sindimetal, 1997). Five suppliers were installed on the plant's own property. It was decided that the following suppliers were to be located within the state of Paraná at the beginning of their operations: Siemens (automobile wires); Bertrand Faure (seats); Valeo (clutches); Peguform (bumpers) and Ecia (exhaust pipes). The suppliers of wheels, axles and dashboards were also eventually to be located within the state. Other components were to be outsourced. According to Santos and Pinhão (1999), the plant was given to obtain flexibility, with the purpose of minimizing the costs of logistics and inventory.

With respect to suppliers, it is important to note that of 100, 24 were located in Curitiba. Of the total components purchased within Brazil, 64% of the Scénic model came from Paraná, 34% from São Paulo and 2% from other states. The suppliers synchronized their output with the assembly plant, and many of these were betting on Mercosul. The main suppliers are shown in Table 4. Renault's plan was to increase the value added within Brazil and Mercosul (Santos and Pinhão, 1999).

Labor Market

Total investments in assembly plants amounted to US$ 4.5 billion, of which 30% was invested in Paraná (Meiners, 1998). The arrival of new suppliers resulted in investments in the state exceeding US$ 5 billion, and these investments created 5,400 jobs. The indirect effect and income generated, respectively, 24,000 and 90,392 jobs. The industrial sector would generate 5,400 direct and 16,200 indirect jobs; the primary and tertiary sectors 1,800 and 6,000 indirect jobs, respectively (see Table 5).

TABLE 3. Total Benefits Granted to Renault, in R$ of 1996

Benefits	R$ of 1996
Budgetary Benefit	165,000.000.00
Land	15,000,000,00
Infrastructure	150,000,000,00
Tax Benefit	188,338,599.00
ICMS Differment	188,338,599.00
Total	353,338,599.00

Source: Alves, 2001

TABLE 4. Main Suppliers for the Renault Assembly Plant

Supplier	Product	Supplier	Product
Bertrand faure	Seats	SAS	Cockpit construction
Borlen	Wheel	Siemens Auto	Injection and interiors
Bosch	Front windshield cleaner	Siemens Cabos	Automotive Wires
Cofap	Shock absorbers	Simoldes	Door panels
Denso	Air-conditioners & heaters	Sommer Aliberti	Dashboards & door linings
DHB	Pumps & power steering	Santa Maria	Windows
Ecia	Steering columns & exhaust pipes	Thera	Stamped components
Goodyear	Tires	Valeo Térmico	Air conditioners & heaters
Koyo/SMI–Perdriel	Steering mounting	Valeo eletronic	Alternaters & starters
Magnetti Mareli	Rearview mirrors & dashboards	Valeo	Clutches & wipers
Michelin	Tires	Valeo cibei	Headlights & taillights
Peguform	Bumpers & mudguards	Vallourec	Suspension mounting
PPG	Painting	Varga	Break systems

Source: Santos and Pinhão (1999)

When the creation of jobs at Renault and some of its suppliers is analyzed directly, one finds that more than 85% of the foreseen vacancies were created. When analyzing the origin of the workers at Renault, Lopes et al. (2004) observed that for the year 2000, 47% of the employees were from the state of Paraná (see Table 6)

Renault's Market

Renault initiated its activities in 1999. In the beginning, its output was concentrated on mixed-use automobiles–the Scenic and Clio mod-

TABLE 5. Generation of Direct and Indirect Jobs, Income Effects According to Programmed Investments for the Automobile Sector for the State of Paraná

	Direct	Indirect	Induced Income Effect	Total
Agriculture		1800	16900	18700
Non-metallic Minerals		600	0	600
Metal Products		500	0	500
Other Metallurgy		1200	0	1200
Machinery and Equipment		400	0	400
Automobiles & other Vehicles	5400	1500	0	6900
Auto parts		6900	0	6900
Rubber		1300	0	1300
Chemicals		600	0	600
Plastic		600	0	600
Lumber & Wood products		1200	1469	2669
Pulp, Paper and Printing		0	735	735
Textiles		600	735	1335
Clothing Products		600	5145	5745
Footwear		0	1469	1469
Foodstuffs		0	2205	2205
Miscellaneous Industries		200	0	200
Public Utilities		0	735	735
Construction		0	735	735
Trade		1800	11756	13556
Transportation		1800	2208	4008
Communications		0	735	735
Financial Institutions		0	735	735
Public Administration		1200	1469	2669
Other Services		1200	13961	15161
Totals	5400	24000	60992	90392

Source: Najberg and Vieira (1996) *apud* Meiners (1998)

els. In the next year, the company increased its product range by producing new versions of these models. In 2002, the production of cargo and mixed-use pickup trucks began. Total production started with 24 thousand units, reaching a peak in 2001, when 71 thousand units were produced (see Table 7).

Analyzing the domestic market, Renault was quite aggressive at first, producing only automobiles of mixed use. In its first year, the company

TABLE 6. Number of Forecast and Generated Jobs at Renault and Selected Suppliers, Year 2000

Company	Forecast	Created	%
Renault	2,000	2,177	109
Copo	400	46	12
Bertrand Faure	300	95	32
Koyo Steering	150	27	18
Thera	110	45	41
Trèves	100	196	196
SNR Roulements	75	75	100
Total	3,115	2,661	85

Source: Motim et al. (2002)

TABLE 7. Renault's Production of Different Types of Automobiles for the Years 1999-2004, in Units

Production	1999		2000		2001		2002		2003		2004*	
	Qty	%	Qty	%	Qty	%	Qty	%	Qty	%	Qty	%
Cars	0	0	6411	11	19981	28	13037	27	16520	28	9332	27
Cars mixed-use	24809	100	51672	89	51127	72	33684	70	40869	70	22797	67
L. Comm. Mixed-use	0	0	0	0	0	0	129	0	775	1	499	1
Light Commercial	0	0	0	0	0	0	1190	2	442	1	1368	4
Total	24809		58083		71108		48040		58606		33996	

Source: Anfavea 1999-2004
*Only the six first months of the year were considered.

acquired a 3% market share in this sector. This share rose to 5% in each of the two subsequent years. From 2002 on, its share was stable at 4%. When it came to passenger cars, the share was unstable. In 2000, its first year, its share was 1%, rising to 8% in the following year, and oscillating between 7% and 6% in the following years. The overall share of the assembly plant began with 2% of the market, peaking at 5% in 2001, and stabilizing at around 4% thereafter (see Table 8).

The assembly plant had a low share of the external market, however. During its first year, it only exported 8% of its domestic output, but this rose in 2000 as exports made up 25% of its production; of these, 48%

TABLE 8. Internal Sales, Renault and Other Assembly Plants, for Different Types of Vehicles for the Years 1999-2004, in Thousands of Units

	1999		2000		2001		2002		2003		2004*	
	Qty	%	Qty	%	Qty	%	Qty	%	Qty	%	Qty	%
Cars	193		212		204		237		233		128	
Renault	0	0	2	1	16	8	15	6	15	7	8	6
Others	193	100	210	99	188	92	223	94	218	93	120	94
Cars mixed-use	706		864		972		926		849		471	
Renault	18	3	40	5	44	5	39	4	36	4	17	4
Others	688	97	824	95	928	95	888	96	814	96	471	100
L.Comm. mixed-use	24		28		24		23		47		29	
Renault	0	0	0	0	0	0	0	1	1	2	1	2
Others	24	100	28	100	24	100	23	99	47	98	28	98
Light Commercial	98		132		134		114		101		61	
Renault	0	0	0	0	0	0	0	0	1	1	1	1
Others	98	100	132	100	134	100	114	100	100	99	60	99
Total	1020		1236		1335		1301		1230		688	
Renault	18	2	42	3	61	5	54	4	52	4	27	4
Others	1002	98	1194	97	1274	95	1247	96	1178	96	679	99

Source: Anfavea 1999-2004
*Only the six first months of the year were considered.

were passenger cars and 22% were mixed-use vehicles. This was the year in which the plant enjoyed its biggest export volume, reaching 14 thousand. In the following years, however, not only did its share of exports decline, but also its volume; in the following two years, its share was 8% and 5%, with a volume of 5 and 2.5 thousand units, respectively. There was a recovery of exports in 2003, chiefly due to pickup trucks, which were mainly being produced for export. Pickup truck exports represented 81% of total pickup production in that year, while exports rose to 12% of total output. Table 9 presents the total output share for exports. When Renault's exports are compared with those of other assembly plants, one observes a small, but stable share. Table 10 presents information on exports by Renault and other assembly plants.

The situation that Renault foresaw for the region was already affected by the closing of the Chrysler plant. Renault's original projection was for the production of 120 thousand units (currently, the assembly plant is

TABLE 9. Exports by Renault and Its Share in Domestic Production for the Years 1999-2004, in Units

	1999		2000		2001		2002		2003		2004*	
	Qty	%	Qty	%	Qty	%	Qty	%	Qty	%	Qty	%
Cars.	0	0	3059	48	2104	11	836	6.4	1571	10	706	8
Cars mixed-use	1903	8	11400	22	3403	7	1650	4.9	4880	12	4314	19
L.Comm. mixed-use	0	0	0	0	0	0	3	2.3	50	6	10	2
Light Commercial	0	0	0	0	0	0	1	0.1	356	81	320	23
Total	1903	8	14459	25	5507	8	2490	5.2	6857	12	5350	16

Source: Anfavea 1999-2004
* Only the six first months of the year were considered.

TABLE 10. Exports by Renault Assembly Plant, by Type, and in Comparison with Other Assembly Plants for the Years 1999-2004

	1999		2000		2001		2002		2003		2004*	
	Qty	%	Qty	%	Qty	%	Qty	%	Qty	%	Qty	%
Cars	30		47		94		101		119		50	
Renault	0	0	3	6	2	2	1	1	2	1	1	1
Others	30	100	44	94	92	98	100	99	117	99	49	99
Cars mixed-use	174		236		227		269		322		165	
Renault	2	1	11	5	3	1	2	1	5	2	4	3
Others	172	99	225	95	224	99	268	99	317	98	161	97
L.Comm. mixed-use	1		2		8		0		22		19	
Renault	0	0	0	0	0	0	0	1	0	0	0	0
Others	1	100	2	100	8	100	0	99	22	100	19	100
Light Commercial	56		71		48		42		50		28	
Renault	0	0	0	0	0	0	1	2	0	1	0	1
Others	56	100	71	100	48	100	41	98	50	99	27	99
Total	262		356		377		412		513		261	
Renault	2	1	14	4	6	1	3	1	7	1	5	2
Others	260	99	342	96	372	99	409	99	506	99	256	98

Source: Anfavea 1999-2004
*Only the six first months of the year were considered

producing just a little more than 50% of this goal, and this situation is not expected to change in the short-run). The domestic market was stagnant until 2004, when it began to grow, especially after the introduction of *bifuel* cars (which could run on either alcohol or gasoline). It is important to remember that in contrast to other automobile companies, especially the older ones, Renault has only one plant in Brazil, and it does not have the flexibility of switching to new products without leaving the country.

FINAL CONSIDERATIONS

The process of Paraná's industrialization began in the 1970s. In the 90s, mainly from the second half on, the state of Paraná started to compete with other states for direct foreign investments. This competition became known as the fiscal war among the states. Paraná attracted three new assembly plants, Renault being one of them. The concessions that were given have been the target of much criticism, since at the beginning they were greater than the total value of the investments. This led to a contract revision. Defenders of the concessions have argued that the incentives will have been worth it in the long-run, since the initial assembly plants will end up attracting more investments. The Renault project is still in its maturation phase. It has, however, attracted investments by supply firms not only from other states but also from abroad. Renault has also fulfilled its goals with respect to job creation.

REFERENCES

Abrix, G. (2000). "Guerra Fiscal e Competição Intermunicipal no Setor Automobilístico Brasileiro." Dados, Vol. 43, No. 1, sp. Available at: <*http://www.scielo.br/ scielo. php?script=sci_arttext&pid=S0011-52582000000100001&lng=en&nrm=iso*>. Accessed on Oct. 07, 2003.

Alves, M.A. de S. (2000). "Guerra Fiscal e Finanças Federativas no Brasil: O Caso do Setor Automotivo." *Master's Thesis*. Campinas: Universidade Estadual de Campinas/ Instituto de Economia.

ANFAVEA–Associação Nacional de Fabricantes de Veículos Automotores. (1999). "Tabelas estatísticas: dados referentes a 1999." Available at: <*http://www.anfavea. com.br/tabelas1999/tabelas.htm*>.

ANFAVEA–Associação Nacional de Fabricantes de Veículos Automotores. (2000). "Tabelas Estatísticas: Dados Referentes a 2000." Available at: <*http://www. anfavea.com.br/tabelas2000/tabelas.htm*>.

ANFAVEA–Associação Nacional de Fabricantes de Veículos Automotores. (2001). "Tabelas Estatísticas: Dados Referentes a 2001." Available at: <*http://www. anfavea. com.br/tabelas2001/tabelas.htm*>.

ANFAVEA–Associação Nacional de Fabricantes de Veículos Automotores. (2002). "Tabelas Estatísticas: Dados Referentes a 2002." Available at: <*http://www. anfavea.com.br/tabelas2002/tabelas.htm*>.

ANFAVEA–Associação Nacional de Fabricantes de Veículos Automotores. (2003). "Tabelas Estatísticas: Dados Referentes a 2003." Available at: <*http://www. anfavea.com.br/tabelas2003/tabelas.htm*>.

ANFAVEA–Associação Nacional de Fabricantes de Veículos Automotores. (2004). "Tabelas Estatísticas: Dados Referentes a 2004." Available at: <*http://www. anfavea.com.br/tabelas2004/tabelas.htm*>.

Fonseca, M. W., and Peris, A. F. (2003). "O Paraná perante o Processo de Desconcentração Industrial Brasileiro." 17 pp. (mimeo) Available at: <*http://www. unioeste.br/cursos/cascavel/economia/artigo.pdf/06_pr_desconcentração.pdf*> Accessed on Oct. 07, 2003.

Lopes, J. C. J. et al. (2004). "Repercussões Sócio-Ambientais Decorrentes da Implantação do Distrito Industrial em São José dos Pinhais–PR." In: II ENCONTRO ASSOCIAÇÃO NACIONAL DE PÓS-GRADUAÇÃO E PESQUISA EM AMBIENTE E SOCIEDADE, Indaiatuba, 2004. Annals. Indaiatuba: ANPPAS, 2004. Available at: <*http://www.anppas.org.br/encontro/segundo/*>

IPARDES–Instituto Paranaense de Desenvolvimento e Social (1982). "Paraná: economia e sociedade." Curitiba: Ipardes. 71pp.

Lourenço, G. M. (2000). "Retaguarda Institucional das Transformações Econômicas no Paraná." *Análise Conjuntural*, Vol. 22, No. 11-12, pp. 2-9.

Lourenço, G. M. (2001). "O Paraná e o Desempenho das Economias Regionais." *Revista F.A.E.*, Vol. 4, No. 2, pp. 1-12.

Macedo, M. M., Vieira, V. F., and Meiners, W. E. M. A. (2002). "Fases de Desenvolvimento Regional no Brasil e no Paraná: De Emergência de um Novo Modelo de Desenvolvimento na Economia Paranaense." *Revista Paranaense de Desenvolvimento*, Curitiba, No. 103, pp. 5-22.

Magalhães Filho, F. (1996). "Evolução Histórica da Economia Paranaense." *Revista Paranaense de Desenvolvimento*, Curitiba, No. 87, pp. 131-148.

Meiners, W. E. M. A. (1998). "Impactos Regionais dos Investimentos Automobilísticos no Paraná." *Revista Paranaense de Desenvolvimento*, Curitiba, No. 94, pp. 29-48.

Motim, B. M., Firkowiski, O. L. C. F., and Araújo, S. M. P. (2002). "Desconcentração da Indústria Brasileira e Seus Efeitos sobre os Trabalhadores: A Indústria Automobilística no Paraná." *Revista Electrónica de Geografía y Ciencias Sociales*, Barcelona, Vol. 6, No. 119, sp. Available at: <*http://www.ub.es/geocrit/sn/sn119-88*>. Accessed on Oct. 02, 2005.

Rodrigues, D. A. (1999). "A Distribuição Setorial e Estadual dos Novos Investimentos no Brasil: 1996/98." *Revista do BNDES*, Rio de Janeiro, June, No. 11, pp. 76-96.

Rodrigues, D. A. (2000). "Os Investimentos no Brasil nos Anos 90: Cenários Setorial e Regional." *Revista do BNDES*, Rio de Janeiro, June, No. 13, pp. 107-135.

Santos, A. M. M. M, and Pinhão, C. M. A. (1999). "Pólos Automotivos Brasileiros." *BNDES Setorial*, Rio de Janeiro, September, No. 10, pp. 173-200.

SEIT–Secretaria de Estado da Indústria, Comércio e do Turismo. Available at: <*http:// www.seit.pr.go.br*> Accessed on Oct. 07, 2003.

Sesso Filho, U. A. *et al.* (2004). "Indústria Automobilística no Paraná: Impactos na Produção Local e no Restante do Brasil." In: XXXII ENCONTRO NACIONAL DE ECONOMIA–ANPEC, João Pessoa, 2004. Annals. Belo Horizonte: ANPEC, 2004. Available at: <*http://www.anpec.org.br/encontro 2004/*>

SINDIMETAL (1997). "Paraná Automotivo: Desafios e Perspectivas para as Empresas Locais." Coord. Téc. Ferro, J. R. Curitiba: SINDIMETAL: SEBRAE/PR. 51pp.

SINDIMETAL (1997). "Paraná Automotivo: Progressos em 1998." Coord. Téc. Ferro, J. R. Curitiba: SINDIMETAL: SEBRAE/PR. 56pp.

Vasconcelos, J. R., and Castro, D. (1999). "Paraná: Economia, Finanças Públicas e Investimentos nos Anos 90." *Texto para discussão*, No. 624, pp. 66, Brasília: IPEA.

Verri, E. J. (2003). "Reestruturação Produtiva no Paraná nos Anos 90: O Papel da Globalização e do Mercosul." São Paulo. Tese de doutorado. São Paulo: Universidade de São Paulo. 111 pp.

doi:10.1300/J140v07n03_04

Structural Change
in the Brazilian Automotive Industry
and Its Regional Impacts

Edmund Amann
Eduardo Haddad
Fernando Perobelli
Joaquim Guilhoto

SUMMARY. From the late 1980s onward, the Brazilian automotive industry has undergone significant change as it has embraced trade liberalization and growing inward FDI. Using an inter-regional input-output model, this paper analyses the evolution of the industry from a spatial perspective. It is shown that new investment has resulted in a more dispersed locational framework for the industry. However, not all the benefits of new investment are garnered by the recipient regions. The paper poses a number of policy questions which center on the issue of inter-regional dependence.

Edmund Amann is affiliated with University of Manchester, UK and Regional Economics Applications Laboratory (REAL), University of Illinois, USA. Eduardo Haddad is affiliated with University of São Paulo, Brazil, Regional Economics Applications Laboratory (REAL), University of Illinois, USA, and is CNPq scholar. Fernando Perobelli is affiliated with Federal University of Juiz de Fora, Brazil. Joaquim Guilhoto is affiliated with University of São Paulo, Brazil, Regional Economics Applications Laboratory (REAL), University of Illinois, USA, and is CNPq scholar.

[Haworth co-indexing entry note]: "Structural Change in the Brazilian Automotive Industry and Its Regional Impacts." Amann, Edmund et al. Co-published simultaneously in *Latin American Business Review* (International Business Press, an imprint of The Haworth Press, Inc.) Vol. 7, No. 3/4, 2006, pp. 97-119; and: *Latin American Business: Equity Distortion in Regional Resource Allocation in Brazil* (ed: Werner Baer, and Geoffrey Hewings) International Business Press, an imprint of The Haworth Press, Inc., 2006, pp. 97-119. Single or multiple copies of this article are available for a fee from The Haworth Document Delivery Service [1-800-HAWORTH, 9:00 a.m. - 5:00 p.m. (EST). E-mail address: docdelivery@haworthpress.com].

RESUMEN. Desde fines de la década de 1980 hasta la fecha, la industria automotriz brasileña ha sufrido importantes cambios al adoptar la liberalización del comercio y atraer más inversiones financieras directas. Basándose en un modelo de entrada-salida interregional, este estudio analiza la evolución de la industria desde una perspectiva espacial. Se ha llegado a la conclusión, que las nuevas inversiones fueron causales de un marco más disperso para el establecimiento de la industria en ciertas localidades. No obstante lo antedicho, también es verdad que no todos los beneficios logrados con estas ventajas fueron atraídas por las regiones receptoras. Consecuentemente, el estudio cuestiona varias políticas que se centralizaban en la problemática de la dependencia interregional.

RESUMO. A partir do final da década de 1980, a indústria automobilística brasileira sofreu uma mudança significativa ao adotar a liberalização comercial e atrair mais investimentos estrangeiros diretos. Usando um modelo de entrada-saída inter-regional, este estudo analisa a evolução do setor em perspectiva espacial. Sabe-se que os investimentos novos resultaram numa estrutura de localização mais dispersa para o setor. Entretanto, nem todos os benefícios dos investimentos novos são obtidos pelas regiões receptoras. O estudo levanta uma série de questões de política, centradas no problema da dependência inter-regional. doi:10.1300/J140v07n03_05 *[Article copies available for a fee from The Haworth Document Delivery Service: 1-800-HAWORTH. E-mail address: <docdelivery@haworthpress.com> Website: <http://www.HaworthPress. com>* © 2006 by The Haworth Press, Inc. All rights reserved.]

KEYWORDS. Automotive industry, input-ouptut models, Brazil, Foreign Direct Investment

1. INTRODUCTION

Over the past two decades, the automotive industry worldwide has been undergoing a profound structural transformation. Driven by declining barriers to trade and investment, an acceleration in the pace of technical change and rising pressure for consolidation, the locational characteristics of the industry have changed radically. In particular, the spread of global production chains[1] and a blurring of the boundary between components suppliers and assemblers have given rise to an increasing internationalization of the production process. To a great extent, it is no longer appropriate to talk in terms of national, vertically integrated automotive industries. Instead, it has become increasingly common to observe a dispersion of distinct elements of the production chain across national borders. This process has perhaps been most elaborately developed in the case of Western Europe and North America, where regional trade arrangements have facilitated the tariff-free intra-regional movement of components as well as finished vehicles.

The automotive industry in Latin America, like its counterparts elsewhere, has not proven immune to these global developments. In particular, the past decade has witnessed the rapid integration of the automotive industries of South America's two largest economies–Argentina and Brazil. With the creation of Mercosul[2] and the signing of a series of bilateral accords, trade in automotive products between Argentina and Brazil has been extensively–though far from totally–liberalized. As a partial result, from the mid-1990s onward, both countries–but most especially Brazil–have experienced a surge in new investment directed at the automotive sector. In the case of Brazil, the expansion of capacity has also been spurred on by a generally healthy growth in domestic demand, itself largely the product of a successful stabilization plan. In addition to these attractive features, a number of automotive producers have been drawn to Brazil by a range of generous fiscal incentives, often originating at sub-national levels of government.

While it is commonly accepted that Brazil's automotive sector is now larger and more "internationalized" than at any time in its history, there have been few attempts to formally assess the implications this has had for the domestic pattern of industrial location and, by extension, the impact on regional development. Over the next few pages, this paper aims to address this somewhat overlooked issue by adopting the following approach. After a brief review of the main recent sectoral and policy developments, an attempt is made to characterize the locational evolution of the Brazilian automotive sector over the past decade. Having established the nature of these locational changes, the paper then goes on to evaluate their implications for the pattern of regional development within Brazil. In order to achieve this objective, an interregional input-output model is prepared and then tested to assess the recent impact of locational change on such variables as regional income levels and employment. Finally, the tractability of these results is discussed before the possible policy implications are reviewed.

2. STRUCTURAL CHANGE IN THE AUTOMOTIVE INDUSTRY: INTERNATIONAL TRENDS

As suggested in the introduction, the international automotive industry has entered a radically new phase in its development. Up until twenty years ago, the development of the industry had been characterized by a curious paradox. While the bulk of global assembly was in the hands of a relatively select group of multinational corporations (MNCs), production activity itself was strongly national rather than global in orientation. Thus, while the major automotive manufacturers owned subsidiaries across North America, Europe, Latin America, Africa and Asia, these subsidiaries frequently had no connection with one another beyond drawing on the same pool of multinational capital and technological expertise.[3]

While assembly activity for the most part took take place within the national market to be supplied, the supply chains underpinning such assembly activity also tended to be domestic rather than international in character. Although a number of multinational components suppliers existed, their production activities tended to be located in the countries for which output was destined. However, by no means was the entire components sector in the hands of MNCs. Instead, a significant portion of component supplies tended to be obtained from domestically owned enterprises in the country of assembly. Taking all of these considerations into account, it becomes obvious that any characterization of the automotive sector as "international" prior to the 1980s would need serious qualification.

Since the beginning of the 1980s, however, the evolution of the automotive sector worldwide has embarked on a distinctively new phase in which the concept of the national has become increasingly subsumed by that of the global. Throughout this period, both developed and less developed economies have significantly lowered barriers to trade and investment, opening up national automotive markets as never before to imports and permitting the entry of new producers. These developments have had the effect of inducing far greater competitive pressures upon automotive producers in whichever national market they operate. However, by the same token, both trade and investment liberalization have granted both incumbent producers and new entrants unparalleled opportunities to gain a competitive advantage by shipping both finished products and components across borders. This process has been lent particular force in the case of Western Europe and North America where, respectively, the deepening of the European Union (EU) and the emergence of the North American Free Trade Agreement (NAFTA) have allowed much greater integration of the production process across national boundaries. Thus, to a great extent, at least in the case of Europe and North America, it seems increasingly anachronistic to talk in terms of national automotive sectors.

In tandem with this regionalization, if not globalization of the automotive industry, two other imperatives have affected its development over the past 20 years. In the first place, it has been possible to observe a far-reaching shift in technological strategy, which has at its core the objective of creating global vehicle platforms upon which local market variants can be produced. With much of automotive assemblers' considerable research and development expenditure being concentrated on the design of the engine, transmission and floor plan layout, it is obvious that such costs (as well as unit production costs) can be defrayed more effectively, the greater the number of units produced using a given platform. In addition, it is equally clear that unit R + D (if not production) costs will tend to fall the fewer the number of platform types in use.

Accompanying the global standardization of platforms, it has also been possible to observe a concurrent shift in the relation between assemblers and their suppliers. To an increasing extent, the major automotive assemblers have been altering their production strategies, aiming to reduce the complexity of the final assembly process and lower their working capital requirements. The result of these developments has been to enhance the role of components suppliers, obliging them to produce more elaborate sub-assemblies and to deliver these to assembly plants on a just in time basis. At the same time, given the increasingly stringent demands of markets around the world, assemblers have been demanding ever-higher standards of quality from their suppliers. Consequently, unprecedented competitive demands have been placed on components suppliers, demands that many traditional single-country based enterprises have been unable to meet. As a consequence, a growing trend within the international automotive industry has been for assemblers to forge global preferred supplier agreements with major multinational components manufacturers such as Lear, TRW and Robert Bosch.

In sum, therefore, as the automotive industry enters its second century of operation, its structural characteristics are changing as rapidly as the technology it embodies. As international production chains supplant their domestic counterparts and components manufacturing becomes dominated by MNCs, automotive manufacturing is at last on the road to becoming a genuinely global undertaking. Under these circumstances, one might well expect profound changes in the locational characteristics of the industry with attendant implications for patterns of regional development. As will be made clear, the experience of Brazil provides ample evidence that this has in fact been the case.

3. STRUCTURAL CHANGE IN THE AUTOMOTIVE INDUSTRY: POLICY DEVELOPMENTS IN THE 1990s AND THE BRAZILIAN EXPERIENCE

Prior to 1990, the Brazilian automotive sector was one of the world's most heavily protected, being surrounded by stringent tariff and non-tariff barriers which applied to both components and assembled vehicles. This protective regime represented the ultimate evolution of almost four decades of official attempts to foster the development of the sector through a policy of import substitution industrialization (ISI). In general terms, the application of ISI policies proved initially highly successful in bringing about the expansion and modernization of Brazil's nascent automotive industry (Shapiro 1994; Addis 1999). However, by the 1980s it had become increasingly clear that the policies of protection that had once guided the sector's development so effectively were now directly associated with mounting inefficiency, poor quality, technological backwardness and low export intensity. With the accession to power of President Fernando Collor de Melo in 1990, policy makers embarked on an ambitious program of trade liberalization, which had as its prime objective the rapid insertion of Brazil into the international economy (Amann, 2000). The impacts of this dramatic shift in policy on levels of protection enjoyed by the automotive sector were profound. As Table 1 indicates, over the first four years of the trade liberalization program, average tariff levels applying to finished vehicles and autoparts fell by 40%. More significantly still, the trade reforms of 1990 abolished quantitative restrictions on imports. For a number of years, these had effectively barred imports of finished vehicles, thereby rendering the heavy tariffs redundant.

However, by the beginning of 1995, a combination of accelerating domestic demand and a strengthening exchange rate had led to a substantial surge in automotive imports, particularly of assembled passenger cars. With this surge in imports strongly contributing toward a sharp deterioration in the trade balance, the authorities elected to partially reverse their policy of trade liberalization, raising tariffs on finished vehi-

TABLE 1. The Evolution of Brazilian Import Tariffs on Automotive Sector Products, 1990-2000 (%)

	1990	1994	1995 (February)	1995 (March)	1996-1999	2000
Finished Vehicles	45	20	32	70	70-35*	35
Autoparts	30	18	18	18	2.4-9.6	14-18

*Manufacturers with assembly facilities or investment projects in Brazil qualified for the 35% tariff. All other importers were required to pay the 70% tariff
Used with permission *BNDES Setorial*. Santos and Gonçalves, 2001, p. 209

cles from 32% to 70%. However, by 1996, with concern over the trade deficit abating, the tariff increase was partially rescinded with a new tariff of 35% established, applying to imports of vehicles by manufacturers with production facilities in Brazil (Bonelli et al., 1997).

The launch of the Brazilian trade liberalization program in the early 1990s coincided with another highly significant development: negotiations for the creation of a regional free trade area embracing Brazil, Argentina, Uruguay and Paraguay. This free trade area, known as Mercosul, formally came into being on January 1, 1995 and should have ushered in completely free trade in automotive products between its members. However, the Argentineans, fearing that their automotive industry would not be able to withstand unrestrained competition from its Brazilian counterpart, set in train negotiations to create a managed trade regime in which quantitative measures would continue to play a role. With the negotiations concluded, toward the end of 1995, the first automotive accord came into force providing for qualified free trade in automotive products between South America's two largest economies.

Under the terms of the accord, automotive products could be traded free of tariffs between Brazil and Argentina provided that neither country ran an automotive product trade deficit or surplus with the other. The agreement also set out the tariffs, which would be applied to imports from outside Mercosul. In the case of Brazil, it was agreed that a tariff of 35% would apply, although, as noted above, a tariff of 70% would be imposed on vehicles whose manufacturers had no production facilities in Brazil. By the end of 2000, a new version of the automotive accord had come into being. This agreement, while retaining the 35% tariff for non-Mercosul vehicle imports, allowed for limited free Argentinean-Brazilian trade in automotive products even in the event that such trade was imbalanced.

To sum up, over the 1990s, despite the existence of a bilateral managed trade accord with Argentina, and the persistent, relatively high tariffs, there is no question but that Brazil did substantially liberalize trade in automotive products. A particular feature of the trade liberalization process has been its emphasis on the creation of a regional, as opposed to a purely national market for vehicles and their components. This, taken together with strong regional growth in the early to mid-1990s provided conditions that proved highly attractive to foreign investors. As a result, the Brazilian automotive industry has recently experienced a surge in investment not seen since its founding in the 1950s. Responding to this promising development, substantial competition has emerged among different localities in Brazil to act as recipients for this investment. Taken together with regional integration and increasing competitive pressure on producers, a radical evolution in locational patterns within the sector has resulted. It is to this issue that the paper now turns.

4. CHANGES IN THE LOCATIONAL CHARACTERISTICS OF THE BRAZILIAN AUTOMOTIVE SECTOR AND THE ROLE OF LOCAL INCENTIVES

Large-scale vehicle assembly in Brazil began at the end of the 1950s with the establishment of assembly plants by Volkswagen, Toyota, Ford (for passenger cars and light commercial vehicles), Mercedes-Benz (for trucks and buses) and General Motors (for all vehicle types). As in the early days of mass production in the United States, the initial growth of the automotive industry in Brazil was characterized by a high degree of geographical concentration. Of the assembly facilities mentioned above, all lay within the confines of metropolitan São Paulo, with the industrial suburb of São Caetano do Sul alone playing host to no fewer than four plants. Accompanying the expansion of automotive assembly came rapid growth in the components sector. Once again, the development of this sector proved highly geographically concentrated at first, with the vast bulk of capacity being located in São Caetano do Sul and the neighboring suburbs of Santo André and Diadema.

In a fashion similar to the United States, as time progressed and the industry matured, a process of geographical dispersion became evident. The origins of this development can be traced to the early 1970s when Ford and Volkswagen, attracted by the fiscal incentives on offer, extended their activities beyond the immediate vicinity of metropolitan São Paulo into the upstate region of Vale do Paraíba. General Motors, too, opted to locate a portion of capacity away from the city of São Paulo, choosing São José dos Campos for its new engine plant. More significantly still, in 1977 Fiat established a major assembly facility well away from São Paulo, in Betim in the heart of Minas Gerais state. Despite these important locational decisions, however, the Brazilian automotive sector still remained largely centered on the city of São Paulo right through the late 1970s and into the 1980s.

Since the beginning of the 1990s, the centrifugal forces underpinning geographical dispersion in the industry have become far stronger. As noted in the previous section, technological change and alterations in the policy environment over the past ten years or so have proven increasingly conducive to the location of production facilities away from the traditional industrial centers. In the first place, the lowering of trade barriers, while by no means as dramatic as for other industrial sectors, has nonetheless placed heightened competitive pressure on both automotive assemblers and components manufacturers.

Against this background, enterprises have become preoccupied with tackling the cost base and improving flexibility of response to changing market demands. Not surprisingly, therefore, the attractions of locating away from São Paulo city, with its relatively high labor costs and levels of unionization, have proved compelling. At the same time, the advent of Mercosul and the signing of automotive trade accords with Argentina have opened up new markets to the South. Aside from providing an enhanced export outlet for finished vehicles, the accords specifically promote the use of Argentinean components in Brazilian vehicles and vice-versa. As a consequence, the opportunities presented by locating both assembly and components production closer to Brazil's southern borders have become far more enticing than was the case previously.

Perhaps of greatest significance in determining new locational patterns in the Brazilian automotive industry has been the role of state and municipal government incentives. While the development of Mercosul and strong growth in the domestic market have proven key determinants for the wave of new investments in the sector since 1990, the importance of the providing of tax breaks, grants, infrastructure and other measures by sub-national governments should not be underestimated. As Table 2 suggests, states and municipalities outside the traditional heartland of the Brazilian automotive industry have proven by far the most aggressive in offering prospective investors generous incentives. In a number of instances, the scale of these incentives has been such so as to substantially outweigh the otherwise obvious locational disadvantages of particular sites.[4]

Taking all of the above factors together, it is hardly surprising that the geographical spread of the Brazilian automotive industry has altered radically over the past few years. As Table 3 attests, besides the state of São Paulo, major assembly facilities now operate in the states of Rio de Janeiro, Minas Gerais, Paraná, Rio Grande do Sul, Goiás and Bahia. Whereas at the beginning of the 1970s 100% of all vehicles were assembled in São Paulo, by the beginning of this decade that state was responsible for just under 50% of total national output (ANFAVEA, 2000). By contrast, automotive assembly plants in Minas Gerais and Rio de Janeiro, non-existent in the early 1970s, now account for around 30% of all vehicles produced in Brazil.

Although the production of automotive components remains concentrated in São Paulo state,[5] the past few years have nevertheless witnessed a process of geographical dispersion similar in direction if not in scale to that affecting the assembly sector. As Table 4 reveals, between 1991 and 2001, both in terms of employees and numbers of enterprises there was a marked tendency toward the movement of component manufacturing outside the traditional heartland of metropolitan São Paulo. Of particular significance, over this ten-year period the percentage of enterprises and employees engaged in component production in states other than São Paulo rose from 9.3% to 20.9% and 10.6% to 29.4%, respectively.[6]

Naturally, this tendency toward geographical dispersion of production activity in the components sector should not be viewed in isolation from the emergence of new locational patterns in the assembly sector. As new assembly facilities were established away from the greater São Paulo metropolitan area, components manufacturers[7] increasingly found it necessary to locate close to their customers. At the same time, as in the case of the assembly industry, with its clients in locations away from its traditional center of production the components industry found itself able to benefit from attractive fiscal incentives on offer, which were often tied into just-in-time relationships.

In the next section, we use an interregional input-output model for the Brazilian economy for purposes of regional impact assessment. The model is to be used to capture the role of interindustrial and interregional relations in the economic development process through the evaluation of the regional impact of new investments in the automobile industry. The use of this modeling approach is very relevant to the Brazilian case. Its ability to handle detail at a disaggregated level is useful for analyzing the evolution of Brazil's productive structure.

TABLE 2. State and Municipal Government Incentives Granted to Automobile Assemblers: Two Case Studies

Incentive	The State of Minas Gerais and Mercedes Benz	The State of Paraná and Renault
Land Donated by State/Municipality	28 million square meters	Purchase of 5 million square meters funded though not donated by the state government
Infrastructure provided	Drainage, road access, vehicle testing roads, electricity connection	Electricity substation and connection (with 25% electricity tariff reduction), railhead and spur, water supply, exclusive berth at Paranaguá docks
Capital participation by state/municipal government	None	40% equivalent to R$300m financed by COPEL (a power utility) share sales and credits from the now extinct BADEP (Paraná State Bank)
Credit granted	R$112m in fixed and working capital finance facilities repayable at a 3.5% annual real rate of interest. Repayment holidays apply to tranches of the borrowing ranging from 12 to 30 months	Value not disclosed but terms are generous (10 year and no interest) according to company balance sheets
Deferment of state sales tax (ICMS) payments	Deferred payment allowed and financed by state-provided credit facilities	Deferment of 48 months granted. The real rate of interest to be charged on the balance due is equivalent to 0%
Tax exemptions granted	None disclosed	None disclosed
State government guarantees for credit facilities provided	R$101.9m in CEMIG (a power utility) shares; a R$3.1m bond	None disclosed

Used with permission. Cavalcanti, C., and Prado, S. "Aspectos da Guerra Fiscal no Brasil." IPEA/FUNDAP (1998, p. 132).

5. ASSESSING THE REGIONAL IMPACTS OF FISCAL INCENTIVES IN THE AUTOMOBILE SECTOR IN BRAZIL

We start by describing the model used to analyze the regional effects of new investments in the automobile industry. The general equilibrium nature of economic interdependence and the fact that the policy impacts in various regional markets differ are considered in the results of the model. Attention is directed to two main issues: (a) the differential impacts in the construction and operation phases, and (b) the differential impacts of investments originating in different regions.

As the simulations try to mimic a "typical investment project," we have selected as our case study the investments undertaken by Mercedes

TABLE 3. Location of Major Production Facilities in the Brazilian Automotive Sector

State	City	Company	Product
São Paulo	São Bernardo do Campo	Ford	Cars, light commercials
		Karmann-Ghia	Tools, welding and assembly of modules and complete bodies, vehicle assembly
		Land Rover	Light commercials
		Mercedes-Benz	Trucks, bus chassis, engines
		Scania	Trucks, buses; industrial and marine engines
		Toyota	Light commercials
		Volkswagen	Cars, light commercials
	São Paulo	Ford	Light commercials, trucks
	Taubaté	Ford	Components, engines, transmissions
		Volkswagen	Cars
	São Caetano do Sul	General Motors	Cars
	Mogi das Cruzes	General Motors	Stamped Components
		Toyota	Tractor Wheels
	Sumaré	Honda	Cars
	Campinas	Mercedes-Benz	Bus platforms
	Indaiatuba	Toyota	Cars
	São Carlos	Volkswagen	Engines
	Pederneiras	Volvo	Articulated trucks, loaders, road graders
Minas Gerais	Betim	Fiat	Cars, light commercials, Engines
	Juiz de Fora	Mercedes-Benz	Cars
	Pouso Alegre	JPX	Light commercials
	Sete Lagoas	Fiat/Iveco	Light commercials, trucks and engines
Rio de Janeiro	Porto Real	Peugeot Citroën	Cars
	Resende	Volkswagen	Trucks, buses
Paraná	Campo Largo	Chrysler	Light commercials
		Chrysler/BMW	Engines
	Curitiba	Volvo	Trucks, truck cabins, bus chassis, engines
	São José dos Pinhais	Renault	Cars, engines
		Volkswagen/AUDI	Cars
Rio G. do Sul	Caxias do Sul	Agrale	Trucks, bus chassis, components manufacturing
	Gravataí	General Motors	Trucks
Goiás	Catalão	MMC	Light commercials
Bahia	Camaçari	Ford	Not available

Source: ANFAVEA–Statistical Yearbook of the Brazilian Automotive Industry (2000)

TABLE 4. Percentage Distribution by Location of Enterprises and Employees in the Automotive Components Sector (1991-2001)

	Enterprises		Employees	
	1991	*2001*	*1991*	*2001*
City of São Paulo	38.9	24.6	30.2	13.0
ABCD Industrial Suburbs*	18.4	16.6	15.8	13.4
Other districts of Greater São Paulo city	16.2	16.8	19.9	15.6
São Paulo state**	17.2	21.1	23.5	28.6
Other states	9.3	20.9	10.6	29.4

*Namely Santo André; São Bernardo do Campo; São Caetano do Sul and Diadema. These suburbs form the industrial core of the greater São Paulo city metropolitan area.
**i.e., São Paulo State excluding the greater São Paulo city metropolitan area.
Used with permission. Sindipeças (2002)

Benz in the State of Minas Gerais. In this chapter, we intend to use the project parameters to simulate different arbitrary locations for the plant, rather than evaluate more properly the impacts of Mercedes Benz itself. Readers interested in the specific impacts of the latter project in Juiz de Fora are directed to the chapter by Perobelli et al. (2006).

5.1. Theoretical Background

The intersectoral flows in a given economy can be represented by the following system:

$$X = AX + Y \tag{1}$$

where X is a $(nx1)$ vector with the value of the total production in each sector, Y is a $(nx1)$ vector with values for the final demand, and A is a (nxn) matrix with the technical coefficients of production. In this model, the final demand vector can be treated as exogenous to the system, such that the level of total production can be determined by the final demand, i.e.,

$$X = BY \tag{2}$$

$$B = (I - A)^{-1} \tag{3}$$

where B is a (nxn) matrix of the Leontief inverse.

According to Miller and Blair (1985), an interregional model for the two regions L and M can have its coefficients matrix represented in matricial terms as:

$$A = \begin{bmatrix} A^{LL} & A^{LM} \\ A^{ML} & MM \end{bmatrix} \tag{4}$$

Vectors X^L and X^M will constitute the total production vector, X

$$X = \begin{bmatrix} X^L \\ X^M \end{bmatrix} \tag{5}$$

The final demand vector, Y, will be composed of vectors Y^L and Y^M

$$Y = \begin{bmatrix} Y^L \\ Y^M \end{bmatrix} \tag{6}$$

As such, the system presented by equation (2) can then be used to represent an interregional system; in this way, it is possible to evaluate the impact of the final demand on total production, and from there, on employment, imports, wages, etc., for each one of the regions considered in the model.

Multipliers

From the multiplier results it is possible to measure the direct and indirect effects of a change in the final demand on production, income, tax, employment, etc. (see Miller and Blair, 1985).

From the Leontief inverse matrix (B) defined above, one sees that the production multiplier of type I for each economic sector is given by:

$$P_j = \sum_{i=1}^{n} b_{ij}$$

$$j = 1, ..., n \tag{7}$$

where P_j is the production multiplier for sector j, and b_{ij} is an element of matrix B.

Using the structure of derivation elaborated below for the employment multipliers, all the other multipliers in the economy can be derived.

The first step is to estimate the coefficients of employment, given by

$$w_j = \frac{e_j}{x_j} \tag{8}$$

where w_j is the coefficient of employment in sector j, e_j is the total employment in sector j, and x_j is the level of production in sector j.

The total employment of type I (E_j), generated in sector j, is given by

$$E_j = \sum_{i=1}^{n} w_i b_{ij} \tag{9}$$

where b_{ij} is an element of matrix B described above.

5.2. Hypotheses for the Simulations

In order to grasp the differential effects associated to different locations of such a "typical project," we will consider six different macro-regional locations for the investment, namely North, Northeast, São Paulo State, Rest of Southeast and South. An interregional input-output model, based on data for 1999 (Guilhoto et al., 2002), will serve as the basis for our simulations. Based on the information provided by the Mercedes Benz project, the project is divided into two phases: (a) the first one is the construction phase, in which the Mercedes Benz production plant is implemented; and (b) the second one is the operational phase, when the the Mercedez Benz A Class is produced by the automobile plant.

In the construction phase, the total investment assumed is R$ 700 million, of which 59% is spent on Machinery, and 30% on Civil Construction, and the remaining value is distributed to the other economic sectors according to their respective shares in the standard unit of investment embedded in the input-output coefficients. In this phase, MB will also buy investment goods from the region in which it is located and from the other regions; how much it buys from its own region and from the other regions will depend on the capacity of those regions to produce capital goods.

In the operational phase, it is assumed that: (a) MB will produce, annually, 12 thousand A Class 160 Classic Mechanics at an average price of R$ 30 thousand, resulting in a total sale of R$ 360 million on final demand; (b) 79.1% of the autoparts are produced in São Paulo; (c) autoparts represent around 17% of the total cost of production; (d) the production technology of the automotive sector for the Northeast is made equal to the one for Brazil as a whole; and (e) when changing the productive structure, it is assumed that a given region buys inputs from itself and from the other regions, according to the capacity of these other regions to produce these kinds of goods.

5.3. Results

Tables 5a and 5b present the results, respectively, for the value added and employment effects in the construction phase, when the plant is located in each one of the six regions being considered in the model. It is clear from the results presented that when the direct and indirect effects are taken into consideration, the region that benefits the most in the process is the state of São Paulo. This benefit, however, is not uniform and will depend on where the plant is located.

In the construction phase, if the plant is located in the Northeast, Midwest, or Rest of the Southeast region, between 43% to 48% of the value added, and between 25% to 33% of the employment generated in the process goes to the state of São Paulo. If the plant is located in the North region, São Paulo gets 32% of the value added and 22% of the employment. However, if the location is in the South region, the share of São Paulo decreases to 14% of the value added and 13% of the employment. This gives an indication of the high level of dependence that the other regions have on São Paulo as a supplier of capital goods.

For the operation phase, the results for value added and employment are presented in Tables 6a and 6b. In this phase, the impacts in the region where the plant is installed are greater than in the construction phase, a fact that can be explained in part by the high concentration of the capital goods industry in the state of São Paulo, and in part by the fact that when a new automobile plant is installed, it brings together a series of satellite industries. However, the results show that between 17% to 23% of the value added, and 13% to 26% of the employment generated stays in the state of São Paulo.

In both phases it also stands out that: (a) after São Paulo, the South region is the one that depends less on the other regions; and (b) the South and Rest of Southeast regions also play an important role as suppliers to the other regions, which is not the case of the North, Northeast and Midwest regions.

The differences in the results are, of course, accounted for by the regional differences and by the hypothesis that the productive structure of the regions is given. Naturally, as the case of Fiat in Minas Gerais has shown, after some time, it is possible that the satellite industries of the automotive complex will move toward the main industry.

FINAL REMARKS

In relation to the discussion above, it is worth making a few additional points. In the first place, the results and estimates so far presented constitute only a partial view of the enormous spatial changes currently affecting the Brazilian automotive sector. Specifically, the analysis only concerned itself with the Brazilian "mega regions" and the state of São Paulo, taking into account their productive interrelationships. From the point of view of a planning exercise at the state level, an interstate model would probably be more suitable when estimating the effects of investment location within the state or the leakage of investment benefits to other regions of the country.

Above and beyond this, such an exercise should also take into account the relationship between the income generating effects of investment and its impact on consumption. Haddad and Hewings (1999) show that such relationships are also important in the assessment of regional impacts of automotive investment, since the income generated in and outside the region transforms itself into distinct patterns of consumption from region to region, a factor which induces new and region-specific rounds of expenditure in the economy.[8] A related point emerges in a study by Perobelli (1999), which highlighted several important regional impacts of investment, drawing on the case study of the Mercedes Benz plant in Juiz de Fora. Taking into account alternate locational configurations of second and third tier suppliers, Perobelli demonstrated that it was municipalities from the state of Rio de Janeiro that had most benefited from the investment despite the fact that it was the government of neighboring Minas Gerais state that had expended all the time, money and effort in attracting Mercedes Benz.[9] In other words, the state of Minas faced a sort of free rider problem as it failed to fully internalize the benefits of the new inward investment.

TABLE 5a. Projected Value Added Effects of New Regional Investments in the Automobile Sector: Construction Phase

	Percentage Distribution					
	N	NE	MW	SP	RES	S
North	47.21	2.63	2.74	1.58	2.16	0.91
Northeast	2.47	25.56	3.23	2.85	2.79	1.83
Midwest	1.41	1.06	20.05	1.08	1.17	1.12
São Paulo	31.69	43.01	43.12	80.48	48.06	14.12
Rest of Southeast	8.31	12.39	13.75	9.55	33.55	6.32
South	8.92	15.34	17.12	4.47	12.28	75.70
Total	100.00	100.00	100.00	100.00	100.00	100.00
	R$ Million					
	N	NE	MW	SP	RES	S
North	271.75	15.38	15.91	9.11	12.59	5.47
Northeast	14.19	149.77	18.73	16.49	16.26	11.06
Midwest	8.10	6.24	116.37	6.22	6.85	6.80
São Paulo	182.39	252.01	250.29	465.42	280.41	85.38
Rest of Southeast	47.85	72.62	79.84	55.25	195.74	38.22
South	51.32	89.86	99.37	25.85	71.65	457.74
Total	575.61	585.87	580.52	578.33	583.50	604.66

Source: Research Results

TABLE 5b. Projected Employment Effects of New Regional Investments in the Automobile Sector: Construction Phase

	Percentage Distribution					
	N	NE	MW	SP	RES	S
North	52.41	2.87	3.03	2.71	3.00	1.38
Northeast	5.38	47.30	6.63	7.09	6.55	4.33
Midwest	4.15	2.34	36.19	2.29	3.48	2.17
São Paulo	21.69	24.97	27.31	70.70	33.26	13.32
Rest of Southeast	7.96	10.63	12.63	9.72	41.66	5.32
South	8.42	11.89	14.22	7.50	12.06	73.47
Total	100.00	100.00	100.00	100.00	100.00	100.00
	R$ Million					
	N	NE	MW	SP	RES	S
North	9940	668	644	487	567	278
Northeast	1021	10999	1411	1276	1239	871
Midwest	787	543	7703	411	657	437
São Paulo	4113	5805	5812	12721	6287	2677
Rest of Southeast	1510	2472	2688	1749	7876	1069
South	1596	2764	3026	1350	2280	14768
Total	18967	23252	21284	17994	18906	20099

Source: Research Results

TABLE 6a. Projected Value Added Effects of New Regional Investments in the Automobile Sector: Operation Phase

	Percentage Distribution					
	N	*NE*	*MW*	*SP*	*RES*	*S*
North	64.96	1.09	1.11	1.63	1.74	0.98
Northeast	2.98	70.80	1.64	3.17	2.50	1.67
Midwest	1.60	0.66	67.32	1.28	1.25	1.04
São Paulo	19.54	17.35	18.47	78.14	22.84	17.65
Rest of Southeast	7.37	6.53	7.24	10.95	66.14	8.00
South	3.55	3.56	4.21	4.83	5.52	70.66
Total	100.00	100.00	100.00	100.00	100.00	100.00
	R$ Million					
	N	*NE*	*MW*	*SP*	*RES*	*S*
North	154.39	2.66	2.71	3.70	4.39	2.55
Northeast	7.09	173.20	4.01	7.21	6.32	4.32
Midwest	3.80	1.60	164.40	2.92	3.15	2.69
São Paulo	46.44	42.45	45.11	177.77	57.66	45.75
Rest of Southeast	17.51	15.98	17.69	24.90	166.96	20.74
South	8.43	8.72	10.28	10.99	13.94	183.16
Total	237.65	244.62	244.20	227.49	252.42	259.21

Source: Research Results

TABLE 6b. Projected Employment Effects of New Regional Investments in the Automobile Sector: Operation Phase

	Percentage Distribution					
	N	*NE*	*MW*	*SP*	*RES*	*S*
North	60.87	1.21	1.20	3.58	2.73	1.44
Northeast	5.81	76.34	2.83	9.10	7.30	4.21
Midwest	3.21	1.00	71.62	2.78	2.98	1.85
São Paulo	19.05	13.05	14.54	65.49	26.18	17.70
Rest of Southeast	6.10	4.59	5.20	10.33	52.10	6.33
South	4.96	3.81	4.62	8.72	8.72	68.46
Total	100.00	100.00	100.00	100.00	100.00	100.00
	R$ Million					
	N	*NE*	*MW*	*SP*	*RES*	*S*
North	4966	136	119	256	202	122
Northeast	474	8528	281	653	540	359
Midwest	262	111	7111	199	221	158
São Paulo	1554	1458	1443	4696	1940	1507
Rest of Southeast	498	512	516	740	3860	539
South	405	426	459	625	646	5828
Total	8159	11171	9929	7171	7409	8513

Source: Research Results

In the second place, it is important to take technological considerations into account. One of the principal concerns of trade unions relates to the adoption of new capital-intensive technologies in the automotive sector. The experience of the recent wave of investment has been that the modernization of existing plants has been accompanied by reductions in the level of employment due to the less labor intensive production techniques embodied in new capital stock. The implications of this are clearly of great significance in terms of regional income-generating effects. Interestingly, preliminary studies have shown that the multiplier effects of the automotive sector and productivity gains associated with technical progress more than compensate for the fall in employment from the perspective of the economy as a whole.[10]

In the third place, the results presented in this chapter constitute an essentially static view of the regional economies. Future studies must move beyond this, highlighting the differences in regional impacts over time. In our study, in the short run the productive structure was taken as a given, and it was also assumed that there would be a failure to fully internalize the benefits of large investments in the peripheral regions. As was demonstrated, currently some 80% of autoparts suppliers in Brazil are located in the state of São Paulo, leading to the supply chain being especially regionally concentrated. However, the recent experience of some automotive assemblers points to a more "optimistic" scenario, in which suppliers are increasingly located in greater proximity to the customer base. The effect of this, given the establishment of car plants in other parts of Brazil, will be to encourage the development of a less regionally concentrated autoparts industry.

Evidence to support this conclusion is offered by the case of Fiat. When that enterprise originally commenced operations in Betim, Minas Gerais in 1976, most of its suppliers were concentrated in São Paulo state, although, it should be stated, the overall level of domestic content was relatively low. With the passing of time, structural changes in the sector (outsourcing, just in time, automation, etc.) created the conditions for an increasing proportion of production to take place in and around the Betim site itself. This tendency was strengthened further through the direct support of the state government. Thus, comparative advantages were progressively created allowing the entrenchment of a viable, integrated automotive sector in a region of the country where previously there had been none.[11] Today, Fiat and its suppliers represent one of the principal sources of state and municipal revenues in Minas Gerais.

In the current context of state government fiscal crises, much criticism has been leveled at financial incentives to attract automakers. Often, but not always, this criticism has had little rational basis. The arguments against the providing of state support span a spectrum ranging from questions of efficiency to doubts surrounding the power of the automotive sector to propel regional development. As is evident from the introduction, however, the current cycle of investment in Brazil forms part of a global process of automotive sector restructuring, one that involves new productive techniques and sales and marketing strategies. Against this background, it can only be expected that regional governments would compete actively for a share of the resulting investment activity.

As has been demonstrated, there is a very real danger that the benefits of new inward investments will not be fully internalized by the states that seek to instigate them. In this regard, from a regional perspective, it is important that effective strategies are devised which minimize this risk. This is especially so given the substantial fiscal resources that are necessary in order to attract automotive assemblers to commence operations in non-traditional areas. The experience of Fiat in Minas Gerais shows that it is possible to more fully internalize the benefits of investment but only if certain conditions are in place. One of the most important such conditions is that there be in place a planning framework aimed at encouraging establishment and maintenance in place of an effective chain of component suppliers. Another important condition is that the creation of new comparative advantages over time requires sustained investment in infrastructure, most especially in energy and telecommunications. Investment in human capital is equally, if not more important. To this effect there should be an active local workforce training program in place.

The increasing emphasis on "economic" rather than "financial" incentives throughout Brazil has given rise to a new form of regional incentive based explicitly on building up dynamic comparative advantages rather than granting fiscal handouts. In this regard, attempts to deepen the regional roots of inward automotive investments should focus on the building up of quality infrastructure and the facilitation of enhanced integration with regional, extra-regional and international markets.

NOTES

1. For a comprehensive discussion of this phenomenon see Gereffi (1993).
2. A customs union founded by the Treaty of Asunción in 1991, which embraces Argentina, Brazil, Uruguay and Paraguay.
3. See Jenkins (1987) for an interesting discussion of these issues.
4. The most noteworthy example here being Ford's decision to invest in Bahia, a coastal state several hundred kilometers north of major concentrations of markets and suppliers.
5. Some 80% of auto components plants are currently located in the state.
6. In absolute terms, for the state of São Paulo, the number of enterprises rose from 506 to 573 between 1991 and 2002, while over the same period the number of employees fell from 255,600 to 170,000.
7. Who are frequently tied into just-in-time relationships with their clients.
8. Haddad, E.A. and Hewings, G.J.D. (1999) 'The short-run regional effects on new investments and technological upgrade in the Brazilian automotive industry: an interregional Computable General Equilibrium analysis,' *Oxford Development Studies*, vol. 27, no. 3.
9. Perobelli, F.S. (1999) 'Uma Análise das potencialidades de desenvolvimento dos municípios da região de Juiz de Fora utilizando análise fatorial,' *Relatório Final de Pesquisa*, NUPE-FEA, Universidade Federal de Juiz de Fora. See also chapter in this volume.
10. Haddad and Hewings, op.cit.
11. In 1989, 26% of Fiat purchases stemmed from suppliers located in Minas Gerais. In 1999 the equivalent figure stood at 75% (Santos, A. and Pinhão, C., 1999) 'Pólos automotivos Brasileiros,' *BNDES Setorial*, Rio de Janeiro, no. 10, pp. 173-200.

REFERENCES

Addis, C. (1999). "Taking the Wheel: Auto Parts Firms and the Political Economy of Industrialisation in Brazil." University Park PA: Pennsylvania State University Press.

Amann, E. (2000). "Economic Liberalisation and Industrial Performance in Brazil." Oxford, New York: Oxford University Press.

Bonelli, P. da M. V. R., and Brito, A. F. de. (1997). "As Políticas Industrial e de Comércio Exterior no Brasil: Rumos e Indefinições." Texto para Discussão, No. 527. Brasília: IPEA.

Cavalcanti, C., and Prado, S. (1998). "Aspectos da Guerra Fiscal no Brasil." Rio de Janeiro: IPEA/FUNDAP.

Guilhoto, J. J. M. et al. (2002). "An Interregional Input-Output System for the Brazilian Economy for 1999." São Paulo: Economics Department, FEA-USP.

Haddad, E. A., and Hewings, G. J. D. (1999). "The Short-Run Regional Effects of New Investments and Technological Upgrade in the Brazilian Automobile Industry: An Interregional Computable General Equilibrium Analysis." *Oxford Development Studies*, Vol. 27, No. 3, pp. 359-383.

Jenkins, R. (1987). "Transnational Corporations and the Latin American Automotive Industry." London & Basingstoke: Macmillan.

Miller R. E., and Blair, P. D. (1985). "Input-Output Analysis: Foundations and Extensions." Englewood Cliffs: Prentice-Hall.

Perobelli, F.S (1999). "Uma Análise das potencialidades de desenvolvimento dos municípios da região de Juiz de Fora utilizando análise fatorial,' Relatório Final de Pesquisa, NUPE-FEA, Universidade Federal de Juiz de Fora–MG.

Perobelli, F. S; Haddad, E. H; Bastos, S Q de A e Pimentel, E. (2006). "Fiscal incentive and regional development projects: Mercedes-Benz at Juiz de Fora (MG)–Brazil 1996/1999." in *Latin American Business Review*. Special Issue.

Santos, A. M. M., and Pinhão, C. M. A. (1999). "Pólos Automotivos Brasileiros." *BNDES Setorial*, September, No. 10, pp. 173-200. Rio de Janeiro: BNDES.

Santos, A. M., and Gonçalves, J. R. J. (2001). "Evolução do Comércio Exterior do Complexo Automotivo." *BNDES Setorial*, March, No. 13, pp. 205-218.

Shapiro, H. (1994). "Engines of Growth: The State and Transnational Auto Companies in Brazil." Cambridge: Cambridge University Press.

doi:10.1300/J140v07n03_05

The Brazilian Automotive Industry in the Nineties

Kerlyng Cecchini
Joaquim Guilhoto
Geoffrey J.D. Hewings
Chokri Dridi

SUMMARY. The aim of this paper is to carry out a study of the importance of the Brazilian automotive industry through the analysis of fuzzy clusters. The main results stress the importance of automotive economic activities located in Sao Paulo and in the South of Brazil, and the diversification of the productive process in the Brazilian economy with less dependence on the automotive sector for its growth. The results also suggest that, from the nineties onwards, with the opening of the Brazilian economy to international commerce, the productive relationships between domestic clusters have become more fragile. Moreover, the results reveal the relatively greater importance of components and other vehicle-related industries in Sao Paulo as a supplier of components for the maintenance of the auto fleet in the Brazilian economy. In addition, it reveals the importance of suppliers for the automotive complex, such as metallurgy, steel, plastics, and electronic components.

Kerlyng Cecchini is affiliated with Technology Institute of Paraná, Tecpar, Brazil. Joaquim Guilhoto, Department of Economics, University of São Paulo, Brazil; REAL, University of Illinois; and CNPq Scholar, U.S.A. Geoffrey J.D. Hewings is affiliated with REAL, University of Illinois, U.S.A. Chokri Dridi is affiliated with the University of Alberta, Canada; REAL, University of Illinois, U.S.A.

[Haworth co-indexing entry note]: "The Brazilian Automotive Industry in the Nineties." Cecchini, Kerlyng et al. Co-published simultaneously in *Latin American Business Review* (International Business Press, an imprint of The Haworth Press, Inc.) Vol. 7, No. 3/4, 2006, pp. 121-150; and: *Latin American Business: Equity Distortion in Regional Resource Allocation in Brazil* (ed: Werner Baer, and Geoffrey Hewings) International Business Press, an imprint of The Haworth Press, Inc., 2006, pp. 121-150. Single or multiple copies of this article are available for a fee from The Haworth Document Delivery Service [1-800-HAWORTH, 9:00 a.m. - 5:00 p.m. (EST). E-mail address: docdelivery@haworthpress.com].

Available online at http://labr.haworthpress.com
doi:10.1300/J140v07n03_06

RESUMEN. En este estudio se analizó la importancia de la industria automotriz brasileña a través del análisis de grupos probabilísticos *fuzzy (fuzzy clusters)*. Los principales resultados obtenidos recalcaron la importancia de las actividades económicas del ramo automotriz en la región de São Paulo y el sur de Brasil, y la diversificación del proceso productivo en la economía brasileña cuya dependencia de la industria automotriz era menor para alcanzar su crecimiento. Además, los resultados también sugirieron que, a partir de los años 90 la relación productiva entre los aglomerados (clusters) domésticos se fragilizó debido a la apertura de la economía brasileña al comercio internacional. Por otra parte, los resultados revelaron el aumento de la importancia relativa de la industria de componentes y otras industrias de vehículos en São Paulo, como proveedores de componentes para el mantenimiento de la flota automotriz en la economía brasileña. El estudio también demostró la importancia que los distintos proveedores tenían para el complejo automotriz, tales como la metalurgia, industria siderúrgica, plásticos, y de componentes electrónicos.

RESUMO. Este estudo teve por objetivo uma análise da importância da indústria automobilística brasileira através da análise de *fuzzy clusters*. Os resultados principais enfatizaram a importância de atividades econômicas automotivas localizadas em São Paulo e no sul do Brasil e a diversificação do processo produtivo na economia brasileira, com menos dependência do setor automobilístico para seu crescimento. Os resultados também indicaram que, a partir da década de 1990, com a abertura da economia brasileira ao comércio internacional, as relações produtivas entre aglomerados (*clusters*) domésticos se tornaram mais frágeis. Além disso, os resultados revelaram a maior importância relativa da indústria de componentes e de outros veículos em São Paulo como fornecedores de componentes para a manutenção da frota de automóveis na economia brasileira. Além do mais, o estudo revelou a importância de fornecedores para o complexo automobilístico, como a metalurgia, indústria metalúrgica, de plásticos e de componentes eletrônicos. doi:10.1300/J140v07n03_06 *[Article copies available for a fee from The Haworth Document Delivery Service: 1-800-HAWORTH. E-mail address: <docdelivery@haworthpress.com> Website: <http://www.HaworthPress. com> © 2006 by The Haworth Press, Inc. All rights reserved.]*

KEYWORDS. Brazil, automotive industry, fuzzy clusters

1. INTRODUCTION

In the 1990s, the automotive industry stood out on the international scene due to investments made in emerging markets such as India, China and Brazil. In the case of Brazil, the macroeconomic and political regime was aimed at modernization, increased productive capacity and greater economic integration of the industry within Mercosur.

With the *Regime Automotivo* (a system of tax breaks for car manufacturers) of 1995, automobile manufacturers benefited from special import tariffs on products from other Mercosur countries. From that period onward, state governments that hoped to capture future investments in the industry broadened their incentives. This resulted in a fiscal war among the states in the late 1990s.

The adoption of incentives to encourage the development of the automobile industry stimulated a much needed debate on the efficiency of recent public policies amidst questions raised concerning the relative importance of this industry for the development of regional economies and their role in the national productive structure.

2. LITERATURE REVIEW

2.2. The Automotive Industry in Brazil

2.2.1. The Role of the State: From Implantation to the Recent Phases of Consolidation and Modernization

The active role of the state was decisive for the development of the Brazilian automobile industry, both during the early stages and consolidation in the 50s and 60s, and more recently during the phases of modernization and expansion to various regions in the 90s. Even with the first vehicle assembly line established in Brazil in 1919, initial efforts to set up the automobile industry in the country were not made until the 1950s during the Getúlio Vargas administration, with the strengthening of steel and other heavy industries (Ferro, 1992).

In the late 50s, there was an effective commitment on the part of the government to develop the sector. This was part of a program called *Plano de Metas*, which included a development program for the automobile industry (Baer, 1995; Orenstein and Sochaczewski, 1990). This program was run by the Executive Group of the Automobile Industry (GEIA). According to Santos and Burity (2002), it was responsible for defining rules of installation, production targets and plans to raise the domestic value added of the industry, with a priority on producing cargo vehicles and attenuating the deterioration of the balance of payments resulting from increased imports of cars and spare parts. By the end of the 1950s, about half of the car production consisted of passenger vehicles and the rest was made up of utility vehicles and trucks (Baer, 1995).

According to Santos and Burity (2002), the granting of quotas for the importation of spare parts that were not produced within the country, an exchange rate favoring imported equipment, and tax exemptions for the importation of components were some of the incentives adopted by the government at that time. In the 70s, the BNDES was responsible for financial support and for numerous restructuring programs for industries without access to affordable long-term credit. The National Development Plan (II PND) also deserves mention. Nevertheless, after the petroleum crises and the II PND, divergences arose between the public and private sectors (Bedê, 1997).

In the early 1990s, the state once again became involved in policies to strengthen the industry. As highlighted by Bonelli and Veiga (2003), in no other industry "was incentive so extensive and industrial policy so explicit" as during this time. With a view to restarting investments and promoting exports via increased competitiveness, the government adopted the *Regime Automotivo* in 1995. When established, this program increased protection for the industry and was reformulated in 1997 to involve less-developed states. Besides a fiscal incentive package for companies to invest in Brazil, there were added incentives for plants to be opened in the northern, northeastern and mid-western states (Bonelli and Veiga, 2003; Laplane and Sarti, 1997; Santos and Burity, 2002).

According to Santos and Burity (2002), the plan allowed a reduction of 50% on import taxes on vehicles for companies that were already producing or involved in producing within the country. Furthermore, there were drastic tax reductions on the import of industrial goods, tools and molds for raw materials. The results of the tax cut were seen in the spare parts industry, affecting its prices. Besides import tariffs, the IPI (tax on industrialized products) on industrial goods, raw materials, spare parts, pneumatics and packaging material were also reduced. In the case of previously established companies, average domestic value added indices of 60% were required. For new companies, this index was 50%, as well as a compensation system for imports and exports. In 1995, when the import tax rate was 70%, the *Regime Automotivo* program reduced it to 35%.

A special trade agreement with Argentina established the Brazil-Argentina Automotive Agreement of 1995. The difficulties of commercial relations between the two countries, however, were made clear with the devaluation of the real against the peso in January, 1999. From 2000 on, a common policy was established between the two countries for the industry to be in force from 2000 to 2005 (Bonelli and Veiga, 2003; Bonelli, 2001).

The granting of incentives, however, was not restricted to the federal government. Among the policies of the states to attract new investments, Santos and Burity (2002) and Bonelli (2001) mentioned measures that varied from the use of direct expenditure with financing and participation of capital, to support in supplying infrastructure and the simplification of bureaucracy. The most widely criticized measures, however, were those which compromised the revenue of the ICMS (Tax on the Circulation of Goods), the main source of income for state governments. It is these last measures that justified the term 'fiscal war' used to characterize the behavior of the governments of several states during that period.

The widespread use of tax reductions and exemptions[1] from the ICMS was accompanied by a variety of other measures. In the case of Rio de Janeiro, Volkswagen's new units were given a five-year deferral on 75% of their ICMS tax, with infrastructure benefits and natural gas, digital telephones, water and electric energy at their disposal. These were practically the same benefits offered for the installation of the bus and truck factory in Resende. The donation of industrial plots of land was the measure adopted by the government of the state of Paraná to entice Renault to open its factory in the state.

The actual effects of the fiscal war, however, have been a matter of debate in the literature. According to Piancastelli and Perobelli (1996), the fiscal war is simply a fiscal renunciation and is harmless. The authors argue that the adoption of a similar set of instruments by states reinforces the question of location as a decisive factor in the flow of investments. Bonelli (2001) suggests that the real beneficiaries of the reduction of the ICMS tax are the multinational companies who assemble cars. According to this author, companies were given an opportunity to set up their plants at an extremely low cost but they would have set up in Brazil anyway, even without all such benefits. He argues that the states may be the losers since, at the time of his study, there were no estimates of the cost-benefit relationship for regions that had given these tax incentives, simultaneously assessing the impact on the creation of jobs and income,[2] along with the cost resulting from the loss of revenue and the expenditure on infrastructure, electricity, water and sanitation, donations of land, etc.

Rodrigues-Pose and Arbix (2001) agree with the former viewpoint by stating that territorial competition has been nothing more than high expenditure. In their view, any well-being that the industry stimulates is neutralized by the direct and indirect costs of attracting investments. From a global standpoint, this territorial competition implies closing other plants, which leads to the reduction of economic activity and increased unemployment nationwide. The set of policies in favor of the automobile industry in the nineties led to the effective widening of production capacity and modernization of the industry.

2.2.2. The Panorama of the Nineties in the Brazilian Automotive Industry

From 1990 to 1993, Brazil's production of vehicles–cars, light commercials, trucks and buses–doubled, rising from 914,000 to 1,800,000 units. Growth was higher in the production of passenger vehicles, which rose from 663,000 units in 1990 to 1,500,000 in 2003. Such growth mostly took place from 1990 to 1997, with a sharp retraction in 1998/1999, picking up again in 2000. This retraction is linked to the slowing of the internal market, and the larger part of production that is destined for domestic consumption.[3]

Increased production reflects in part the modernization and increased production capacity in this sector. Besides higher levels of production, the outcome of modernization has also been less use of labor. In 1990, the production of vehicles provided 117,396 jobs, but by 2002 that number had fallen to 81,737. The reduction in the number of people employed is largely a result of automation and robotization. The industry has also undergone intense internal restructuring for production.[4]

According to the estimates given by Anfavea (2004), in 2003 the automobile industry was made up of 48 plants in seven states and 27 cities and towns. Of these 48 plants, around 22 were inaugurated between 1996 and 2002. With a capacity to produce 3.2 million vehicles per year, this industry accounted for around R$10 billion in direct taxes and R$1.5 billion in indirect taxes. According to Anfavea, the automobile industry, including agricultural machinery and automotives, was responsible for creating 92,000 direct jobs, and in that year established inter-industrial relations with over 200,000 companies and 3,700 show-rooms. Its GDP, including the spare parts industry, accounted for around 13.5% of the industrial GDP and 4.5% of the GDP on the whole.

The spare parts industry grew until 1997. In the following years, the volume of sales in the industry slowed. Exports grew by 82% from 1990 to 1992. However, the installation of new foreign companies and the global strategies adopted by these companies led to a significant increase in imports for the sector, from US$837 million in 1990 to US$3.9 billion in 2002.

2.2.3. Investments and Recent Regional Configuration

In the nineties, worldwide companies announced investments in the Brazilian economy with a view to establishing new plants or restructuring old ones. Fiat, Ford, General Motors and Volkswagen increased their presence in the domestic market, while others, such as Mercedes and Renault, set up new plants. The huge investments in this industry in the nineties were similar to those seen during the initial period of their installation (Rodrigues-Pose and Arbix, 2001). The amount invested in the production of vehicles from 1990 to 1992 was over US$18 billion, with 80% of this total made after 1993 (Anfavea, 2004). The regional distribution of these investments, however, varied a great deal. The data from Anfavea (2004) and from Santos and Pinhão (1999) make it possible to analyze the investments by region, as shown in Table 1.

There are several reasons that can explain the regional deconcentration of this industry. Rodrigues-Pose and Arbix (2001) emphasize that in the past the availability of skilled labor and superior infrastructure in the Southeast led to greater development of this region. More recently, the lower cost of labor in other regions of the country and improvement in the availability of skilled labor have led to deconcentration. Also contributing to the latter was the better organization of trade unions in the Southeast, which raised labor costs in the industrial ABC region of São Paulo, and the effects of pollution and traffic congestion in the city of São Paulo. Even with the recent regional deconcentration moves, the volume of production in the state of São Paulo is still higher than that of other states. According to Anfavea (2004), around 53.4% of Brazilian car production takes place in this state. Minas Gerais, Paraná and Bahia are next in line with 20.1%, 7.6% and 7.5%, respectively, in volume of production.

TABLE 1. Regional Distribution of Direct Foreign Investment in Automobile Assembly Plants in Brazil 1996-2001

Location	Company	Country of Origin	Date of investment	Minimum planned investment (in millions of US$)	Planned annual capacity (in thousands)
São Paulo					
São Bernardo do Campo	BMW/ L.Rover	UK	1998	150	150
São Carlos	Volkswagen	Germany	In operation	250	300*
Indaiatuba	Toyota	Japan	1999	150	15
Sumaré	Honda	Japan	In operation	100	30
Paraná					
São José dos Pinhais	Renault	France	1999	750	100/110
São José dos Pinhais	Audi	Germany	1999	600	120
Campo Largo	Chrysler/ BMW	USA/ Germany	1999	600	120
Minas Gerais					
Juiz de Fora	Mercedes	Germany	1999	820	70
Betim	Fiat	Italy	1998	500	5,000*
Sete Lagoas	Iveco	Italy	1998	250	20
Belo Horizonte	Fiat	Italy	1999	200	100
Rio Grande do Sul					
Gravataí	GM	USA	1999	600	120
Caxias do Sul	Navistar	USA	1998	50	5
Rio de Janeiro					
Porto Real	PSA-Peugeot	France	2000	600	1,000
Resende	Volkswagen	Germany	In operation	250	50
Bahia					
Camaçari	Ford	USA	2001	1,300	250

Source: Anfavea (2004), Santos and Pinhão (1999)

3. METHODOLOGY[5]

The core of the analysis in this paper is done through the use of input-output models applied in the identification of economic clusters. This section presents an overview of the methodology used.

3.1. Input-Output Model

The input-output model was originally developed by Wassily Leontief. The model displays the information of flows of input and output for each of the sectors of an economic region during a determined period of time (Feijó et al., 2001; Leontief, 1986). In mathematical terms, the relationship between sectors may be represented by a system of linear equations in the form of a matrix so that each of the equations describes within the economy the distribution of a product from a certain industry or sector. The economic interpretations to be had from the use of the model come from the resolution of this system of equations by way of an inverse matrix and other algebraic derivations of the model (Miller and Blair, 1985).

According to Miller and Blair (1985), the fundamental aspect of the model can be expressed by the equation:

$$X = (I - A)^{-1} Y \tag{1}$$

in which,

$(I - A)^{-1}$ represents the Leontief inverse matrix;
X represents the production vector;
Y represents the final demand vector;
A represents the matrix of technical coefficients of the sectors.

Equation (1), by multiplying the final demand vector Y by the Leontief inverse matrix, allows us to measure the total impacts caused by exogenous shocks resulting from the variations of the final demand components (consumption by families, exports and private investment).

The interregional input-output models are more suitable when the intention is to analyze the interactions between economic regions. According to Miller and Blair (1985), an interregional model for two regions L and M can have its coefficients matrix represented in matricial terms as:

$$A = \begin{bmatrix} A^{LL} & A^{LM} \\ A^{ML} & A^{MM} \end{bmatrix} \tag{2}$$

Vectors X^L and X^M will constitute the total production vector X

$$X = \begin{bmatrix} X^L \\ X^M \end{bmatrix} \tag{3}$$

The final demand vector, Y, will be composed of vectors Y^L and Y^M

$$Y = \begin{bmatrix} Y^L \\ Y^M \end{bmatrix} \qquad (4)$$

3.2. Fuzzy Clusters[6]

One of the more relevant contributions concerning the methods for identifying clusters based on input-output theory can be found in Czamanski and Ablas (1979). These authors discuss and analyze four-teen studies that seek to identify clusters and industrial complexes. Other works also deserve to be mentioned, such as Streit (1969), Bergsman et al. (1972, 1975), Roepke et al. (1974), Blin and Cohen (1977), Hewings et al. (1998), Oosterhaven et al. (1999) and Hoen (2002).

One aspect in which the method used in this paper differs from most of the methods used in the literature is the type of cluster identified. Most methods allow for the identification of clusters formed by a limited number of sectors, identifying crisp clusters. In these analyses, the sectors belong to only one cluster and it is not possible to allow participation in more than one cluster at a time, which leads to analyses that are far from economic reality.

To this end, Czamanski (1974) utilizes four different coefficients in one of the first attempts to evaluate clusters according to the most important sectors. More recently, Dridi and Hewings (2002a, 2002b) utilize the analysis of fuzzy clusters, seeking to take into consideration the complexity of the productive relationships in the establishment of sector groupings. The method does not require the researcher to arbitrarily choose the values of restrictions required by other methods. It is crucial to add that the groupings are identified in such a way that all sectors of the economy belong to a certain cluster in varying degrees. These characteristics were preponderant in the choice of method used in this paper, which will be dealt with in further detail later.

The sector groupings, or clusters as they are called in this paper, do not restrict their relationships to the purchase and sale of inputs to a small number of activities in the productive structure, even when there is great similarity between them. On the contrary, the sectors establish input purchase and sale relationships with a high number of sectors. In other words, it is possible that some activities, when grouped together according to the input purchase and sale relationships, belong to more than one cluster at a time.

Utilizing the fuzzy set theory, it is possible to carry out an analysis that takes this fluidity of the productive structure into consideration. Dridi and Hewings (2002a) present the utilization of the analysis of fuzzy clusters resulting from this theory as a methodological proposal for assessing sector clusters, and they perform an exercise using the matrix of the American economy. By recognizing the limitations of the traditional crisp approach, the fuzzy approach aims to analyze the complexity of the productive structure more coherently.

An application of this method in a study of the Brazilian economy can be found in Simões (2003). The author utilizes the fuzzy cluster approach to identify spatial industrial complexes in the state of Minas Gerais, applying the method in a way that is similar to its use in this study. This paper, by utilizing use matrix data, requires a decomposition of that matrix in order to obtain distances between sectors. This method, called dual scaling, will be outlined in item 3.2.2 of the following section, which seeks to specify the methodology utilized.

3.2.1. Identification of Fuzzy Clusters

The method for identifying fuzzy clusters is described below, as demonstrated by Dridi and Hewings (2002a).

Considering X as a finite set of points, and a generic point, x, a fuzzy subset of X, denominated A, will be characterized by a function of membership, $\mu_A(x)$, that will associate, at each x point, a coefficient within a real interval of [0.1].

Thus, subset *fuzzy A* is a set of ordered pairs $\left\{ \left(x \middle| \mu_A(x) \right); \forall x \in X \right\}$,

in which $\mu_A(x)$ is the membership coefficient of the x element in A.

If we let $A_{k,}$ $\forall k = 1, ...K$, all the subsets of a universal set X have the following properties:

$$\mu_{A_K}(x) \in [0,1]; \forall x \in X, \forall k = 1, ...K$$

$$\sum_{k=1}^{K} \mu_{A_K}(x) = 1 \tag{5}$$

The authors mention controversies concerning the format of the membership function, especially because this type of function is determined *ad hoc*, and adopt the proposal of Kaufman and Rosseeuw (1990). According to this alternative, the clusters are obtained by minimizing the following objective function:

$$\min_{\mu_{ik}} \sum_{v=1}^{K} \frac{\sum_{i,i'}^{r} \mu^2{}_{iv} \mu^2{}_{i'v} d_{i,i'}}{2\sum \mu^2{}_{i'v}} \tag{6}$$

restricted to:

$$\mu_{iv} \geq 0; \forall i = 1,\ldots,r, \forall v = 1,\ldots,k$$

$$\sum_{v=1}^{k} \mu_{iv} = 1; \forall i = 1,\ldots,k$$

in which:

μ_{iv} represents the values of the membership coefficients of each of the i sectors in relation to the v clusters, which will minimize the function;

$d_{i,i'}$ represents the Euclidian distance calculated between the sectors of the matrix submitted to the cluster analysis.

To the authors, this method has advantages over the other models of fuzzy cluster analysis. This is because this method minimizes errors by utilizing a unitary distance exponent, whereas in other methods the distance is squared.

The fanny algorithm classifies r objects (in this case sectors) into k clusters based on the observation of s characteristics, or observations of a variable. Obtaining the s characteristics requires a decomposition of the use matrix by using a dual scaling technique. This method is a descriptive, multivaried analysis technique introduced by Nishisato (1994). Its application in the input-output matrix allows for the decomposition of the complexity of associations that are established between the sectors of the productive structure and allows us to determine a vector of rows weight and a vector of columns weight.

The resulting matrixes are utilized to calculate the Euclidean distance between the rows and columns. The next step consists of the realization of the cluster analysis based on the distances calculated from the matrixes weight. The number of clusters analyzed must be the highest possible (Simões, 2003). For this work, S-PLUS software was used, whose fuzzy cluster analysis is obtained by the fanny algorithm and allows for a maximum number of clusters, so that $k = \dfrac{s}{2} - 1$, where s is the number of solutions found, as described in the dual scaling procedure.

Thus, the result of the cluster analysis consists of a matrix formed by vectors expressing the membership coefficients of each of the sectors that form the clusters identified in the economy. These matrixes are called membership matrixes.

The membership information subsidizes a preliminary analysis of the productive clusters. Other measures, like those given below, can be employed to better characterize the importance of the sectors in each of the clusters identified.

3.2.2. Involvement of the Sectors

According to Dridi and Hewings (2002b), the relative importance of a cluster can be obtained through the coefficient called involvement, defined as:

$$Inv_A(x_i) = \frac{\mu_A(x_i)}{card(A)}; \forall i = 1, \ldots, n; \tag{7}$$

where,

$\mu_{A_A}(x_i)$ represents the membership coefficient of the sector to the cluster;

$card(A_K) = \sum \mu_{A_A}(x_i); \forall k \in C$ represents the cardinality of the sectors

X is a set of points, in this case, secorts x_i finite and countable; $\forall i \in I = \{1, \ldots, N\}$;

A_k are the fuzzy X sets;

$;\forall k \in C = \{1, \ldots, K\}.$

Thus, the highest values of this involvement coefficient indicate the most important sectors of the cluster, with leadership of the cluster in question. In their turn, the lower values indicate the sectors with secondary importance in the cluster; in other words, the sectors that supply support to the main activity of the cluster.

3.2.3. Subsethood

This is an indicator for assessing how much a fuzzy set is present in another fuzzy set. It is defined as:

$$D(B,A) = \frac{card(B \cap A)}{card(B)} = \frac{\sum_i min(\mu_A(x_i), \mu_B(x_i))}{\sum_i (\mu_B(x_i))} \quad (8)$$

Therefore, $D(B,A)$ expresses the subsethood of cluster A in relation to cluster B. The subsethood matrix expresses the mutual dependence of the clusters in the productive structure.

4. RESULTS AND DISCUSSION

The clusters identified in this paper are called fuzzy clusters because the participation of all economic activities in a productive grouping are considered. The most important activities in a cluster are called leader activities, while the others are called support activities for the production of the final goods of the cluster.

The first step in the identification of clusters consists of decomposing the use matrix into a similarity matrix using the dual scaling method. This procedure results in two similarity matrixes: one referring to the relations of purchase and the other to the relations of sales in the economy. The two resulting matrixes have $m \times n$ dimensions, where m is the number of sectors in the economy and n the number of variables of solutions found in the decomposition of the original use matrix. The vectors that constitute these matrixes, therefore, match each of the similarity variables found in the decomposition of the matrix into the different economic activities. The number of variables found will be utilized to define the maximum number of clusters in the economy.[7]

The resulting matrixes are submitted to a fuzzy cluster analysis and as a result produce membership matrixes, $m \times c$ dimensions, in which m represents the number of sectors in the economy and c is the number of clusters identified. These matrixes present the degree of relationship of each of the sectors of the economy to the clusters. The sum along the row that represents each sector of this matrix is one.

Based on the information of the membership matrix, we obtain the involvement matrix. This matrix has $m \times c$ dimensions, where m represents the number of sectors in the economy and c is the number of clusters, as in the original matrix. Contrary to the previous matrix, the values along each column add up to one, so that the degree to which an economic activity belongs to or is involved with a cluster can be measured in relation to the other economic activities belonging to the same cluster. According to Dridi and Hewings (2002a), this information is a more precise measurement for assessing the relationship of economic activities in established clusters. Once the clusters have been identified, the subsethood between clusters is measured.

In this paper, the clusters were identified from the viewpoint of an interregional and isolated region system for 1999, and consisted of six Brazilian regions: North (N), Northeast (NE), Central West (CW), São Paulo State (SP), Rest of the Southeast region (RSE), and South (S), in addition to national input-output systems for 1990 and 2002. The results are discussed in more detail below.

4.1. Interregional System

The decomposition of the interregional system utilized, composed of 186 economic activities (31 activities in each region), allows us to identify a maximum number of 91 clusters. Table 2 shows each of the clusters identified according to the purchase profiles and according to the activities that show the larger membership coefficient. These activities are called leader activities of the cluster. The clusters are shown in the order in which they are identified by the method. Thus, the first cluster shown is led by the activity of Food products in the North.

In Table 3, we see economic activities that lead the clusters, considering the sales profiles of the interregional system. This table can be read in the same way as Table 1. In this way, the first cluster identified according to the purchase profile of the interregional system is the cluster led by the Crops and Livestock activity in São Paulo. The analyses according to the two viewpoints show the same leader activities for the clusters of the automotive industry. They highlight the region of São Paulo, where automotive activity (cars, spare parts and other vehicles) lead the different clusters. It is also worth mentioning that the com-

TABLE 2. Clusters According to Purchase Profiles in the Interregional System, 1999

	Leader Activities		Leader Activities		Leader Activities
1	N–Food Products	31	NE–Plastics	61	SP–Public administration
2	N–Mineral extraction	32	NE–Clothing and footwear	62	SP–Clothing and Footwear
3	N–Commerce	33	NE–Various industries	63	S–Crops and Livestock
4	N–Non-metallic minerals	34	NE–Sale Vehicles/spare parts	64	SP–Various industries
5	SP–Man. Machinery and tractors	35	NE–Communications	65	SP–Sales of Vehicles and parts
6	N–Steelworks	36	SP–Crops and Livestock	66	SP–Communications
7	N–Electrical/Electronic Equipment	37	CW–Mineral extraction	67	RSE–Food products
8	N–Trucks and buses	38	CW–Private services	68	RSE–Private services
9	N–Wood and furnishing	39	CW–Non-metallic minerals	69	RSE–Non-metallic minerals
10	N–Private services	40	CW–Steelworks	70	RSE–Steelworks
11	N–Rubber industry	41	CW–Electrical/Electronic equip.	71	RSE–Electrical/electronic equip.
12	N–Oil refinery	42	CW–Trucks and buses	72	RSE–Trucks and buses
13	SP–Various chemicals	43	CW–Wood and furnishing	73	RSE–Wood and furnishing
14	N–Pharmacy and veterinary	44	CW–Rubber industry	74	RSE–Rubber industry
15	SP–Plastics	45	CW–Food products	75	RSE–Oil refinery
16	N–Textile industry	46	CW–Oil refinery	76	RSE–Pharmacy and veterinary
17	N–Public Utilities	47	CW–Pharmacy and veterinary	77	RSE–Textile industry
18	N–Transport	48	CW–Textile industry	78	RSE–Public Utilities
19	NE–Crops and Livestock	49	S–Clothing and Footwear	79	RSE–Transport
20	NE–Public administration	50	CW–Public Utilities	80	S–Public administration
21	NE–Ext. oil, gas, coal	51	CW–Commerce	81	S–Ext. oil, gas, coal
22	NE–Construction	52	CW–Transport	82	S–Construction
23	NE–Steelworks	53	RSE–Ext. minerals	83	S–Steelworks
24	NE–Man. Machinery/tractors	54	SP–Ext. oil, gas, coal	84	S–Man. Machinery/tractors
25	NE–Cars	55	SP–Construction	85	S–Cars
26	NE–Parts and other vehicles	56	SP–Steelworks	86	S–Parts and other vehicles
27	NE–Cellulose, paper and printing	57	SP–Cars	87	S–Cellulose, paper and printing
28	NE–Chemical elements	58	SP–Parts and other vehicles	88	S–Chemical elements
29	RSE–Commerce	59	SP–Cellulose, paper and printing	89	S–Plastics
30	NE–Diverse chemicals	60	SP–Chemical elements	90	S–Diverse chemicals
				91	S–Various industries

The Ford project, initially set up in Guaíba, Rio Grande de Sul, expected investments of half a million dollars and a capacity for 100,000 vehicle units (Cavalcante and Uderman, 2003). Other investments such as those announced by Mitsubish, Ásia and Hyundai were not made owing to the Asian crisis.

TABLE 3. Clusters According to Sales Profiles in the Interregional System, 1999

	Leader Activities		Leader Activities		Leader Activities
1	SP–Crops and Livestock	31	NE–Plastics	61	SP–Sale vehicles/parts
2	N–Ext. mineral	32	NE–Clothing and Footwear	62	SP–Public administration
3	NE–Ext. oil, gas, coal	33	NE–Various industries	63	No activity
4	N–Non-metallic minerals	34	NE–Public administration	64	RSE–Mineral ext.
5	SP–Mach and tractors	35	NE–Sale vehicles/spare parts	65	RSE–Non-metallic minerals
6	N–Steelworks	36	No activity	66	RSE–Steelworks
7	N–Commerce	37	CW–Mineral ext.	67	RSE–Commerce
8	N–Electrical/electronic equip.	38	CW–Non-metallic minerals	68	RSE–Electrical/electronic equip.
9	N–Trucks and buses	39	CW–Steelworks	69	RSE–Trucks and buses
10	N–Wood and Furnishing	40	CW–Private services	70	RSE–Wood and Furnishing
11	N–Rubber industry	41	CW–Electrical/electronic equip.	71	RSE–Rubber industry
12	SP–Diverse chemicals	42	CW–Trucks and buses	72	RSE–Oil refinery
13	N–Oil refinery	43	CW–Wood and Furnishing	73	RSE–Pharmacy and Veterinary
14	N–Pharmacy and Veterinary	44	CW–Rubber industry	74	RSE–Textile industry
15	N–Textile industry	45	CW–Oil refinery	75	RSE–Public Utilities
16	N–Food products	46	CW–Pharmacy and Veterinary	76	RSE–Transport
17	N–Public Utilities	47	CW–Textile industry	77	RSE–Private services
18	N–Private Services	48	CW–Public Utilities	78	S–Crops and Livestock
19	N–Transport	49	CW–Commerce	79	S–Mach and tractors
20	NE–Crops and Livestock	50	CW–Transport	80	S–Ext. oil, gas, coal
21	SP–Plastics	51	SP–Ext. oil, gas, coal	81	S–Construction
22	NE–Steelworks	52	SP–Construction	82	S–Steelworks
23	NE–Mach and tractors	53	SP–Steelworks	83	S–Plastics
24	NE–Cars	54	SP–Cars	84	S–Cars
25	NE–Parts and other vehicles	55	SP–Parts and other vehicles	85	S–Parts and other vehicles
26	NE–Communications	56	SP–Cellulose, paper and printing	86	S–Cellulose, paper and printing
27	NE–Cellulose, paper and printing	57	SP–Chemical elements	87	S–Chemical elements
28	NE–Chemical elements	58	SP–Communications	88	S–Diverse chemicals
29	NE–Diverse chemicals	59	SP–Clothing and Footwear	89	S–Clothing and Footwear
30	NE–Construction	60	SP–Various industries	90	S–Various industries
				91	S–Public administration

merce of spare parts and vehicles in São Paulo as seen in the automotive industry also leads a cluster in the system. Other leader activities in the clusters are: trucks and buses in the rest of the Southeast; cars, parts and other vehicles in the South; trucks and buses in the Central West; cars and parts and other vehicles in the Northeast; trucks in the North.

It is worth highlighting that the clusters identified according to the purchase profiles of the North, Central West and Northeast regions (N–Trucks and buses, CW–Cars, and NE–Parts and other vehicles) are characterized as support activities for these very regions. In general, the clusters of São Paulo (SP–Cars, SP–Parts and other vehicles and SP–Commerce of vehicles and parts) in their turn are those belonging to the region of São Paulo, the South and the rest of the Southeast and are shown to be main support activities. The cluster of cars in the South shows the importance of the activities in that region and the rest of the Southeast. The clusters with the highest degree of regional diversity in support activities are parts in the South, and trucks and buses in the rest of the Southeast. When it comes to sales, the presence of support activities in the North, Northeast and Central West in the clusters of the automotive industry is much more expressive, especially in the cluster led by the Commerce of vehicles and parts.

It is worth mentioning that the identification of a cluster in the North, Northeast and Central West must be assessed with caution, since the method identifies clusters according to similarity in inter-sector relations, not taking into account the value of the total production of the sector. In these regions, the results may indicate the potential for development of a cluster.

A fundamental aspect is that the productive relevance of the automotive industry in the rest of the Southeast and São Paulo is not captured by the method when using the interregional system. In other words, the automotive industry of the rest of the Southeast is not among the activities that present the highest values for the involvement of sectors in the automotive clusters in the North, Northeast and Central West. This behavior is expected since involvement is a measure of the importance of sectors in the clusters. However, the method does not consider the value of the total production of the sector, but rather the input values.

In order to observe how clusters relate to one another, it is possible to assess their subsethood. The subsethood results in a matrix of $c \times c$ dimensions, where c represents the number of clusters identified in the economy. The main diagonal shows values equal to 1, expressing the maximum subsethood of the sector in relation to itself. The other cells in the matrix show values that vary from zero to one, equaling the mutual subsethood of clusters.

As suggested by Dridi and Hewings (2002b), the option was to consider the subsethood of those values that were above the average, i.e., over 0.5. Thus, seeking to observe the dependence between clusters in

Baer, W. (1995). "Economia Brasileira." São Paulo: Nobel.

Bedê, M. A. (1997). "A Política Automotiva nos Anos 90." In G. Arbix and M. Zilbovicius (Orgs.), *De JK a FHC: A Reinvenção dos Carros.* São Paulo: Scritta.

Bergsman, J., Greenston, P., and Healy, R. (1972). "The Agglomeration Process in Urban Growth." *Urban Studies,* Vol. 9, No. 3, pp. 263-288.

Bergsman, J., Greenston, P., and Healy, R. (1975). "A Classification of Economic Activities Based on Location Patterns." *Journal of Urban Economics,* Vol. 2, No. 1, pp. 1-28.

Blin, J. M., and Cohen, C. (1977). "Technological Similarity and Aggregation in Input-Output Systems: A Cluster-Analytic Approach." *Review of Economic & Statistics,* Vol. 59, No. 1, pp. 82-91.

Bonelli, R. (2001). "Políticas de Competitividade Industrial no Brasil: 1995/2000." *Discussion Paper,* 810, 44 pp. Brasília: IPEA.

Bonelli, R., and Veiga, P. M. (2003). "Dinâmica das Políticas Setoriais no Brasil na Década de 1990: Continuidade e Mudança." *Revista Brasileira de Comércio Exterior,* Vol. 17, No. 75, pp. 1-24.

Cavalcante, L. C., and Uderman, S. (2002). "The Cost of a Structural Change: a Large Automobile Plant in a Brazilian Less Developed Region." *Discussion Paper,* 04-T-5. Urbana: University of Illinois, Regional Economics Applications Laboratory.

Cecchini, K. (2005). "Setor Automotivo Brasileiro: Evolução da Estrutura Produtiva e sua Importância Regional nos Anos 90." Master's Thesis. Escola Superior de Agricultura "Luiz de Queiroz," Universidade de São Paulo. Piracicaba.

Czamanski, S. (1974). "Study of Clustering of Industries." Halifax: Dalhouse University, Institute of Public Affairs.

Czamanski, S., and Ablas, L. A. Q. (1979). "Identification of Industrial Clusters and Complexes: A Comparison of Methods and Findings." *Urban Studies,* Vol. 16, pp. 61-80.

Dridi, C., and Hewings, G. J. D. (2002a). "Toward a Quantitative Analysis of Industrial Clusters I: Fuzzy Clusters vs. Crisp Cluster." *Discussion Paper,* 02-T-1. Urbana: University of Illinois, Regional Economics Applications Laboratory.

Dridi, C., and Hewings, G. J. D. (2002b). "Toward a Quantitative Analysis of Industrial Clusters II: Shapley Value, Entropy, and Other Fuzzy Measures." *Discussion Paper,* 02-T-6. Urbana: University of Illinois, Regional Economics Applications Laboratory.

Feijó, C. A. et al. (2001). "Contabilidade Social: O Novo Sistema de Contas Nacionais do Brasil." Rio de Janeiro: Editora Campus.

Ferro, J. R. (1992). "A Produção Enxuta no Brasil." In: J. P. Womack et al. *A Máquina que Mudou o Mundo.* pp. 311-337. Rio de Janeiro: Campus.

Guilhoto, J. J. M., and Sesso Filho, U. A. (2005). "Estimação da Matriz Insumo-Produto a Partir de Dados Preliminares das Contas Nacionais." *Economia Aplicada,* April-June, Vol. 2, No. 9, pp. 277-299.

Hewings, G. J. D., Schindler, G. R., Israilevich, P. R., Sonis, M. (1998). "Agglomeration, Clustering, and Structural Change: Interpreting Changes in the Chicago Regional Economy." In M. Steiner (Ed.), *Clusters and Regional Specialization.* Heidelberg: Springer Verlag.

Hoen, A. R. (2002). "Identifying Linkages with Cluster Based Methodology." *Economic Systems Research*, Vol. 14, No. 2, pp. 131-146.

Kaufman, L., Rosseeuw, P. J. (1990). "Finding Groups in Data: An Introduction to Cluster Analysis." New York: Wiley

Laplane, M. F., and Sarti, F. (1997). "The Restructuring of Brazilian Automobile Industry in the Nineties." *Actes du GERPISA*, No. 20, pp. 31-48.

Leontief, W. (1986). "Input-Output Economics." 2. ed. New York: Oxford University Press.

Miller, R. E., and Blair, P. D. (1985). "Input-Output Analysis: Foundations and Extensions." New Jersey: Englewood Cliffs.

Nishisato, S. (1994). "Elements of Dual Scaling: An Introduction to Practical Data Analysis." New Jersey: Lawrence Erlbaum Associates.

Oosterhaven, J., Eding, G. J., and Stelder, D. (1999). "Clusters, Forward and Backward Linkages, and Bi-Regional Spillovers: Policy Implications for the Two Dutch Mainport Regions and the Rural North." In *Proceedings of the XXXIX European Congress of the Regional Science Association*, Dublin. Dublin: Carfax.

Orenstein, L., and Sochaczewski, A. C. (1990). "Democracia com Desenvolvimento." In M. Abreu (Org.). *A Ordem do Progresso: Cem Anos de Política Econômica 1889-1989*. 10. ed. Rio de Janeiro: Campus.

Piancastelli, M., and Perobelli, F. (1996). "ICMS: Evolução Recente e Guerra Fiscal." Discusssion Paper, 402. Brasília: IPEA.

Rodriguez-Pose, A., and Arbix, G. (2001). "Strategies of Waste: Bidding Wars in the Brazilian Automotive Sector." *International Journal of Urban and Regional Research*, Vol. 25, No. 1, pp. 134-154.

Roepke, H., Adams, D., and Wiseman, R. (1974). "A New Approach to the Identification of Industrial Complexes Using Input-Output Data." *Journal of Regional Science*, Vol. 14, pp. 15-29.

Santos, A. M. M. M., and Burity, P. (2002). "Complexo Automotivo." In: Banco Nacional de Desenvolvimento Econômico e Social, *BNDES 50 Anos: Histórias Setoriais*. Rio de Janeiro: BNDES.

Santos, A. M. M. M., and Pinhão, C.M.A. (1999). "Pólos Automotivos Brasileiros." *BNDES Setorial*, No. 10, September, pp. 173-200.

Simões, R. F. (2003). "Complexos Industriais no Espaço: Uma Análise de *Fuzzy Cluster.*" *Discussion Paper*, 209. Belo Horizonte: Universidade Federal de Minas Gerais (UFMG)/Cedeplar (*Discussion Paper*, 209).

Streit, M. E. (1969). "Spatial Association and Economics Linkages between Industries." *Journal of Regional Science*, Vol. 9, No. 2, pp. 177-188.

doi:10.1300/J140v07n03_06

Pernambuco's Fiscal Incentives Program: An Evaluation of Recent Performance

André Matos Magalhães
Liedje Siqueira

SUMMARY. This paper presents the current fiscal incentives program of the state of Pernambuco and its results over the last eight years. The empirical discussion uses data on planned investment and planned jobs to focus on projects approved from 1996 on. In our analysis of the data on projects, planned investment and jobs, we found that the program was capable of attracting a significant number of projects, most of them concentrated in the sector that the state considers as a priority. When the low costs of the program are taken into account, it is possible to consider PRODEPE a successful program. It is difficult, however, to believe that the incentives provided will be able to attract large projects without a more aggressive package (land donation, loans at interest rates below market, etc.). When the geographical aspect of the program is considered, however, the results are clearly unsatisfactory. The incentives have not been able to make a significant impact on the spatial allocation of economic activities in the state, with most of the projects being concentrated in Recife's metropolitan area.

André Matos Magalhães is Professor, Economics Department at Federal University of Pernambuco, Brazil and Research Associate, Regional Economics Applications Laboratory (REAL), U.S.A. Liedje Siqueira is Professor, Economics Department at the Federal University of Paraíba, and PhD student, Federal University of Pernambuco, Brazil.

[Haworth co-indexing entry note]: "Pernambuco's Fiscal Incentives Program: An Evaluation of Recent Performance." Magalhães, André Matos, and Liedje Siqueira. Co-published simultaneously in *Latin American Business Review* (International Business Press, an imprint of The Haworth Press, Inc.) Vol. 7, No. 3/4, 2006, pp. 151-179; and: *Latin American Business: Equity Distortion in Regional Resource Allocation in Brazil* (ed: Werner Baer, and Geoffrey Hewings) International Business Press, an imprint of The Haworth Press, Inc., 2006, pp. 151-179. Single or multiple copies of this article are available for a fee from The Haworth Document Delivery Service [1-800-HAWORTH, 9:00 a.m. - 5:00 p.m. (EST). E-mail address: docdelivery@haworthpress.com].

RESUMEN. Este estudio presenta el actual programa de incentivos del estado de Pernambuco, y los resultados que obtuvo durante los últimos ocho años. La discusión empírica se basa en datos inherentes a la inversión y empleos programados para focalizar su atención en proyectos aprobados desde 1996 en adelante. Nuestros análisis de los datos existentes sobre los proyectos, las inversiones y empleos programados, demostraron que el programa era capaz de atraer un número significativo de proyectos, la gran mayoría concentrados en el sector considerado prioritario por el estado. Si tomamos en cuenta los bajos costos del programa, podemos considerar que el PRODEPE es un programa exitoso. Sin embargo, resulta difícil creer que los incentivos otorgados podrán realmente atraer grandes proyectos si no incluyen un paquete más agresivo (donación de tierras, préstamos a tasas más bajas que las del mercado, etc.) Por otra parte, cuando tomamos en consideración el aspecto geográfico del programa, los resultados son claramente insatisfactorios. Los incentivos fueron incapaces de provocar un impacto importante en la asignación espacial de las actividades económicas en el estado, y la gran mayoría de los proyectos se concentraron en el área metropolitana de Recife.

RESUMO. Este estudo apresenta o programa atual de incentivos fiscais do estado de Pernambuco e seus resultados nos últimos oito anos. A discussão empírica usa dados de investimentos planejados e empregos planejados para focalizar projetos aprovados de 1996 em diante. Em nossa análise dos dados sobre projetos, investimentos planejados e empregos, descobrimos que o programa foi capaz de atrair um número significativo de projetos, a maioria concentrados no setor que o estado considera prioritário. Quando se levam em conta os custos baixos do programa, é possível considerar o PRODEPE um programa bem-sucedido. É difícil, porém, acreditar que os incentivos fornecidos serão capazes de atrair projetos grandes sem um pacote mais agressivo (doação de terrenos, empréstimos com taxas de juros abaixo do mercado, etc.). Entretanto, quando se considera o aspecto geográfico do programa, os resultados são claramente insatisfatórios. Os incentivos não conseguiram ter um impacto significativo na alocação espacial das atividades econômicas do estado, a maioria dos projetos concentrados na área metropolitana de Recife. doi:10.1300/J140v07n03_07 *[Article copies available for a fee from The Haworth Document Delivery Service: 1-800-HAWORTH. E-mail address: <docdelivery@haworthpress.com> Website: <http://www.HaworthPress.com>*

KEYWORDS. Prodete, fiscal incentives, Pernambuco

1. INTRODUCTION

Since the 1960s, Brazil's states have participated in what is called a fiscal war. Over these 45 years, many of the rules have changed and the incentives have evolved, but the basic idea is still to attract new companies to the states and generate faster economic growth (Tendler, 2000 and Rocha, 2000). The state of Pernambuco is no exception in this scenario. The attempts to use fiscal incentives also began in the 1960s. The first laws were written with the objective of attracting new firms that would produce goods that were new to the state's productive capacity. Since then the program has been altered many times.

In its current version, the basic mechanism of providing fiscal incentives operates in the following manner: companies that benefit from the program pay only a fraction of the required state taxes (the ICMS–Value-Added Tax on Sales and Services), since the state government assumes that part of these taxes has already been paid. Legal issues aside,[1] and different from the current programs of the states of Ceará and Bahia, this mechanism does not imply any costs to the state treasury and can be effective in attracting new companies (Pedrosa et al., 2000).

The incentives are available to different economic sectors, to new companies and those already installed in the state. Clearly, the main goal of the policy is to attract new companies. However, already-installed companies can request fiscal incentives starting from the moment that they feel harmed by incentives granted to arriving firms. The state has issued a list of a few strategic sectors that would be eligible for the largest benefits. The state has also explicitly mentioned that it has an interest in seeing new companies establish themselves in the state's interior, thus reducing the already large concentration of economic activities in the metropolitan region of the capital, Recife.

This paper presents the current fiscal incentives program of Pernambuco and analyzes its main results over the last eight years (1996 through 2003). We shall focus on projects approved from 1996 on, and will be working with data on planned investments and planned jobs creation, not with actual numbers. Although we realize that this is not ideal, we believe that the data on approved projects can provide a fairly reasonable picture of the program's effectiveness. Moreover, since for most of the projects the state does not at first incur any costs when it provides these incentives, the project numbers will give us the best case scenario.

2. A HISTORICAL BACKGROUND OF PERNAMBUCO'S FISCAL INCENTIVES PROGRAMS

2.1. From the 1960s to the 1980s

Fiscal incentives as a form of attracting new investment–a practice in all Brazilian states–started around the 1960s. Following other northeastern states, the first incentive polices of the state of Pernambuco also started around this time. In the beginning, incentives were used timidly more as a way of not losing out to other states in the region (Bahia, Ceará, Paraíba, among others), which were already employing more aggressive fiscal incentives.

Law 3831/61 made it possible to grant fiscal incentives. At the time, the criteria for incentives were based on the production of goods that were dissimilar to those already produced in the state (Lima, 1997).

By the end of the 1960s, there was a change in the federal government's position towards the states. The tax reform of 1966 established fiscal centralization in the federal government, and the states lost autonomy in setting the rates of their main tax, the ICMS, which was to be set by the Senate. This was the way in which the federal government tried to control the indiscriminate use of fiscal incentives as instruments of regional development policies. At the same time, the National Tax Code, together with Supplementary Law 34/67, established a mechanism for reducing the fiscal conflicts among states. Regional councils were established for the purpose of creating an incentive policy common to each region, as well as unifying the ICMS among its member states. Several benefits were unanimously agreed to by representatives of the northeastern states (Alves, 2001).

The position of Pernambuco during the 60s and 70s was highly defensive and the Secretariat of Finance at times positioned itself against the fiscal incentives granted for attracting new industries. This was clear when the state, in Agreement ICMS 28/81, suggested a series of new bureaucratic rules that made new incentives unfeasible. According to Lima (1997), Pernambuco's position could be explained by the position of the Secretariat of Finance, who feared a tax loss through the use of unregulated tax exemptions. There was also general skepticism with regard to the true effectiveness of this type of instrument to bring about the desired regional development.

The little interest displayed by Pernambuco could be associated with the strong presence of the federal government in the investment policies for the Northeast region. It was during this period that the Superintendence for the Development of the Northeast (SUDENE) was created. Through federal fiscal incentives policies, the government tried to promote a regional redistribution of industry, which had been concentrated in the South/ Southeast regions. The best-known instrument used at that time was FINOR 34/18.

In the 1980s, there was a reduction in inter-regional disputes. According to Cavalcanti and Prado (1998), during this period there were no indications of significant fiscal conflicts among the states. The authors suggest that the explanation for this peaceful period could lie in the stagnation of private investment and the spatial stabilization of industry. Alves (2001), on the other hand, points out that little attention has been given to the fiscal war that actually did take place during this period. It was a time in which state governments increased their creativity and intensity in the development of incentives programs. Since total investments were insignificant, they did not stimulate disputes among states.

For Pernambuco, the 1980s displayed contradictory behaviors with regard to fiscal incentives for the industrial sector. Initially, giving in to internal pressures, the state government decided to implement, between 1983 and 1986, a program of support for the industrial sector and three more financial incentives were granted: The Industrial Development Fund of SUAPE–FDS, the Computer Science Development Fund of Pernambuco–FDIP and the Small Business Development Fund.

With the election of a new government in 1987 in opposition to the previous one, there were changes in the position with respect to the granting of incentives. Among the first measures taken by the newly elected government was one that suspended the financial incentives already established for some companies and stopped new agreements on fiscal incentives altogether. The idea was to reduce to zero any fiscal cost that the state treasury could possibly incur (Lima, 1997).

2.2. The 1990s

With the new Brazilian Constitution of 1988, there was an increase in the autonomy of the states. From the fiscal standpoint, one of the main taxes going to the states was renamed the ICMS. As the states received more financial and political autonomy, a void was left by the central government in terms of regional policies, and new competition among states for investment became stronger than ever, especially with the use of the ICMS as the main attracting instrument (Varsano, 1996).

From 1994 on, the number of incentives multiplied in all states, becoming one of the main national economic issues of the time. The fiscal war started to appear in the media, especially when the disputes were related to the automobile sector.[2] Most of the incentive packages for the automobile sector included tax breaks, land donations and the construction of infrastructure by the states, giving the impression of a complete subordination of state governments to the interests of the automobile companies they were seeking to attract and raising doubts about the real benefits of such policies.[3]

Nowadays, the federal government is attempting to impose limits on the fiscal war by proposing a tax reform which foresees a process of ICMS unification and forbids any use of fiscal incentives. Moreover, there is a discussion about replacing the existing mixed collection system, where part of the tax is paid to the state where the producer is located and part is paid to the state where the product is consumed, with a system where the tax is fully paid in the state of destination of the goods and services. This last modification would solve the whole fiscal dispute around the ICMS, since the producing states would cease to have legislative power over this tax.[4]

3. THREE CHARACTERISTICS OF THE CURRENT INCENTIVES ADOPTED BY THE STATE OF PERNAMBUCO

Starting in 1991, Pernambuco decided to seek new investments in a more active way through mechanisms of financial incentive. At that time, Pernambuco followed the same path as other states and presented a package with all possible incentives. The program was named the Pernambuco Growth Fund (*Fundo Cresce Pernambuco*–FUNCRESCE), and was designed to support production in a general way without restrictions on the production of similar goods, in spite of trying not to harm already existing enterprises. New companies could use up to 60% of the owing ICMS to finance their operations for a period of 24 months, with repayment over a 10-year period, and a two-year grace period. Interest payments were set at 3% a year, with 0% indexation. The low cost of loans placed Pernambuco among the top contenders in the dispute for investments, especially because of the subsidy given through the exemption from indexation, which represented a significant sum in a period of high inflation (Lima, 1997, Piancastelli and Perobelli, 1996).

Besides this fund, the state reactivated the Development Fund for SUAPE,[5] which had been suspended in the previous administration, allowing for the appropriation of credits due during the suspension period. Through Law 11.180/94, the state created PROBATEC, an institution to promote the technological development of firms. The fiscal benefit granted by this program consists of the postponement of the payment period of ICMS owed by firms as a result of acquiring products with a higher technological content. PROBATEC was meant to last for 10 years and was scheduled to end in December of 2004.

In 1995, FUNCRESCE, through Law 11.152 of 12/12/94, became the Program for the Development of the State of Pernambuco (PRODEPE). It has gone through changes since it was implemented, and is now supported by Law no. 11.937, of January 4, 2001. Through the granting of fiscal and financial incentives, PRODEPE seeks to benefit not only the state's industrial sector but also its commercial sector. Moreover, there was the concern of not only granting the incentive to non-similar goods, but also taking into consideration the nature of the activity, the specification of the products, the geographical location of the enterprise within the state, and the priority of the economic activities of Pernambuco.

3.1. PRODEPE III

PRODEPE is in its third version. Firms eligible to participate are industrial companies or trade wholesalers. Special attention, however, is given to the notion that the incentives granted by PRODEPE do imply reductions in the level of tax collected by the state. In other words, they will only be granted to new enterprises. In the case of companies already present in the state, they will cover only the production resulting from a proven increase in installed capacity of at least 20%. Also, they can be granted in the recovery process of companies that have been paralyzed for at least 12 uninterrupted months.[6]

The fiscal incentives of PRODEPE are applicable in five different circumstantial groups, and the sectors and the instruments available vary considerably among them. The five groups are:

Group A–Industrial companies belonging to strategic groups, producers of products subject to incentives specified by law and companies belonging to one of the following production chains:

- Agro-industry, except sugarcane products and wheat mills;
- Metal-mechanics and transportation materials;
- Electronics;
- Pharmaceuticals-chemicals;
- Beverages;
- Non-metallic minerals, except cement and red ceramics;
- Textiles;
- Plastics.

For these products the following benefits are offered:

1. Presumed credit: in state and interstate operations, a presumed credit of 75% of the tax for which the taxpayer is directly responsible, incurred in each fiscal period. The benefit can be extended for a period of 12 years.
2. Compensation for freight costs:[7] for the commercialization of products outside the Northeast Region there will be an additional credit corresponding to 5% of the total value of exits in the fiscal period, limited to the value of the freight.

These benefits may be expanded if the company decides to locate in SUAPE or in areas outside the Recife metropolitan area, and if the decisive factor for its location is not inherent to the nature of the respective activity, relative to the source of mineral resources. In this case, the value of the credit can reach a value of 85% of the tax due in the first four years of benefits. During those four years, however, the company cannot make use of the freight benefits, and after four years it will begin to use the credit of 75% of the tax due.

Group B–Companies belonging to strategic industrial sectors, and which manufacture products not subject to incentives. In this case, a firm can obtain the benefits meant for companies whose activity the state considers as important (see below).

Group C–Industrial companies which manufacture products not receiving the incentives provided in A. Nevertheless, benefits will not be granted for the following industrial activities:

- Construction;
- Extractive industry;
- Sugarcane agro-industry;
- Gas Industry;
- Wheat mills.

There are a few different features between these incentives and those given to the group in A. The incentives are, once again, given as a credit for state and interstate operations. The values, however, are smaller than in the former case: the incentives go up to 47.5% in the case of a dissimilar product in the state, and up to 25% in the case of a similar product. The benefit can be granted for a maximum of eight years. The neutral freight mechanism also applies to this group of companies, and for those that produce similar goods there is a possibility of increasing the benefits up to 47.5% in the first four years if they decide to locate outside the Recife metropolitan area or in SUAPE.

Group D–Importers: this group can also be stimulated by means of the granting of ICMS fiscal benefits. These are basically the postponement of payment of the ICMS related to the import operation until the moment the products are sold by the importers, and also the use of the credit mechanism at the time of sale. The amount of the credit cannot be greater than 47.5% of the taxes due.[8]

Group E–Distribution Centers: industrial or commercial companies that promote the outflow of goods. The only goods subject to benefits are those acquired from the producer, or those that are transfers from other states.

The benefits granted to this group are, in the case of outflow, a credit of 3% for 15 years, and in the case of inflow of goods through transference from an industrial site located outside the state the same 3%, limited to the freight value, up to the same 15 years.

TABLE 1. Planned Investment and Planned Jobs Creation for Beneficiary Companies of PRODEPE, 1996-2003

Date	Project	% of projects	Investment (R$1,000)	% on total investment	jobs	% on jobs
1996	39	6%	457,449	8%	7,795	14%
1997	67	9%	538,786	9%	7,451	13%
1998	118	17%	935,262	16%	12,278	22%
1999	156	22%	1,055,017	18%	8,787	16%
2000	100	14%	463,747	8%	7,725	14%
2001	160	23%	1,172,206	20%	8,797	16%
2002	64	9%	1,116,754	19%	3,391	6%
2003	2	0%	-	-	-	-
Total	706	100%	5,739,224	100%	56,224	100%

Used with permission. AD/DIPER. The data for 2003 are preliminary.

It is worth noting that the benefits can be suspended at any time if the company alters the characteristics of the product without proper authorization from the state, if there is a reduction in the installed production capacity, or if there is a reduction in the level of taxes on products not subject to incentive with the simultaneous increase in the production of the product subject to incentives.

4. RECENT YEARS OF PRODEPE

In this section, we present some of the results of the fiscal incentive program, PRODEPE. The data were obtained from the Development Agency of the State of Pernambuco (AD/DIPER). In its first version, the program began to approve incentives in 1996, which gives us eight years of information.[9] The data contains information on 706 projects that were eligible for some type of incentive. It is worth noting that since the incentives changed over time, similar companies were most likely subjected to different levels of incentives in different years. This makes it difficult to track down each particular incentive, and this will therefore not be attempted here.[10] The analysis will concentrate on companies that received the incentives, their economic sectors, their location within the state, and the planned levels of investment and job creation. For confidentiality reasons, and also for practical ones, the data will not be presented by specified company.

Table 1 presents the data for planned investment and job creation since the beginning of PRODEPE. It is important to note that actual figures for investment and jobs may be different from planned figures. Most likely, the actual numbers will turn out to be smaller that those presented in the projects, since there is an incentive to inflate them at the project level.[11] Also, the dates correspond to the approval of the project. While many companies will need a short period of time to start production, there will be cases where a considerable amount of time will be needed; that is, part of the investment and jobs included in Table 1 are yet to be realized, especially for those approved after 2001.

With these remarks in mind, we can analyze the data in Table 1. The data reveal that in its eight years of existence PRODEPE approved a total of 706 projects for companies that planned to invest a little less than six billion Reals and create 56 thousand jobs. It should be clear that the number of projects do not necessarily correspond to the number of companies, since one company can apply more than once for different types

TABLE 2. Number of Approved Projects, Planned Investment and Planned Jobs by Sector, 1996-2003

Sectors	projects	% projects	Investment (R$1,000)	% on total investment	Jobs	% on jobs
Agro-industry	2	0.28%	1,497	0.03%	62	0.11%
Beverages	72	10.20%	669,042	11.66%	4,662	8.29%
Chemical products	40	5.67%	995,665	17.35%	2,827	5.03%
Clothing	16	2.27%	136,826	2.38%	1,558	2.77%
Distribution Centers	61	8.64%		-		-
Electro-mechanicals	1	0.14%	12,000	0.21%	200	0.36%
Electrical materials	31	4.39%	252,076	4.39%	2,649	4.71%
Foodstuffs	70	9.92%	686,819	11.97%	8,771	15.60%
Furniture	7	0.99%	46,465	0.81%	736	1.31%
Natural Gas Distribution	1	0.14%	365,000	6.36%	50	0.09%
Imports	72	10.20%		-		-
Leather	4	0.57%	33,096	0.58%	339	0.60%
Machinery and equipment n,e,c	15	2.12%	69,008	1.20%	1,259	2.24%
Metal-mechanicals	5	0.71%	11,425	0.20%	347	0.62%
Basic metals	39	5.52%	458,948	8.00%	5,019	8.93%
Non-metallic minerals	85	12.04%	285,343	4.97%	4,949	8.80%
Paper and Pulp	14	1.98%	93,681	1.63%	794	1.41%
Pharmaceuticals	9	1.27%	93,972	1.64%	819	1.45%
Plastics	84	11.90%	654,528	11.40%	5,900	10.49%
Printing	2	0.28%	75,899	1.32%	30	0.05%
Rubber	3	0.42%	40,575	0.71%	289	0.51%
Footwear	14	1.98%	89,605	1.56%	6,498	11.56%
Textiles	47	6.66%	558,920	9.74%	6,722	11.96%
Transportation equipment	4	0.57%	39,933	0.70%	586	1.04%
Wood products (excluding furniture)	1	0.14%	38	0.00%	9	0.02%
Non-specific	7	0.99%	68,863	1.20%	1,149	2.04%
Total	706	100.00%	5,739,224	100.00%	56,224	100.00%

Used with permission. AD/DIPER

of benefits, as will be seen below. In fact, since 1996, PRODEPE has approved benefits for approximately 540 companies.

The program started small, with only 39 projects approved in its first year. The number of projects almost doubled in the second year, although the number of jobs created did not increase, and rose again in 1998 and 1999. In 2001, after a relatively slow year, the number of projects reached the maximum (160). The behavior of planned investment

TABLE 3. Formal Employment by Sector in Pernambuco According to RAIS, Selected Years

Sectors	1994		1998		2002	
	Jobs	Distribution	Jobs	Distribution	Jobs	Distribution
Mineral mining	1,321	0.16%	1,798	0.22%	1,241	0.13%
Non-metallic mineral products	8,243	1.02%	8,649	1.05%	9,760	1.03%
Basic metals	6,169	0.76%	5,803	0.71%	7,021	0.74%
Machinery and equipment n,e,c	2,033	0.25%	1,223	0.15%	1,495	0.16%
Electrical machinery and communication equipment	3,828	0.47%	4,413	0.54%	4,443	0.47%
Transportation equipment	3,535	0.44%	1,290	0.16%	1,654	0.18%
Wood products	2,821	0.35%	3,301	0.40%	3,439	0.36%
Paper and pulp	6,056	0.75%	6,267	0.76%	6,555	0.69%
Rubber, tobacco, leather and similars	3,290	0.41%	1,994	0.24%	2,227	0.24%
Pharmaceuticals	10,088	1.25%	10,371	1.26%	11,041	1.17%
Textiles	22,077	2.74%	15,380	1.87%	15,727	1.67%
Footwear	1,530	0.19%	1,817	0.22%	1,446	0.15%
Beverages and Foodstuffs	75,874	9.41%	68,482	8.32%	68,444	7.25%
Electricity, gas, steam and hydrothermal	14,386	1.78%	9,429	1.15%	14,238	1.51%
Construction	31,759	3.94%	41,586	5.05%	44,897	4.76%
Retail trade	73,389	9.10%	93,661	11.38%	120,683	12.79%
Wholesale trade	19,014	2.36%	18,818	2.29%	20,937	2.22%
Financial intermediation	19,514	2.42%	11,921	1.45%	11,606	1.23%
Real estate	49,589	6.15%	64,361	7.82%	91,382	9.68%
Health and social work	36,736	4.56%	39,591	4.81%	40,733	4.32%
Hotels and restaurants	42,479	5.27%	63,852	7.76%	81,217	8.60%
Health and social work	25,598	3.17%	43,642	5.30%	31,431	3.33%
Education	11,143	1.38%	25,619	3.11%	27,321	2.89%
Public administration	230,676	28.60%	235,389	28.61%	278,084	29.46%
Agriculture, hunting and forestry	53,874	6.68%	43,528	5.29%	46,873	4.97%
Others	51,413	6.38%	543	0.07%	-	0.00%
Total	806,435	100.00%	822,728	100.00%	943,895	100.00%

Used with permission. RAIS.

follows that of the number of projects very closely. Planned jobs, on the other hand, presented a slightly different pattern, reaching their peak in 1998 but falling considerably in 2002.

These differences in behavior should not come as a surprise since some sectors are more labor intensive than others. Tables A1 through A3 in the Appendix help in understanding these variations. The 1998 numbers are mainly explained by the strong participation of six sectors, namely, foodstuffs, beverages, electrical materials, metallurgy, chemical products and textiles. Four of these sectors (beverages, electrical materials, manufacture of basic metals and chemicals) were especially high in that year in terms of planned jobs (see table A2). In 2002, the number of projects fell drastically, but the number of planned jobs fell even more. The projects approved in that year were smaller than in the previous years, both in terms of jobs and planned investment. The one exception was a project in the chemical sector that had a planned investment of R$ 720 million, but has yet to be started.[12]

Table 2 presents the numbers of approved projects, planned investment and jobs by sector for the entire period. Tables A1 through A3 present the same numbers by years. In Table 2 one observes that nine sectors (non-metallic minerals, plastics, imports, beverages, foodstuffs, distribution centers, textiles, chemical products and basic metals) account for 80% of the projects, 75% of the planned investment and 69% of the planned jobs. With the exception of three sectors (imports, foodstuffs and distribution centers), this list corresponds to the strategic sectors defined by the program, i.e., those which receive the largest incentives.

It is worth noting that, as shown in the previous section, given the nature of their activities and the form that the incentive provided, imports and the distribution centers are not required to report planned investments and planned jobs.

A question that could arise when one looks at Table 2 is whether the projects had any impact on the state's economy. We try to take a first glance at this question by examining the employment distribution by sector in Pernambuco before and after the program.

Table 3 presents employment by sector. It is possible to note that the 56,224 potential jobs of PRODEPE would represent approximately 7% of total employment in 1994. One also observes that total formal employment rose by 17% from 1994 to 2002. However, the data indicate that this increase in employment had little to do with PRODEPE incentives. The sectors that contributed the most to the increase in formal employment in the state were wholesale trade, education, construction, real

TABLE 4. Distribution of Projects by Category, 1996-2003

Category	Projects	% projects	Investment (R$ 1,000.00)	% on total investment	Jobs	% on jobs
Expansion	161	22.80	1,088,433	18.96	13,483	23.98
New Plant	283	40.08	3,840,897	66.92	34,249	60.92
Restoration	8	1.13	39,540	0.69	881	1.57
Replacement	6	0.85	46,753	0.81	980	1.74
Competitiveness	19	2.69	128,157	2.23	918	1.63
Change of status	24	3.40	49,225	0.86	1,066	1.90
Isonomy	13	1.84	96,673	1.68	1,037	1.84
Migration	36	5.10	208,501	3.63	888	1.58
Imports	63	8.92	-	-	-	-
Distribution Centers	45	6.37	-	-	-	-
Expansion/New Plant	26	3.68	212,140	3.70	2,540	4.52
Others*	22	3.12	28,907	0.50	182	0.32

"Others" represents 18 combined categories.
Used with permission. AD/DIPER

estate and hotels, and restaurants. On the other hand, a sector like food-stuffs and beverages, which is strongly present in PRODEPE, displays a 10% decrease in employment from 1994 to 2002. Similar results are found for the other sectors in PRODEPE. The sectors that received the fiscal benefits from PRODEPE and presented a positive growth in formal employment are relatively small in Pernambuco.[13]

How can one explain this small impact of the program on employment, despite the 56 thousand planned jobs? One possible explanation is that most of the projects were not yet implemented; that is, most of impacts are yet to be realized. On the other hand, it is possible that part of the projects did not represent new plants at all; i.e., part of the incentives went to firms that were already installed in the state. In that sense, one aspect of the program that is worth analyzing is related to the category of incentives that have been approved over the years. Table 4 presents these numbers.

As previously stated, the main goal of the incentives program is to attract new companies to the state. There is also a possibility that companies that are already in the state receive incentives while increasing their production capacity. The program was, however, also designed to maintain competitiveness among companies already operating in the state with respect to arriving companies and those which operate in other states.

TABLE 5. Regional Distribution of Formal Jobs in Pernambuco, 2000

Region	Jobs	Distribution
Recife Metropolitan Area	621,354	70.70%
Mata Pernambucana	104,158	11.80%
Agreste Pernambucano	88,453	10.02%
Sertão Pernambucano	35,672	4.04%
São Francisco	33,395	3.78%
Total	883,032	100.00%

Used with permission. MTE/RAIS, 2000

TABLE 6. Number of Approved Projects, Planned Investment and Planned Jobs by Location, 1996-2003

Region	projects	% projects	Investment (R$1,000)	% on total investment	Jobs	% on jobs
Recife Metropolitan Area	528	74.79	4,651,949	81.06	38,462	68.41
Agreste Pernambucano	53	7.51	346,145	6.03	7,557	13.44
Mata Pernambucana	53	7.51	306,520	5.34	5,228	9.30
Sertão Pernambucano	52	7.37	165,070	2.88	2,805	4.99
São Francisco	20	2.83	269,539	4.70	2,172	3.86
Total	706	100.00	5,739,224	100.00	56,224	100.00

Used with permission. AD/DIPER

There are only three possible ways to obtain incentives from the state government. Table 4 presents the distribution of the projects by type. As can be observed, there are several possible categories for projects. Imports, Distribution Centers, and Migration are examples of other categories that present a significant number of projects. In fact, the three categories mentioned previously (New plants, Expansion and Competitiveness) represent only 65% of the projects, when considering only the simple categories. This percentage increases when the combined categories are considered.[14] New companies alone represented 40.08% of the approved projects or 283 cases.[15]

The share of these three categories increases significantly when planned investment or planned jobs are considered. Together, they represent 80% of the investment and 77% of the jobs. The category "New Plants" by itself represents 66.92% of the investments and more than half of the jobs. From these numbers it seems reasonable to argue that, at least in terms of incentive distribution, the program managed to accomplish its main goal, i.e., focusing on the attraction of new investments and new jobs. If these jobs are not yet accounted for in official statistics, it is probably because most of the projects are not operating at full capacity or did not start production until 2002.

As pointed out previously, one of the goals of PRODEPE is to promote the distribution of economic activity throughout state, reducing its large geographical concentration around the Recife's metropolitan area. Table 5 shows that 70.7% of the formal jobs in Pernambuco were located in the Recife metropolitan area in 2000, leaving the rest of the state with a little less than 30%. Even the latter were concentrated in the Mata Pernambucana and Agreste Pernambuco areas. It seems only natural to seek ways to spread the economic activity throughout the state, leading to more balanced economic and social growth.

Table 6 presents the geographical distribution of approved projects within the state. As can be observed, 75% of the projects were planned to be located in the Recife metropolitan area. This number is even higher when planned investment is considered (81%). The concentration in terms of jobs, on the other hand, is smaller when compared to the other two indicators. This difference is mainly due to the projects approved for the Agreste and Mata regions.

One would hope that this trend in jobs could lead to a more equal regional distribution of employment. However, a closer analysis of the distribution of jobs among regions and years (see table in the appendix) shows that during the most recent years of the program, planned jobs have been highly concentrated in the metropolitan area of the state capital; that is, most of the jobs created outside the Recife metropolitan area were approved in the first years of the program but new projects tend to concentrate even more around the state's capital.[16]

Summing up, these numbers seem to indicate that, at least until 2002, PRODEPE's incentives were not able to make a significant impact on the spatial allocation of economic activities in the state. This suggests that the incentives offered so far have not been attractive enough to overcome the agglomeration economies provided by the state's capital and its surrounding areas.

CONCLUSION

PRODEPE has undergone several changes over the last few years. As presented in this paper, in its latest version the incentives can be provided for a variety of sectors. The state was also careful enough to create a list of sectors that would be of greatest interest to its economy.

From the analyses of the data on projects, planned investment and jobs, we have seen that the program has been capable of attracting a significant number of projects, most of which are concentrated in the sector considered as a priority by the state. It was noted that approximately 60% of the projects were related to new plants or expansions of plants already present in the state, creating new jobs and bringing new investment to Pernambuco.

When the low costs of the program are considered, i.e., the fact that the state does not incur losses of ICMS and does not provide companies with funds, it is possible to regard PRODEPE as a success. It is difficult, however, to believe that incentives provided in this fashion will be able to attract big projects without a more aggressive package (land donation, loans at interest rates below market value, etc.).

Moreover, when the geographical aspect of the program is considered, the results are clearly not satisfactory. The incentives have not been able to make a significant impact on the spatial allocation of economic activities in the state, with most of the projects being concentrated in the Recife metropolitan area. The incentives offered so far have not been strong enough to overcome the agglomeration economies provided by the state's capital and its surrounding areas.

NOTES

1. This kind of fiscal incentive has already been ruled illegal in court on several occasions (see Alves, 2001).

2. See, for instance, Tendler (2000).

3. See Cavalcanti and Prado (1998) for further discussion on these packages.

4. This would not, however, necessarily put an end to the disputes among the states. Some of the current programs are adapting to a new format where it would still be possible to "fight" for new investments. This seems to be the case of Ceará's investment fund.

5. SUAPE is nowadays the main port of the state.

6. See Oliveira.

7. This mechanism is call neutral freight.

8. For instance, if the taxes due are 7%, the credit is around 3.5%.

9. The information on the projects approved in 2003 is preliminary and includes only two projects.

10. The state government publishes this information in the "Diário Oficial" on a case by case basis. This means that to recover the information on the incentives for each company it would be necessary to consult the last eight years of this publication.

11. It can be argued that in cases like this, companies will behave as if presenting bigger numbers would increase the probability of receiving benefits.

12. This represents 99% of the planned investment in the chemical sector and 65% of total planned investment in 2002.

13. For instance, this is the case of paper and pulp.

14. For instance, 26 projects were approved for "Expansion/New plant."

15. Projects of new companies (New Plant) are concentrated in six sectors (Foodstuffs, Beverages, Non-metallic minerals, Plastics, Chemicals and Textiles).

16. 74% of the projects approved in 2001 are to be located in the Recife metropolitan area.

REFERENCES

Alves, M. A. da S. (2001). "Guerra Fiscal e Finanças Federativas no Brasil: O Caso do Setor Automotivo." *Master's Thesis.* Campinas: Universidade Estadual de Campinas, Instituto de Economia.

ADDIPER–Agência de Desenvolvimento de Pernambuco.

Cavalcanti, C. E, and Prado, S. (1998). "Aspectos da Guerra Fiscal no Brasil." São Paulo: IPEA/FUNDAP.

Lima, A. A. (1997). "A Questão dos Incentivos Fiscais em Pernambuco." *Tributação & Desenvolvimento,* Recife, Vol. 1, No. 1.

Oliveira, A., S. "Incentivos ficais e Financeiros." Available at: <http://www.sefaz.pe.gov.br/sefaz2/outros/incentivos_fiscais.asp>.

Piancastelli, M., and Perobelli, F. (1996). "ICMS: Evolução Recente e Guerra Fiscal." *Discussion Paper* n. 402. Brasília: IPEA.

Pedrosa, I. V., Carvalho, M. R. de, and Oliveira, M. C. de A. (2000). "Renúncia Fiscal do Estado de Pernambuco: Estimativa referente ao ICMS de 1996." *Revista de Administração Pública,* Vol. 34, No. 1, pp. 229-58.

MTE/RAIS (2000). Relação Anual de Informações sociais (RAIS)–Ministério do Trabalho e Emprego. CD-ROM.

Rocha, A. G. (2000). "Velhos Instrumentos, Enfoque Inovador: Combinando Subsídios Fiscais e Desenvolvimento Local: O Caso do Ceará." INPECE. Available at: *<http://www.inplance.ce.gov.br/publicacoes/artigos/ART_5.pdf>.*

Tendler, J. (2000). "The Economic Wars between the States." *Report for the Banco do Nordeste/MIT Project.*

Varsano, R. (1996). "A Guerra Fiscal do ICMS: Quem Ganha e Quem Perde." *Text for discussion,* No. 500. Brasília: IPEA.

doi:10.1300/J140v07n03_07

APPENDIX

TABLE A1. Distribution of Projects by Sector and Year of Approval

Sector	1996	1997	1998	1999	2000	2001	2002	2003
Agro-industry						1	1	
Foodstuffs	6	3	10	15	7	22	7	
Beverages	4	10	18	16	10	12	2	
Rubbers		1	1				1	
Distribution Centers				13	18	18	12	
Footwear	2	2	3	3	1	3		
Leather		2				2		
Electro-mechanicals							1	
Natural gas distribution						1		
Printing				1			1	
Imports			3	26	10	19	13	1
Wood products (excluding furniture)				1				
Electrical materials	2	4	6	10	4	3	2	
Transport material			1	2		1		
Machinery and equipment n,e,c	2	2	1	3	4	1	2	
Metal-mechanicals						5		
Basic metals	2	5	8	4	8	7	5	
Non-metallic minerals	9	15	23	13	13	9	3	
Furniture			4	2		1		
Paper and Pulp	2	3	2	3	2	1	1	
Plastics	3	7	13	19	7	27	7	1
Pharmaceuticals			1		1	6	1	
Chemical products	3	3	11	8	6	6	3	
Textiles	4	6	6	12	8	10	1	
Clothing		2	5	4	1	4		
Non-specific		2	2	1		1	1	

APPENDIX (continued)

TABLE A2. Number of Planned Jobs by Sector and Year of Approval

Sector	1996	1997	1998	1999	2000	2001	2002
Agro-industry							62
Foodstuffs	658	545	1623	1624	893	2356	1072
Beverages	261	1420	1118	553	542	602	166
Rubber		68	153				68
Distribution Centers							
Footwear	2024	652	478	494	2500	350	
Leather		208				131	
Electro-mechanicals							200
Natural gas distribution						50	
Printing				13			17
Imports							
Wood products (excluding furniture)				9			
Electrical materials	757	346	860	480	68	73	65
Transportation materials			250	300		36	
Mechanicals	463	206	12	109	388	41	40
Metal-mechanicals						347	
Electro-mechanicals	808	440	1578	731	581	634	247
Non-metallic minerals	688	1301	1123	973	470	311	83
Furniture			293	243		200	
Paper and Pulp	94	200	236	211	42	11	
Plastics	191	513	971	1194	749	1465	817
Pharmaceuticals			38		105	652	24
Chemical products	318	185	1462	206	138	86	432
Textiles	1533	662	1161	1005	1172	1189	
Clothing		18	833	607	77	23	
Non-specific		687	89	35		240	98

TABLE A3. Planned Investment by Sector and Year of Approval (R$ 1,000.00)

Sector	1996	1997	1998	1999	2000	2001	2002
Agro-industry							1,497
Foodstuffs	114,917	30,607	79,235	95,067	66,755	224,731	75,507
Beverages	56,387	141,708	120,549	129,345	50,448	141,915	28,689
Rubber		1,360	7,215				32,000
Distribution Centers							
Footwear	19,077	30,504	5,737	10,535	18,753	5,000	
Leather		9,299				23,797	
Electro-mechanicals							12,000
Natural gas distribution						365,000	
Printing				2,198			73,702
Imports							
Wood products (excluding furniture)				38			
Electrical materials	14,945	40,027	60,671	104,915	1,472	1,305	28,740
Transportation equipment			1,870	10,463		27,600	
Machinery and equipment n,e,c	14,236	10,799	3,856	5,520	31,281	2,365	950
Metal-mechanicals						11,425	
Basic metals	8,677	16,859	196,220	44,574	28,835	104,886	58,897
Non-metallic minerals	36,586	50,684	47,812	117,810	20,484	10,681	1,285
Furniture			33,243	11,416		1,807	
Paper and Pulp	31,114	8,949	17,490	24,918	10,312	897	
Plastics	62,072	20,116	86,019	253,386	57,435	116,156	59,344
Pharmaceuticals			690		30,557	62,060	665
Chemical products	48,781	20,200	131,069	40,450	15,143	4,384	735,638
Textiles	50,658	79,495	72,616	164,075	131,811	60,265	
Clothing		45,451	67,749	22,576	459	590	
Non-specific		32,729	3,223	17,731		7,340	7,840
Total	457,450	538,786	935,263	1,055,018	463,747	1,172,206	1,116,755

Used with permission. AD/DIPER

APPENDIX (continued)

TABLE A4. Distribution of Projects by Category and Year of Approval

Category	1996	1997	1998	1999	2000	2001	2002	2003
Expansion	15	30	50	23	14	17	12	
New Plant	13	32	48	55	56	62	17	
Restoration	3	2	2	1				
Replacement		1	3	2				
Competitiveness		1	4	9		4	1	
Change of Status	4		6	11		2	1	
Isonomy			1	2		6	4	
Migration		1		16	5	13	1	
Imports				21	6	20	14	2
Distribution Centers				13	8	13	11	
Expansion/New Plant	4		1	2	4	14	1	
Others			3	1	7	9	2	

Used with permission. AD/DIPER

TABLE A5. Number of Planned Jobs by Category and Year of Approval

Category	1996	1997	1998	1999	2000	2001	2002
Expansion	1,928	2,599	4,410	1,998	401	1,706	441
New Plant	4,061	4,413	6,805	5,158	7,020	4,896	1,896
Restoration	232	206	363	80			
Replacement		233	566	181			
Competitiveness				507		411	
Change of Status	968			.			98
Isonomy				105			932
Migration				455	65	368	
Imports							
Distribution Centers							
Expansion/New Plant	606		111	144	239	1,416	24
Others			23	159			

Used with permission. AD/DIPER. Note: there are no planned investment values for the projects approved in 2003.

TABLE A6. Planned Investment by Category and Year of Approval (R$ 1,000.00)

Category	1996	1997	1998	1999	2000	2001	2002
Expansion	204,666	180,587	275,685	129,478	51,421	183,037	63,558
New Plant	162,202	300,026	567,467	697,405	373,797	782,861	957,138
Restoration	5,045	10,758	23,717	20			
Replacement		2,019	29,554	15,179			
Competitiveness			30,161	77,897		20,099	
Change of Status	22,462						26,762
Isonomy				28,041			68,632
Migration		45,396		76,427	1,588	85,090	
Imports							
Distribution Centers							
Expansion/New Plant	63,075		630	9,711	36,941	101,119	665
Others			8,049	20,858			

Used with permission. AD/DIPER. Note: there are no planned investment values for the projects approved in 2003.

TABLE A7. Number of Projects Approved by Region and Year

Region	1996	1997	1998	1999	2000	2001	2002	2003
Sertão Pernambucano	4	10	7	10	9	9	3	.
São Francisco	1	.	4	6	2	7	.	.
Agreste Pernambucano	3	6	10	13	6	8	7	.
Mata Pernambucana	3	5	8	16	6	13	2	.
Recife Metropolitan Area	28	46	89	111	77	123	52	2

TABLE A8. Planned Investment by Region and Year (R$ 1,000)

Region	1996	1997	1998	1999	2000	2001	2002
Sertão Pernambucano	16,016	31,103	17,597	85,831	3,442	9,796	1,285
São Francisco	3,320	.	61,495	78,970	17,300	108,455	.
Agreste Pernambucano	41,461	43,631	99,233	58,658	56,937	16,091	30,133
Mata Pernambucana	30,615	50,654	65,062	98,262	16,985	39,283	5,660
Recife Metropolitan Area	366,037	413,399	691,876	733,297	369,083	998,581	1,079,677

Note: there are no planned investment values for the projects approved in 2003.

TABLE A9. Planned Jobs by Region and Year

Region	1996	1997	1998	1999	2000	2001	2002
Sertão Pernambucano	250	601	545	831	265	230	83
São Francisco	24		568	583	272	725	.
Agreste Pernambucano	265	517	1,465	1,447	3,013	588	262
Mata Pernambucana	264	1088	1655	978	431	757	55
Recife Metropolitan Area	6,992	5,245	8,045	4,948	3,744	6,497	2,991

Note: there are no planned jobs values for the projects approved in 2003.

APPENDIX (continued)

TABLE A10. Number of Projects Approved by Sector and Region

Sector	Sertão Pernambucano	São Francisco Pernambucano	Agreste Pernambucano	Mata Pernambucana	Recife Metropolitan Area
Agro-industry					2
Foodstuffs	4	4	9	4	49
Beverages		11	6	6	49
Rubber				1	2
Distribution Centers				1	60
Footwear			4	7	3
Leather	1		1	2	
Electro-mechanicals					1
Natural gas distribution					1
Printing					2
Imports			4	3	65
Wood products (excluding furniture)					1
Electrical materials			7	4	20
Transportation equipment					4
Machinery and equipment n,e,c				1	14
Metal-mechanicals				1	4
Basic metals			1	3	35
Non-metallic minerals	41		3	10	31
Furniture					7
Paper and Pulp				2	12
Plastics			3	2	79
Pharmaceuticals		1			8
Chemical products			1	1	38
Textiles	5	3	5	3	31
Clothing	2		8		6
Non-specific			1	2	4

TABLE A11. Planned Investment by Sector and Region (R$ 1,000)

Sector	Sertão Pernambucano	São Francisco Pernambucano	Agreste Pernambucano	Mata Pernambucana	Recife Metropolitan Area
Agro-industry					1,497
Foodstuffs	9,241	50,426	83,025	1,497	542,630
Beverages		96,976	44,290	14,761	513,015
Rubbers				1,360	39,215
Distribution Centers					
Footwear			24,314	49,089	16,201
Leather		22,250	5,199	5,647	
Electro-mechanicals					12,000
Natural gas distribution					365,000
Printing					75,900
Imports					
Wood products (excluding furniture)					38
Electrical materials			66,937	40,074	145,064
Transportation equipment					39,933
Machinery and equipment					68,778
Metal-mechanicals				5,917	5,509
Basic metals			4,300	60,444	394,204
Non-metallic minerals	47,698		2,395	16,706	218,544
Furniture					46,465
Paper and Pulp				29,253	64,428
Plastics			11,565	13,198	629,765
Pharmaceuticals		45,270			48,701
Chemical products			5,032	1,392	989,241
Textiles	97,082	54,618	49,304	41,881	316,035
Clothing	11,049		48,016		77,760
Non-specific			1,767	25,071	42,025

Used with permission. AD/DIPER

APPENDIX (continued)

TABLE A12. Planned Jobs by Sector and Regions

Sector	Sertão Pernambucano	São Francisco Pernambucano	Agreste Pernambucano	Mata Pernambucana	Recife Metropolitan Area
Agro-industry					62
Foodstuffs	255	592	1285	93	6546
Beverages		752	370	352	3188
Rubber				68	221
Distribution Centers					
Footwear			3015	1335	2148
Leather		30	83	226	
Electro-mechanicals					200
Natural gas distribution					50
Printing					30
Imports					
Wood products (excluding furniture)					9
Electrical materials			518	66	2065
Transportation equipment					586
Machinery and equipment n,e,c				13	1246
Metal-mechanicals				11	336
Basic metals			224	1266	3529
Non-metallic minerals	1737		172	449	2591
Furniture					736
Paper and Pulp				47	747
Plastics			114	188	5598
Pharmaceuticals		346			473
Chemical products			93	30	2704
Clothing	280		1065		213
Non-specific			73	275	801

Used with permission. AD/DIPER

TABLE A13. Number of Projects by Sector and Category of Incentive

Sector	Expansion	New Plant	Imports	Distribution Centers	Competitiveness	Others
Agro-industry		1				1
Foodstuffs	22	29			1	18
Beverages	20	31	2		2	17
Rubber	1	2				0
Distribution Centers	1	13	1	45		1
Footwear	3	6			1	4
Leather	2	2				0
Electro-mechanicals		1				0
Natural gas distribution		1				0
Printing	1	1				0
Imports	3	11	58			0
Wood products (excluding furniture)	1					0
Electrical materials	4	15				12
Transportation equipment		3				1
Machinery and equipment n,e,c	4	8				3
Metal-mechanicals		5				0
Basic metals	10	18			1	10
Non-metallic minerals	42	29			2	12
Furniture	2	5				0
Paper and Pulp	5	3			1	5
Plastics	18	46	1		3	16
Pharmaceuticals	1	5				3
Chemical products	12	19	1			8
Textiles	5	18			7	17
Clothing	3	6			1	6
Non-specific	1	5				1
Total	161	283	63	45	19	135

Used with permission. AD/DIPER

APPENDIX (continued)

TABLE A14. Planned Investment by Sector and Category of Incentive (R$ 1,000.00)

Sector	Expansion	New Plant	Distribution Centers	Competitiveness	Others
Agro-industry		1,497			-
Beverages	125,744	511,431			28,547
Chemical products	164,585	828,490			2,590
Clothing	1,124	59,516		30,161	46,026
Distribution Centers					-
Electrical materials	44,015	154,221			52,889
Electro-mechanicals		12,000			-
Foodstuffs	278,650	193,668			171,252
Footwear	15,570	68,856			4,612
Furniture	919	45,547			-
Natural gas distribution		365,000			-
Imports					-
Leather	26,350	6,747			-
Machinery and equipment n,e,c	4,932	61,214			2,862
Basic metals	150,689	167,537			140,722
Metal-mechanicals		11,425			-
Non-metallic minerals	49,076	195,008			36,085
Non-specific	1,991	49,141			17,731
Paper and Pulp	35,748	26,514		3,275	22,540
Pharmaceuticals	690	61,241			32,041
Plastics	124,502	514,312			14,940
Printing	2,198	73,702			-
Rubber	1,360	39,215			-
Textiles	60,253	364,369		74,622	59,675
Transportation equipment		30,247			9,686
Wood products (excluding furniture)	38				-
Total	1,088,434	3,840,898	-	128,157	642,198

Used with permission. AD/DIPER

TABLE A15. Planned Jobs by Sector and Category of Incentive

Sector	Expansion	New Plant	Competitiveness	Others
Agro-industry		62		-
Beverages	1,282	3,163		217
Chemical products	992	1,792		43
Clothing	138	1309		111
Distribution Centers				-
Electrical materials	1,073	1,228		348
Electro-mechanicals		200		-
Foodstuffs	3,643	2,609	411	2,108
Footwear	779	5,496		223
Furniture	62	674		-
Natural gas distribution		50		-
Imports				-
Leather	155	184		-
Machinery and equipment n,e,c	97	1,100		62
Basic metals	848	2,394		1,777
Metal-mechanicals		347		-
Non-metallic minerals	1,887	2,349		713
Non-specific	68	1,046		35
Paper and Pulp	243	199	34	318
Pharmaceuticals	38	636		145
Plastics	1,589	4,174		137
Printing	13	17		-
Rubber	68	221		-
Textiles	499	4413	473	1,337
Transportation equipment		586		-
Wood products (excluding furniture)	9			-
Total	13,483	34,249	918	7,574

Used with permission. AD/DIPER

Industrial Development
from Tax Incentives:
With Special Application to Ceará

Marcos Costa Holanda
Francis Carlo Petterini

SUMMARY. This work seeks to show that a fiscal incentives policy should be based on an analysis of both costs and benefits. When such an analysis is well-prepared, fiscal incentives can be a strong policy for industrial development. In order to illustrate the logic of this reasoning, the case of recent industrial development in the Brazilian state of Ceará is analyzed.

RESUMEN. Este estudio busca demostrar que una política de incentivos fiscales debe basarse en el análisis de costos y beneficios. Cuando el análisis se traza correctamente, los incentivos fiscales pueden convertirse en una poderosa política de desarrollo industrial. Para ilustrar la lógica de este razonamiento, se analiza el caso del reciente desarrollo industrial ocurrido en el estado brasileño de Ceará.

Marcos Costa Holanda is Professor of Economics, Federal University of Ceara Graduate School of Economics, and General Director, Economic Research Institute of Ceara, IPECE. Francis Carlo Petterini is Public Policy Annalist, Economic Research Institute of Ceara, IPECE.

[Haworth co-indexing entry note]: "Industrial Development from Tax Incentives: With Special Application to Ceará." Holanda, Marcos Costa, and Francis Carlo Petterini. Co-published simultaneously in *Latin American Business Review* (International Business Press, an imprint of The Haworth Press, Inc.) Vol. 7, No. 3/4, 2006, pp. 181-194; and: *Latin American Business: Equity Distortion in Regional Resource Allocation in Brazil* (ed: Werner Baer, and Geoffrey Hewings) International Business Press, an imprint of The Haworth Press, Inc., 2006, pp. 181-194. Single or multiple copies of this article are available for a fee from The Haworth Document Delivery Service [1-800-HAWORTH, 9:00 a.m. - 5:00 p.m. (EST). E-mail address: docdelivery@haworthpress.com].

Available online at http://labr.haworthpress.com
doi:10.1300/J140v07n03_08

RESUMO. Este trabalho procura mostrar que uma política de incentivos fiscais deve ser baseada na análise de custos e benefícios. Quando bem desenhada esta análise, os incentivos fiscais podem ser uma forte política de desenvolvimento industrial. Para ilustrar a lógica deste raciocínio é analisado o caso do recente desenvolvimento industrial no estado brasileiro do Ceará. *[Article copies available for a fee from The Haworth Document Delivery Service: 1-800-HAWORTH. E-mail address: <docdelivery@ haworthpress.com> Website: <http://www.HaworthPress. com> © 2006 by The Haworth Press, Inc. All rights reserved.]*

KEYWORDS. Industrial development, tax incentives, market failures

1. INTRODUCTION

The present federal government tax reform proposal has revived an old debate about tax incentives in Brazil. Unfortunately, this debate has concentrated on "allow" or "do not allow" tax incentives in the country's states, while important points like the efficacy, efficiency and fiscal sustainability of these incentives have been regarded as being of secondary importance.

Contrary to what some may think, tax incentives are not "free money" from the government to firms, nor are they "corporate welfare" (Hartzheim, 1997). Actually, when they are well designed and well implemented, tax incentives play an important role in correcting market failures (Barro and Sala-I-Martin, 1992; Laffont and Tirole, 1993; Nogueira, 2002).

We can point out at least two types of market failures that may be corrected. The first one is related to the absence of a well-defined national policy for compensating for the unequal distribution of production factors and income among the country's states.

The second one is related to the inability of the market to price the positive externalities created by private investments. For many investments, there are other benefits besides those priced by the investor. These additional benefits are transmitted to the region, but they are not considered in the private investment decision. In this case, the tax incentive is simply the state's pricing of the social benefits created by the investment.

The validity of tax incentives for attracting investments is defined the same way as the validity of the investments themselves, which are based on costs-benefits analysis.

For the state, the benefits are the positive externalities created by these investments (jobs, technology absorption, attraction of productive factors to the region, taxes, new markets, etc.). On the other hand, costs would be the amount of taxes forgiven and direct costs such as land donation, personnel training, etc.

Therefore, the main point is not "allow" or "do not allow" tax incentives, but to establish rules for "grant" or "do not grant" incentives for a specific investment. Furthermore, once this decision is made, it is necessary to define how they will be given and how much.

The decision on how to grant incentives should be based on some variables that are correlated with the capacity of the investment to generate positive externalities. The decision on how much to grant should be based on an analysis of the social benefits and the costs of the incentive. The costs are reflected mainly in the government's renouncement of its taxes. The private investments, job creation and technological innovation reflect the benefits.

From the above explanation, the reasoning for not allowing tax incentives in order to avoid a "fiscal war" between states is very simplistic. Other factors should be taken into consideration before condemning the tax incentives given by states.[1]

In the next section, we present the economic logic for tax incentives, and also an analytic model that enables evaluating a tax incentive program. This model is utilized in an empirical evaluation of the state of Ceará's tax incentive program in Brazil.

2. THE LOGIC OF TAX INCENTIVES

The decision to grant tax incentives always involves a trade-off between fiscal costs and economic benefits.[2] For the sake of analysis, let us consider the state's value-added tax. In Brazil this tax is called the ICMS (Value-Added Tax on Sales and Services), which may be regarded as being comprised of three parts. The first part could be called the *Pure ICMS* (ICMSP), which is the tax paid by companies that are not participants in the tax incentive program. The second one could be called the *Foreign ICMS* (ICMSF), which is the tax paid by foreign company participants in the program, and the third and last one could be called the *Local ICMS* (ICMSL), which is the tax paid by local company participants in the tax incentives program.

Only companies that do not receive tax incentives pay the entire ICMS. The other companies, which do receive tax incentives, pay less ICMS.

As showed in Diagram 1, "C" is the group of companies located in the state. These companies are classified into two groups. Sub group

"C*" represents the companies which are local but which receive tax incentives. They generate ICMSL, while the others generate ICMSP. The group classified as "A" includes companies from other states and other countries that are attracted by the tax incentive program–they will generate ICMSF. Finally, Group "B" entails companies within the state that migrate because they are attracted by other state programs. These companies used to generate ICMSP.

We can observe that the companies included in Group "A" should not have a negative impact on the state's net collection of taxes. The ICMSF paid by them is less than the ICMSP but they did not come into existence until the creation of the tax incentives program and the attraction of the foreign firm. On the other hand, companies in Group "C*" have a negative impact on the state's collection of taxes, since they pay tax on incentives, the ICMSL, but not the ICMSP.

The basic logic for renouncing fiscal revenues is that attracting new investments will improve the economy's dynamics, which will in turn allow for high growth and high consumption in the future. This leads us to the following two questions: How much of the ICMS can be renounced? Which companies will receive incentives and in what amount?

Taking into consideration that the ICMS is the state's main source of tax revenue, the incentives are restrained by the net revenue needed to finance the state's budget. In the state of Ceará, the renouncement of the ICMS has a limit of 10% of the total collected during a fiscal year. Regarding the second question, the state has created a scoring system to define the tax incentives (See Dias, Holanda and Amaral Filho, 2003). This system defines the amount of tax credit based on variables such as the value of the investment, job creation, location, and inputs purchased from local firms.

There is furthermore a third question, and we can use the example of Ceará to answer it empirically. In the analysis of Diagram (1), the dynamics of the *Pure ICMS* after the movement of firms in and out of the state is not clear. Is the ICMSP positively or negatively affected by the fiscal renouncement? After the incentives are granted, is there an increase in the ICMSP that can compensate for the fiscal renouncement? That is, is the program fiscally sustainable?

To answer this question, monthly series of ICMSP, ICMSL and ICMSF were analyzed for the period from January 1995 through May 2003 (see Graph 1). The series are in Brazilian Reals and are stationary in level.[3]

From these series, a VAR can be estimated and the following impulse–response analysis can be established: (1) Does a positive shock in

DIAGRAM 1

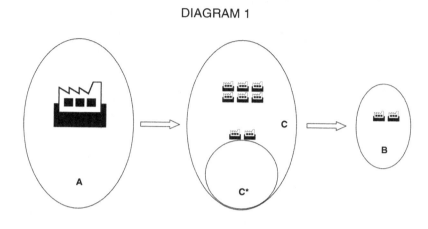

GRAPH 1

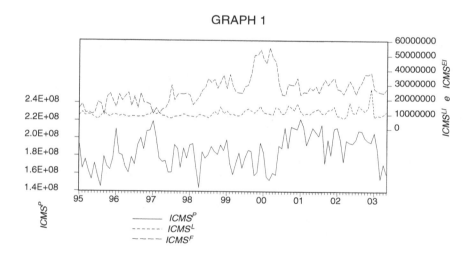

the ICMSL make the ICMSP respond positively? (2) Does a positive shock in the ICMSF make the ICMSP respond positively? The answer to both questions is yes, as illustrated in Graph 2.

The impulse–response analysis shows that the *ICMSP* is positively affected by the fiscal renouncement. It also shows that the answer of the

GRAPH 2. *ICMS^P* Reaction to a Standard Deviation in *ICMS^L* and *ICMS^F*

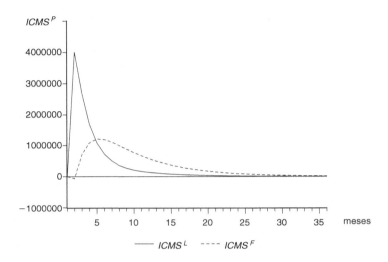

ICMSP to a shock in the *ICMSF* has a higher level of persistency than that to a shock in the *ICMSL*. This fact may be linked to the higher capability of foreign companies to create positive externalities.

3. AN ANALYTICAL MODEL

In general, tax incentive programs follow the same logic. A company pays an amount of taxes, herein defined as ICMS *f*. From this amount paid to the state, the company has a restitution of "$\alpha_f \times ICMS_f$" ($\alpha_f \in [0,1]$) as a non-refundable loan.

Defining the balance of the program (S) as the difference between benefits and costs, and dividing the foreign companies by their national or international origin we have:

$$S = \sum_{i=1}^{3} S_i \qquad i = \text{State, Brazil, World} \tag{1}$$

The firms that originate from the state are local companies; from Brazil, they are companies from other states; and from the World, companies from other countries. The balances are defined by the difference between the benefits and costs created by each firm that receives the tax incentives.

Assuming that the state would renounce part of the ICMS as a non-refundable loan, two benefits are defined by the program. The first one is denominated Cash *(Ci)* and represents the net amount of ICMS paid to the state by the firm. The second benefit is denominated Amplified Benefit *(Bi)*. It represents the benefits created by the investment such as jobs, technology, new ICMS (for example, taxes resulting from the electricity the new companies will consume), etc.

On the other hand, two costs are defined. The first one is denominated Loan *(Li)* and represents the ICMS amount that the firm does not pay to the state. The second cost is called Expenditures *(Gi)* and represents other costs the state incurs with the program (personnel training, land donation, etc).

Each balance may be represented with the following equation:

$$S_i = C_i + B_i - L_i - G_i \tag{2}$$

Now, we will define the structure of each component of (3). The *Cash* variable may be defined as the following equation:

$$C_i = (1 - \alpha_i) \times ICMS_i \tag{3}$$

Observe that $(1 - \alpha_i)$ is the marginal tax paid by the firm attracted to the program and it is limited to between zero and one.

The *Amplified Benefit* is a function of a vector Γ of benefits brought to the state by the program and the ICMS, as expressed in (4):

$$B_i = f_B(\Gamma, ICMS_i) \tag{4}$$

The variable *Loan* comes directly from (4) and is expressed in (5):

$$L_i = \alpha_i \times ICMS_i \tag{5}$$

The *Expenditure (Gi)* is defined as a function of a vector Ω of various costs related to the program and the ICMS, as expressed in (6):

$$G_i = f_G(\Omega, ICMS_i) \tag{6}$$

Placing definitions from (3) to (6) into equation (2) and assuming that the tax incentives program is only valid if all partial balances of (2) are positive, we get to the following condition:

$$S_i > 0 \quad e \quad \frac{\partial S_i}{\partial ICMS_1} > 0 \quad \Leftrightarrow$$

$$\frac{\partial f_B}{\partial ICMS_i} - \frac{\partial f_G}{\partial ICMS_i} > \alpha_i - (1 - \alpha_i) \qquad \forall\, i \qquad (7)$$

$$BLMg > CLMg$$

Equation (7) means that the program is only valid if its Net Marginal Benefit (*BLMg*) is larger than its Net Marginal Cost (CLMg). The validity of the tax incentive program is defined by the relationship between cost and benefit, like any other public or private investment.

In (7), the left side defines the Net Marginal Benefit of the program (*BLMg*) and the right side the Net Marginal Cost (*CLMg*). The sign of *BLMg* may not be observed in the short run, but as the program progresses into maturity it would be revealed. The *CLMg* represents how much income the state renounces with an infinitesimal increase of ICMS generated by the firm. It is observed in the short run.

A key point here is that while the costs of the tax incentive program can be observed in the short run, the benefits cannot. Therefore, there is an implicit risk in any tax incentive program.

4. THE PROGRAM OF THE STATE OF CEARÁ

The Ceara tax incentive program is operated through a fund called the Industrial Development Fund (FDI), which was created in 1979 to promote the development of certain industrial activities in Ceará. Its basic role is to finance the program's subsidized loans.

Since then, the FDI has proven quite effective in attracting companies to the state (Graph 3).

Presently the FDI has three types of programs: PROVIN, directed to industrial firms; PROAPI, directed to exporting firms; PDCI, directed to retail firms.

Table 1 shows disbursements by program and by origin of firms contracted.

GRAPH 3. Number of FDI Contracts Signed Per Year

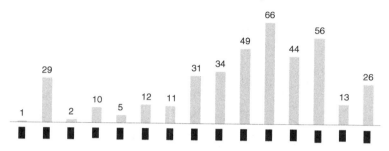

Source: Economic Development Secretariat of the State of Ceará

TABLE 1. Firms Contracted by the FDI

YEAR	ORIGIN OF FIRM CONTRACTED %							TOTAL
	Ceará		Rest of Brazil			Rest of world		
	PROVIN	PROAPI	PROVIN	PROAPI	PDCI	PROVIN	PROAPI	
1995	39.43	-	55.89	-	-	4.68	-	100
1996	29.98	-	66.11	0.32	-	3.60	-	100
1997	31.18	0.05	61.88	3.46	0.99	2.44	-	100
1998	26.65	0.44	64.07	5.98	0.37	2.48	-	100
1999	25.65	0.22	64.13	6.79	0.29	2.03	0.88	100
2000	25.29	0.01	62.12	6.63	0.17	2.42	3.36	100
2001	24.40	0.04	55.58	10.55	0.34	3.55	5.53	100
2002	24.75	0.01	56.72	9.31	0.09	3.48	5.63	100

Source: Economic Development Secretariat of the State of Ceará.

The main industrial sectors that have received incentives are as follows: Shoes and Leather–20.4% of total contracts; Clothes and Accessories–14.9%; Textiles–10.1%; Food and Beverages–9.7%; Chemical Products–8.5%.

As per geographic distribution, 70% of all the companies are located in the metropolitan area of Fortaleza (Ceará's capital).

Graph 4 presents the behavior of the gross private capital formation in Ceará in relation to its PIB for the 1990s. Notice that from 1990 through 1996 this variable oscillated between 10.5% and 12% of PIB, expanding to 14.7% in the year 2000.

GRAPH 4. Gross Private Capital Formation in Relation to PIB–Ceará

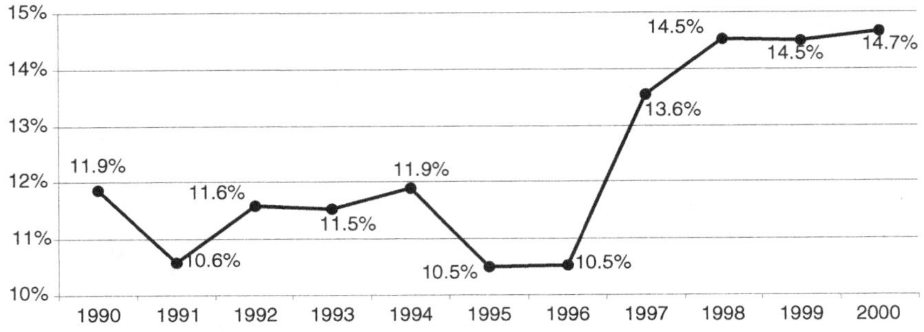

Used with permission. IPECE

From the behavior presented in Graph 4, it is possible to conclude that FDI does not negatively affect gross private capital formation in Ceará. On the contrary, as the largest contracts were signed between 1995 and 1996, and since it takes around two years to convert such contracts into production, it seems the incentives have contributed to Ceará's capital accumulation.

Notice that the way tax incentives contribute to economic welfare is by increasing future consumption. This is achieved when the net total investment of the economy increases.

Table 2 presents the ICMS subsidized loans, private investments and jobs created by the FDI in the period 1995-2002.

Table 2 shows that Ceara's tax incentive program generated over three billion Brazilian Reals in investments and created more than 57 thousand jobs in the period of 1995-2002.[4]

The amounts expressed in Table 2 also allow us to deduct the cost of creating jobs through the FDI. Observe that the state renounced taxes of R$ 2,371 million to generate 57,335 jobs over the eight-year period. This is equivalent to R$ 5,170 or US$ 1,720 per year per employee (around 2 Brazilian minimum wages per month). On the other hand, the private sector invested R$ 3,148 million to generate these same jobs. This is equivalent to R $6,900 or US$ 2,300 per year per employee (around 2.4 Brazilian minimum wages per month).[5]

A direct benefit of the tax incentives can be estimated from the income these jobs generate. Table 3 reveals the expenditure profile of Ceara's families by type of expense. Knowing this profile and knowing that an

TABLE 2. *ICMS Subsidized Loans*, Private Investments and Jobs Created–
R$ 1,000.00

		1995	1996	1997	1998	1999	2000	2001	2002	1995-2002 (Total)
Ceará	ICMS	111.4	106.1	111.2	115.1	137.5	151.8	143.9	157.7	1,034.7
	Sub. Loans	69.2	66.6	71.5	79.0	99.9	108.4	102.7	110.1	707.4
	Investment	33.4	19.4	109.2	119.0	1,039.4	11.7	11.9	394.6	1,738.6
	Jobs	1,214	843	5,650	3,709	3,686	3,571	1,351	1,060	21,084
Brazil	ICMS	180.5	227.9	215.6	308.9	385.4	397.6	270.7	292.7	2,279.3
	Sub. Loans	97.4	146.6	143.8	190.9	249.9	268.1	235.0	254.6	1,586.3
	Investment	94.6	61.5	113.8	475.5	67.4	230.6	0.3	302.1	1,345.8
	Jobs	343	5,746	6,320	15,957	2,734	2,219	126	1,339	34,784
World	ICMS	11.4	10.8	7.4	9.7	10.3	13.6	18.7	19.4	101.3
	Sub. Loans	8.2	7.9	5.6	7.3	7.9	10.3	14.9	15.5	77.6
	Investment	3.1	24.7	0	3.8	11.9	19.9	0.8	0	64.2
	Jobs	108	560	0	269	157	343	30	0	1,467
Total	ICMS	303.3	344.8	334.2	433.7	533.2	563.0	433.3	469.8	3,415.3
	Sub. Loans	174.8	221.1	220.9	277.2	357.7	386.8	352.6	380.2	2,371.3
	Investment	131.1	105.6	223.0	598.3	1,118.7	262.2	13.0	696.7	3,148.6
	Jobs	1,665	7,149	11,970	19,935	6,577	6,133	1,507	2,399	57,335

Source: Economic Development Secretariat of the State of Ceará.

TABLE 3. Type of Expenditure in the Total Budget and Its Respective ICMS
Rate

Type of Family Expense	Percentage of each expense in the Family Budget %	ICMS rate charged over each expense %
Food	38.04	7.00
Housing	14.63	17.00
Household goods	6.27	17.00
Clothing	6.21	17.00
Transportation	14.39	8.13
Health and personal grooming	8.54	17.00
Personal expenses	6.79	2.93
Education	3.01	1.55
Communication	2.12	17.00
Average ICMS Rate %		10.5%

Source: IPECE, IBGE

ICMS rate is charged on each expenditure, we can estimate the amount of ICMS that is generated when this income goes to consumption.

Therefore, 10.5% of the payroll generated by the jobs created by the tax incentive program returns to the state's treasury. This amount will reduce the fiscal loss generated by the program. As pointed out earlier, the CLMg differs from the BLMg, because it can be observed and estimated in the short run. Observe that the loans from FDI are the sum of the ICMS generated by each one of the *F firms* multiplied by the established incentive rate ($\alpha_{f,i}$). Suppose there is one representative rate (α_i). The loans for firm *i* in period *t* is equal to this rate multiplied by the total ICMS generated by the firm, added by a random term ($u_{i,t}$), as described in (8).

$$L_{i,t} = \sum_{f=1}^{F}\left\{\alpha_{f,i} \times ICMS_{f,i,t}\right\} = \alpha_i \times ICMS_{i,t} + u_{i,t} \qquad (8)$$

Based on the estimate of Equation (8), and taking into consideration the concepts discussed in the former section, Table 4 presents the CLMg, α-(1-α), and the tax incentive rate ($\hat{\alpha}$) for the FDI.

We can observe in Table 4 that in general the *CLMg* increases until 1999. From there the estimated *CLMg* stabilizes at R$0.30 per R$1.00 of ICMS in the case of local companies, at R$0.60 per R$1.00 of ICMS in the case of outside firms from the world, and at R$0.80 per R$1.00 of ICMS in the case of outside firms from Brazil. The latter says that the

TABLE 4. FDI: *RLMg* and α Estimated by Origin of Firm

YEAR	CEARÁ		BRAZIL		WORLD	
	CLMg	α	CLMg	α	CLMg	α
1995	0.07	0.54	−0.54	0.23	0.50	0.75
1996	0.07	0.54	−0.24	0.38	0.50	0.75
1997	0.12	0.56	−0.22	0.39	0.59	0.80
1998	0.21	0.61	−0.12	0.44	0.59	0.80
1999	0.31	0.66	−0.02	0.49	0.60	0.80
2000	0.30	0.65	0.80	0.90	0.62	0.81
2001	0.29	0.65	0.80	0.90	0.63	0.82
2002	0.27	0.64	0.80	0.90	0.64	0.82
2003	0.31	0.66	0.80	0.90	0.63	0.82

tax incentive to outside firms from Brazil is equivalent to 80% of the tax due.

These results show that, as expected, it takes fewer incentives to attract local firms than to attract outside firms.

Observe that it is cheaper to attract firms from other countries than from other states. This probably happens because in foreign firms' planning the tax incentive is the least important factor in their decision to invest.

5. CONCLUDING REMARKS

This paper has aimed to contribute to the tax incentive debate. In Brazil, this debate focuses on the dilemma "allow" or "do not allow" the incentives by the states to avoid the so-called "fiscal war."

The fiscal war argument tends to look only to the fiscal costs of the program. From a state's point of view, however, what matters is the balance of benefits and costs of the program.

An empirical analysis of the state of Ceara's tax incentive program was performed. The data showed that since its advent, private gross capital formation in the state has increased. It was observed that the program generated over three billion Brazilian Reals in private investments and around 57 thousand direct jobs.

Regarding costs, it was verified that the incentives could average up to 80% of the tax due.

It should be pointed out that tax incentive policies such as the one developed by the state of Ceará originated from the lack of a well-defined national policy for regional development.

As discussed, it seems extremely simplistic to condemn the incentives only to avoid the "fiscal war." Usually, private investments create significant positive social benefits that should be priced. Tax incentives are no more than the state recognizing and pricing these benefits.

In sum, instead of condemning tax incentives, the more reasonable approach is to find ways to validate these incentives as instruments of a national regional development policy. The issue should not be "condemn" or "do not condemn" the tax incentives, but how to structure regional development policies based on tax incentives.

NOTES

1. For empirical investigations on tax competition in Brazil see Holanda (2001) and Mendes (2000).

2. For an extensive survey on the literature of tax incentives see Buss (2001).

3. The stationariness was tested using the Dickey and Fuller technique (see Patterson, 2000), utilizing variables in level, intercept and level of significance of 5%.

4. These figures were given by the State Secretariat. They were not audited.
5. Considering the Brazilian Real/US Dollar exchange rate of 3:1 as in November 2004.

REFERENCES

Amaral Filho, J. (2003). "Incentivos Fiscais e Políticas Estaduais de Atração de Investimentos." *Texto para Discussão, nº 8*. Ceará: Instituto de Pesquisa e Estratégia Econômica do Ceará (IPECE).

Barro, R., Sala-I-Martin, X. (1992). "Public Finance in Models of Economic Growth." *Review of Economic Studies*, Vol. 59, No. 201, pp. 645-661.

Buss, T. F. (2001). "The Effect of State Tax Incentives on Economic Growth and Firm Location Decisions: An Overview of the Literature." *Economic Development Quarterly* Vol. 15, No. 1, pp. 90-105.

Dias, R., Holanda, M., Amaral Filho, J. (2003). "Base Conceitual dos Critérios para Concessão de Incentivos para Investimento no Ceará." *Nota Técnica nº 3*, Instituto de Pesquisa e Estratégia Econômica do Ceará (IPECE).

Hartzheim, L. A. (1997). "State Tax Incentives: headed in the right direction." *Journal of State Taxation*, Vol. 15, No. 4, pp. 51-64.

Holanda, M. (2000). "Competição Fiscal no Brasil, Uma Análise Empírica Agregada." *Revista Econômica do Nordeste*, Vol. 31, No. especial, pp. 594-603.

Laffont, J., Tirole, J. (1993). "A Theory of Incentives in Procurement and Regulation." Cambridge: MIT Press.

Mendes, C. (2000). "A Política Regional nas Renúncias Fiscais Federais: 1995/1998." *Texto para Discussão nº 697*. Brasília: IPEA.

Nogueira, C. (2002). "Tax Incentives and Entry Promotion." In: *Anais do XXX Encontro Nacional da ANPEC*.

Patterson, K. (2000). "An Introduction to Applied Econometrics." New York: St. Martin's Press.

doi:10.1300/J140v07n03_08

Economic Effects of Regional Tax Incentives: A General Equilibrium Approach

Alexandre Porsse
Eduardo Haddad
Eduardo Pontual Ribeiro

SUMMARY. Regional governments often adopt tax incentive programs to attract private investments to their jurisdictions. This behavior is no different in Brazil, where such incentive policies have been growing in the last few years due to a combination of factors. This paper uses a general equilibrium approach to evaluate the effects of a regional tax incentive program for attracting investments. The analysis focuses mainly on the financing of new private investments through tax revenue relief and public investment expenditures by regional and federal governments. The interregional general equilibrium model used to run the simulations captures the effects of regional interdependence and of vertical relationships between the governments. The results show that the effects on the employment and household welfare of consumers have been positive for the region implementing such an incentive policy, namely the State of

Alexandre Porsse is affiliated with Fundação de Economia e Estatística do Estado do Rio Grande do Sul. Eduardo Haddad is affiliated with the Universidade de São Paulo. Eduardo Pontual Ribeiro is affiliated with the Universidade Federal do Rio Grande do Sul.

[Haworth co-indexing entry note]: "Economic Effects of Regional Tax Incentives: A General Equilibrium Approach." Porsse, Alexandre, Eduardo Haddad, and Eduardo Pontual Ribeiro. Co-published simultaneously in *Latin American Business Review* (International Business Press, an imprint of The Haworth Press, Inc.) Vol. 7, No. 3/4, 2006, pp. 195-216; and: *Latin American Business: Equity Distortion in Regional Resource Allocation in Brazil* (ed: Werner Baer, and Geoffrey Hewings) International Business Press, an imprint of The Haworth Press, Inc., 2006, pp. 195-216. Single or multiple copies of this article are available for a fee from The Haworth Document Delivery Service [1-800-HAWORTH, 9:00 a.m. - 5:00 p.m. (EST). E-mail address: docdelivery@haworthpress.com].

Rio Grande do Sul. However, the effect on real GDP may not follow the same course, which could occur mainly because of the specialized pattern of production in the State.

RESUMEN. Los gobiernos regionales adoptan programas de incentivo fiscal con el propósito de atraer inversiones a sus jurisdicciones. Este comportamiento no cambia en Brasil, donde dichas políticas de incentivo han crecido en los últimos años debido a un conjunto de factores. Este estudio se basa en el enfoque del equilibrio general, para evaluar los efectos de un programa de incentivo fiscal implementado para atraer inversiones. El modelo del equilibrio general interregional usado para realizar simulacros capta los efectos de la interdependencia regional, y de una relación vertical entre los gobiernos. Los resultados muestran que los efectos sobre el empleo y el bienestar doméstico de los consumidores son positivos para la región que implementa este tipo de política de incentivos como ocurre, por ejemplo en el estado de Río Grande do Sul. Sin embargo, el efecto sobre el PIB no sigue el mismo camino, lo que podría ser resultado, principalmente, del patrón de producción especializado del Estado.

RESUMO. Os governos regionais adotam com freqüência programas de incentivo fiscal a fim de atrair investimentos privados para suas jurisdições. Este comportamento não é diferente no Brasil, onde tais políticas de incentivo têm crescido nos últimos anos devido a uma combinação de fatores. Este estudo usa uma abordagem do equilíbrio geral para avaliar os efeitos de um programa regional de incentivos fiscais para atrair investimentos. A análise enfoca principalmente o financiamento de investimentos privados novos através da redução da arrecadação fiscal e do investimento público pelos governos regionais e federal. O modelo do equilíbrio geral inter-regional usado nas simulações capta os efeitos da interdependência regional e de relacionamentos verticais entre os governos. Os resultados mostram que os efeitos sobre o emprego e o bem-estar doméstico dos consumidores são positivos para a região que implementa tal política de incentivo, a saber, o estado do Rio Grande do Sul. Entretanto, o efeito sobre o PIB real pode não seguir o mesmo caminho, e isto ocorreria sobretudo devido ao padrão de produção especializado no estado. doi:10.1300/J140v07n03_09 *[Article copies available for a fee from The Haworth Document Delivery Service: 1-800-HAWORTH. E-mail address: <docdelivery@haworthpress.com> Website: <http://www.HaworthPress.com> © 2006 by The Haworth Press, Inc. All rights reserved.]*

KEYWORDS. Tax competition, fiscal incentives, computable general equilibrium models, regional analysis

INTRODUCTION

Regional governments often adopt tax incentive programs to attract private investment to their jurisdictions. This behavior is no different in Brazil, where such incentive policies have been growing over the last few years due to a combination of factors. The inducement role of the federal government subsided noticeably during the 1990s in the context of the stabilization policies carried out in the country. This federal governmental behavior resulted in the lack of a national agenda for industrial policy and regional development for Brazil and opened the way for an active regional developmental policy by the local and state governments. The improvement in Brazil's competitiveness after a technological upgrade due to trade liberalization, the stability engendered by the Real Plan and the expansionary cycle of foreign capital investment in the second half of the 1990s, especially in the automobile industry, led Brazilian state governments to engage in a true fiscal war in order to influence private decisions surrounding the spatial allocation of new investment.

Tax incentive programs are mainly fueled by expectations of welfare gains by means of an increase in the region's level of employment and income, but the controversy surrounding their efficiency is far from being cleared up due to the difficulty in determining the effects on the economic system as a whole. On the one hand, supporters highlight the positive impacts on the creation of jobs and income, whereas on the other hand, opponents draw attention to possible costs arising from the loss of tax revenue and, consequently, inefficient allocation of public goods.[1]

A consistent analysis of the effects of tax incentives for attracting investments should consider not only the aspects related to the creation of jobs and income in an isolated fashion, in contrast to the necessary supply of public goods for the population, but also the specific characteristics of the environment in which this competition takes place. An important aspect is concerned with the context in which this "dispute" occurs; that is, regional dimension and asymmetries can be a relevant factor, since regional production specialization and interregional trade patterns can determine a regional interdependence that affects the allocation of investments. The government's vertical relationships are also important, especially when the federal system uses mechanisms for the transfer of tax revenues to regional governments,[2] as is the case of Brazil.

However, an important issue is the type of investment targeted by the tax incentive program. In the real world, incentive programs can be used to attract new investments when they do not seek to influence–at least not directly–the allocation of investments already made and distributed across regions.[3] This situation involves the granting of specific incentive packages negotiated at the firm level (e.g., large investments intended for the installation of a new production plant), strongly resembling the behavior of regional governments regarding the competition for the allocation of investments by automobile industries. Nevertheless, regional governments can also implement permanent incentive programs that can either be used to encourage new investments or to influence the regional reallocation of investments. The latter case may be faulty because it implies direct competition for existing capital stock, and its application within a context of strategic interactions between regions can lead to a zero-sum game and to an inefficient allocation of public resources.

This study focuses on the first type of tax incentive, whose aim is to attract new investments by offering tax relief. The objective is to show that the computable general equilibrium (CGE) approach can be an appropriate method for assessing the economic effects of tax incentives to attract new investment to a given region. Our proposal consists in using an interregional computable general equilibrium (ICGE) model developed for two Brazilian regions (State of Rio Grande do Sul and Rest of Brazil) and in simulating the economic effects of an increase in the capital stock of manufacturing industries in Rio Grande do Sul, an increase that is fully granted by the regional government; that is, by the tax revenue yet to be collected. We pay attention to the effects on GDP, employment and the change in tax revenue collection induced by new investment. The theoretical framework of this model is based on the B-MARIA model (Haddad, 1999) and its advantage is the integration between an interregional economic database and a public finance module for regional and federal governments that take into account the structural characteristics of Brazilian fiscal federalism.

The B-MARIA-RS Model

B-MARIA-RS (*Brazilian Multisectoral and Regional/Interregional Analysis–Rio Grande do Sul*) is an interregional computable general equilibrium model developed for analyzing the economy of Rio Grande do Sul and of Brazil. Its theoretical framework is similar to the

B-MARIA model (Haddad, 1999) and follows the Australian tradition of general equilibrium models.[4]

The B-MARIA-RS model divides the Brazilian economy into two regions–Rio Grande do Sul and Rest of Brazil–and identifies a single foreign market (Rest of the World). The calibration data are those for 1998, and 25 productive sectors and investment goods are specified for each region. The productive sectors use two local primary factors (capital and labor). Final demand consists of household consumption, investment, exports, and regional and federal governmental consumption. The regional governments are sources of exclusively local demands and expenditure, comprising the state and municipal levels of public administration in each region. The whole model contains 60,323 equations and 1,475 exogenous variables.[5]

The main innovation in the B-MARIA-RS model is the detailed treatment of public finances. As will be described below, this modification consists in the introduction of alternative closures for the governments regarding public finance policies. The core module of the model comprises blocks of equations that determine the relationship between supply and demand derived from optimization theories and market equilibrium conditions. The indirect taxes at the core of the model are decomposed in order to separate the state's indirect tax from the other federal and municipal indirect taxes. In addition, several regional and national aggregates are defined, such as level of aggregate employment, balance of trade and price indices. Next, we present the main theoretical aspects of the model.

Production Technology

Figure 1 illustrates the production technology encountered in the B-MARIA-RS model, a usual specification in regional models. This specification defines three levels of optimization for the productive process of firms. The dashed lines indicate the functional forms specified in each stage. Fixed proportion combinations of intermediate inputs and primary factors are assumed at the first level, through the Leontief specification. The second level involves substitution between domestically produced and imported inputs on one side, and substitution between capital and labor on the other side. A constant elasticity substitution (CES) function is used for the combination of inputs and primary factors. At the third level, bundles of domestically produced and imported intermediate inputs are formed as combinations of inputs from different sources. Again, a CES function is used to combine goods from different sources.

FIGURE 1. Nested Structure of Regional Production Technology

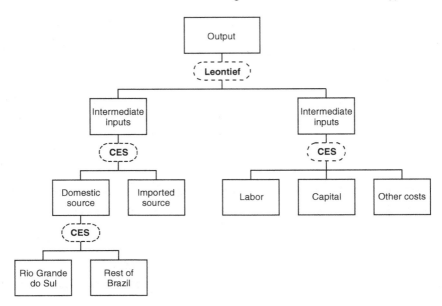

The use of CES functions in production technology implies the adoption of the so-called Armington assumption (Armington, 1969) for product differentiation. This hypothesis regards goods from different sources as imperfect substitutes. For instance, agricultural and livestock products from Rio Grande do Sul are different from agricultural and livestock products from the Rest of Brazil with regard to their use in the productive process (third level in Figure 1). This treatment enables the model to exhibit non-specialized intrasectoral market patterns, an important empirical regularity described in the literature.[6]

Household Demand

Each region has a group of representative households, which buy domestic goods (either locally produced or from other regions) and imported goods. The specification of household demand in each region is based on a CES/linear expenditure system (LES) preference function. The demand equations are derived from a utility maximization problem, whose solution follows hierarchical steps similar to the ones shown in

Figure 1. At the bottom level, substitution occurs across different domestic and imported sources of supply. At the subsequent upper level, substitution occurs between domestic composite and imported goods. The utility derived from the consumption of domestic and imported composite goods is maximized according to a Stone-Geary utility function. This specification gives rise to the linear expenditure system (LES), in which the expenditure share above the subsistence level for each good represents a constant proportion of the total subsistence expenditure of each regional household.[7]

Demand for Investment Goods

Investors are a category of use of final demand, and are held responsible for capital formation in each regional sector. They choose the inputs used in the capital formation process through cost minimization by using a hierarchically structured technology. This technology is similar to production technology, but with some adaptations. As occurs with production technology, the capital good is produced by domestic and imported inputs. At the third level, an aggregate bundle of intermediate goods (domestic and imported) is formed as the combination of inputs from different sources. A CES function is used in the combination of goods from different sources. Differently than production technology, primary factors are not used directly as input for capital formation, but are used indirectly through inputs in sectoral production, especially in the civil construction sector. The level of regional investment in capital goods per sector is determined by the capital accumulation block.

Export and Government Demand

All export goods have downward sloping demand curves for their own prices in the world market. A vector of elasticity defines the response of foreign demand to changes in the FOB price of regional exports.

The government demand for public goods is based on the isolation of the consumption of public goods by the regional and federal governments, obtained from the input-output matrix. However, productive activities carried out by the public sector cannot be dissociated from those performed by the private sector. Thus, the government's entrepreneurial behavior is dictated by the same cost minimization assumptions adopted by the private sector. This hypothesis may be considered more appropriate, at first, for the Brazilian economy, since the privatization process implemented in the 1990s substantially reduced the participation of the government in the productive sector (Haddad, 1999). Public goods consumption is set to maintain a constant proportion with (1) regional private consumption, in the case of regional governments, and (2) with national private consumption, in the case of the federal government.

Capital Accumulation and Investment

Capital stock and investment relationships are defined in this module. There are two comparative static versions for the model that allow its use in short-run and long-run simulations. The use of the comparative statics model implies no fixed relationship between capital and investment; this relationship is selected on the basis of the requirements of the specific simulation. For example, in typical long-run comparative static simulations, growth of investment and capital is assumed to be identical (see Peter et al., 1996). Some qualifications are necessary for the specification of capital formation and investment in the model. As discussed in Dixon et al. (1982), the modeling of these components is basically concerned with how investment expenditures are allocated both per sector and per region, and not with the aggregate private investment in construction, machinery and equipment. On top of that, the temporal conception of investment used is not endowed with a correlation with a precise timetable; this would be a necessary characteristic if the model aimed at explaining the investment expansion path over time. Therefore, the main concern regarding the investment modeling is to capture the effects of the shocks on the allocation of current investment expenditure across sectors and regions.

Labor Market and Regional Migration

In this module, the population in each region is defined exogenously through the interaction of demographic and interregional migration variables, and there is also a connection between regional population and labor supply. Given the specification of the labor market functioning, labor supply can be determined by interregional wage differentials or by regional unemployment rates, along with demographic variables, often defined exogenously. In sum, both labor supply and wage differentials may determine unemployment rates or, alternatively, labor supply and unemployment rates will determine wage differentials.

Other Specifications

The government finance module incorporates equations determining the gross regional product for each region through the decomposition and modeling of its components on both the expenditure and income sides. Budget constraints on the regional and federal governments are also defined,[8] as well as the aggregate household consumption functions in each region (disaggregated into the main sources of income and in the respective tax duties). Other definitions in the model include tax rates, basic prices, and purchase prices of commodities, tax revenues, margins, components of the gross domestic product (GDP) and gross regional product (GRP), regional and national price indices, factor prices, aggregate employment and money wage settings.

Closures

The B-MARIA-RS model can be used for short-run and long-run comparative static simulations. The basic distinction between these two types of closure lies in the treatment given to the microeconomic approach to capital stock adjustment. Capital stocks are held fixed in the short run, whereas in the long run, policy changes may affect capital stocks in each region.[9] In a short-run closure, besides the hypothesis of interindustry and interregional immobility of capital, the regional population and labor supply are fixed, the regional wage differentials are constant and the national real wage is fixed. Regional employment is driven by assumptions about wage rates, which indirectly determine regional unemployment rates. On the demand side, investment expenditures are exogenous–firms cannot reassess investment decisions in the short run. Household consumption follows household disposable income, and government consumption at both regional and federal levels is fixed (alternatively, government deficit can be set exogenously, allowing government expenditures to change). Finally, the technology variables are exogenous, given that the model does not present any endogenous growth theory.

In a long-run closure, capital and labor are mobile across sectors and regions. The major differences from short-run closure lie in the configuration of the labor market and capital accumulation. In the former case, aggregate employment is determined by population growth, labor force participation rates, and the natural rate of unemployment. The distribution of the labor force across regions and sectors is totally determined endogenously. Labor is attracted to more competitive sectors in more favorable geographical areas. Likewise, capital is directed towards more attractive sectors. This movement keeps the rates of return at their initial levels.

MODELING STRATEGY

The simulation design is based on the observation of several tax incentive packages established by Brazilian state governments in the mid-1990s in order to attract new investment in the automobile sector to their jurisdictions.[10] These incentives consisted of tax exemptions, mainly from the value-added tax on sales and services (ICMS[11]), direct infrastructure expenditures, provision of plots of land and direct financing in the form of subsidized credit for fixed capital and shareholders in some cases. The simulation strategy encompasses two aspects. First, it considers that the values of new investments are totally paid by the regional (state) government's indirect tax revenue; that is, it is assumed that the total value of new investments is deducted from the collection of ICMS, the major state indirect tax. This is equivalent to a tax exemption policy that fully covers private expenditures with the capital stock expansion of regional firms.[12] Second, it considers that the regional government's public expenditures with investment goods are endogenous and follow the growth of private investments. This allows capturing the effects of public investments in infrastructure needed to support the private investments.

To apply this strategy, we use a similar procedure applied in Haddad and Hewings (1999). It is assumed that the effects of new investments can be assessed under the hypothesis of the technological upgrade of industries. Specifically, a 1% shock is attributed to the current capital stock of manufacturing industries of Rio Grande do Sul. To include the tax relief in the simulation, the monetary value[13] corresponding to the shock in the current capital stock is deducted from the tax revenue collected through indirect taxes charged by Rio Grande do Sul's governments. The simulation is performed under a long-run closure and, therefore, it accepts interregional and intersectoral mobility of capital and labor.

The government's closure plays a key role in this simulation. In the B-MARIA-RS model, governmental revenues and expenditures are itemized and sorted out according to the level of regional government, including state, municipal and federal government. The federal government has vertical relationships with regional governments through current transfers and capital transfers.[14] Most of the public expenditure components are determined endogenously by aggregate variables of the macroeconomic, demographic and labor market modules. For instance, public investments follow the variation in private investments in order to accommodate the needs of infrastructure investments; personal benefit payments evolve positively with labor supply and population growth, and negatively with the employment variation; subsidies follow the performance of indirect tax revenue, and payment of interests are contingent upon the GDP variation. Despite its endogenous determination, this mechanism implies that the government spending policy is exogenous–governments should meet the demand for public goods–and that the pressures on such expenditures should be accommodated by tax revenue increases.

Tax revenue can grow if there is a positive effect of the new investments on the tax base, or because of changes in tax rates, or both. Then we allow the federal government to respond to public goods pressures by endogenously adjusting the income tax rate if the income tax base effect is not so high. For the regional governments we assume an endogenous adjustment in payroll tax rates. However, it is worth noting the effects on federal income and indirect tax revenues that also have effects on regional government revenues due to the fiscal transfer mechanism. Table 1 summarizes the government's closure regarding the degree of freedom to implement public finance policies in the government's view.

SIMULATION RESULTS

The simulation was implemented using Euler's method to correct linearization errors and the results are reported in percentage change rates, except for the equivalent variation. Table 2 summarizes the main effects of the increase in current capital stock in the manufacturing industry of Rio Grande do Sul for some regional and national variables. The GDP components were deflated by their respective price indices. By observing the results for Rio Grande do Sul, the increase in demand generated by new investments produces positive effects on employment and on the equivalent variation, indicating that it is necessary to increase the number of employed individuals to guarantee the productive growth of manufacturing sectors, and that the representative household of the model has a superior level of utility. The welfare effect is strengthened by the decrease in the price of final consumer goods and

TABLE 1. Government's Closure for the Public Finance Policy

Components of public finances	Regional Gov.	Federal Gov.
Government's revenue	Mixed	Mixed
Direct taxes	Exogenous	Mixed
Income taxes	-	Endogenous
Other direct taxes	Exogenous	Exogenous
Indirect taxes	Mixed	Exogenous
Tariff revenue	Exogenous	Exogenous
Commodity taxes	Exogenous	Exogenous
Payroll taxes	Endogenous	Exogenous
Property taxes	Exogenous	-
Land taxes	-	-
Other indirect taxes	Exogenous	Exogenous
Interests received	Exogenous	Exogenous
Federal transfers	Exogenous	Exogenous
Other revenues	Exogenous	Exogenous
Discrepancy	Exogenous	Exogenous
Public deficit	Exogenous	Exogenous
Government's expenditure	Exogenous	Exogenous
Expenditures on goods and services	Exogenous	Exogenous
Government consumption	Exogenous	Exogenous
Government investment	Exogenous	Exogenous
Personal benefit payments	Exogenous	Exogenous
Subsidies	Exogenous	Exogenous
Interest payments	Exogenous	Exogenous
Federal transfers to regions	Exogenous	Exogenous
Other outlays	Exogenous	Exogenous

by the increase in household disposable income due to the positive impact on primary factors income.

Nevertheless, the effect on real GDP is negative because of the sharp increase in the general price level (GDP deflator) caused by the demand shock. As Rio Grande do Sul's economy is highly specialized in the production of final consumer goods, especially in the agroindustrial sectors, but poorly specialized in the production of investment goods and of some basic inputs, the shock tends to produce a noticeable increase in the prices of these goods. Price increases mainly affect the competitive position of goods traded in interregional and foreign mar-

TABLE 2. Long-Run Percentage Effects: 1% Increase in Current Capital of the Manufacturing Industry of Rio Grande do Sul

Variables	Rio Grande do Sul	Rest of Brazil	Brazil
GDP components			
Real household consumption	0.630	0.031	0.073
Real aggregate investment	4.355	−0.012	0.273
Real aggregate regional government demand	-	-	-
Real aggregate federal government demand	-	-	-
Interregional export volume	−1.331	1.184	-
International export volume	−2.488	−1.006	−1.151
Interregional import volume	1.184	−1.331	-
International import volume	0.737	0.341	0.362
Prices			
Consumer price index	−0.071	0.457	0.419
Investment price index	1.558	0.445	0.519
Regional government price index	0.485	0.537	0.534
Federal government price index	0.485	0.537	0.535
Interregional export price index	2.070	0.435	-
International export price index	1.709	0.418	0.544
Interregional import price index	0.435	2.070	-
International import price index	-	-	-
GDP deflator (expenditure side)	1.117	0.463	0.513
Primary factors			
Aggregate payments to capital	4.506	0.428	0.727
Aggregate payments to labor	0.543	0.481	0.486
Aggregate capital stock	2.712	−0.018	0.184
Welfare indicators			
Equivalent variation*	1,305	1,281	2,585
Real GDP	−0.219	−0.005	−0.021
Employment	0.118	−0.008	0.001

Source: calculated by the authors.
Note: *values in R$ million.

kets, resulting in a substitution effect that exceeds the gains induced by the real increase in investments and in household consumption. The benefits of the incentive program are absorbed by investors and households, whereas the costs are absorbed by interregional and international export agents.

The effects on GDP and employment in the Rest of Brazil are negative and relatively small. Although this region has a competitive advantage in the interregional market, regional mobility of production factors exerts pressure on the cost of production and on the general price level of goods in the region. Interregional relationships concentrate the absorption of price increases in this region. Thus, the reduction in GDP is contingent on the real reduction in investments and on the loss of competitiveness in the foreign market, which also produces a substitution effect between domestically produced and imported goods. Quite surprisingly, real household consumption and equivalent variation show a positive variation in the Rest of Brazil. In this case, the effect results from a nominal increase in the primary factors income–especially labor, which is higher than the increase in the prices of household consumer goods.

The aggregate effects in both regions determine positive results for the Brazilian economy in terms of job creation and a higher level of utility for households, but the negative effect on GDP persists. Considering Brazil as a whole, it is clear that the gains from the tax incentive program for attracting investments to the manufacturing industry of Rio Grande do Sul tend to benefit investors and consumers, whereas the costs related to the increase in the domestic price level determine a substitution between domestically produced and imported goods, which has a negative effect on the balance of trade.

Now we can look at the implications for governmental public finances. Table 3 shows the effects on tax revenue, expenditures and public deficit of the regional and federal governments in real growth rates obtained from the difference between nominal variations and the GDP deflator. It should be pointed out that the change in indirect tax revenue of Rio Grande do Sul is already adjusted; that is, it represents the net revenue after deduction of the monetary values of the shocks in the current capital stock.

The rise in the level of investment in the manufacturing sectors of Rio Grande do Sul increases the demand for investment by the government of Rio Grande do Sul and by the federal government, placing some pressure on their expenditures. For the federal government, the shock of investment in Rio Grande do Sul has a low impact on the tax base associated with the collection of indirect taxes, and there is a real negative effect on tax collection because the nominal variation is lower than changes in the general price level. Considering the effects on the production factors income, the impact on the income tax base is also low. Therefore, the federal government's investments are financed through a

TABLE 3. Long-Run Percentage Effects on Public Finances: 1% Increase in Current Captial of the Manufacturing Industry of Rio Grande do Sul

Variable	Government		
	Rio Grande do Sul	Rest of Brazil	Federal
Government's revenue	0.002	0.057	0.105
Tax revenue	0.293	0.106	0.820
Direct taxes	−0.222	−0.005	3.692
Income taxes	-	-	5.033
Other direct taxes	−0.222	−0.005	−0.022
Indirect taxes	0.691	−0.096	−0.030
Tariff revenue		-	−0.136
Commodity taxes	1.091	−0.042	−0.021
Payroll taxes	−2.618	−1.348	−0.022
Property taxes	−0.222	−0.005	-
Land taxes	-	-	-
Other indirect taxes	−0.222	−0.005	−0.022
Interest received	−0.222	−0.005	−0.022
Federal transfers	2.896	3.550	-
Other revenues	−0.222	−0.005	−0.022
Discrepancy	−0.633	0.074	0.021
Public deficit	-	-	-
Government's expenditure	0.002	0.057	0.105
Expenditures with goods and services	0.006	0.061	0.156
Government consumption	−0.633	0.074	0.021
Government investment	4.864	−0.030	1.825
Personal benefit payments	−0.579	−0.052	−0.089
Subsidies	0.957	−0.044	0.043
Interest payments	−0.222	−0.005	−0.022
Federal transfers to regions	-	-	3.500
Other outlays	0.002	0.057	0.105

relatively high increase in the income tax rate, since part of this revenue is transferred to regional governments in compliance with constitutional rules.[15] So, the adjustment of the federal government on the revenue side tends to benefit the revenue of regional governments.

The pressures on public investments are more noticeable for the regional government of Rio Grande do Sul and are financed by an increase in the indirect tax revenue (exclusively due the tax base growth) and by the increase in revenues from federal transfers. Two aspects related to effects on the tax base of Rio Grande do Sul should be noted: first, since the regional government comprises the state and its municipalities, the tax base growth extends to the indirect tax collection of municipal governments; second, even though the international export sector absorbs a significant amount of the price increase, the decrease in the volume of international exports does not substantially affect the collection of indirect taxes at the state government level because the Kandir Law exempts exporters from paying the ICMS.[16]

The reallocation effect on the economy of the Rest of Brazil, especially regarding capital, contributes to a reduction in the region's real tax base, but on the other hand, it originates less demand for public investments. Even so, the government's revenue in this region benefits from the increase in federal transfers, and this allows for elevating the provision of public goods or creating new expenses. If, on the one hand, the region loses in terms of job creation and GDP, on the other hand, it can have public revenue gains due to vertical governmental relationships.

Two final remarks are also necessary. The combined effect of a tax base growth in Rio Grande do Sul and the increases in regional government revenues established by vertical governmental relationships allow for a reduction in payroll tax rates. The high negative effects on the collection of payroll taxes from regional governments, albeit influenced by a general price increase, also result from an endogenous reduction in tax rates caused by the increase in the indirect tax revenue (only for Rio Grande do Sul) and in the transfer revenues. Finally, on the expenditure side, the real variations in the government consumption arise from the relative effect between the price of these goods and the GDP deflator.

DECOMPOSITION OF RESULTS

In the previous section, we could observe that an increase in the current capital stock in the manufacturing industry of Rio Grande do Sul within a context of a tax incentive program causes demand pressures that result in a general price increase that produce negative effects on real GDP all over the country, and in Rio Grande do Sul more significantly. This section explores the sources of this effect through the sectoral decomposition of those sectoral shocks. In order to do so, each sectoral shock was simulated separately assuming the investments in other sectors of the manufacturing industry of Rio Grande do Sul remain constant.[17] The results for both regions are described in Graphs 1 and 2.

We can clearly see that the increase in the implicit GDP deflator is a general effect, both at the sectoral and interregional levels, resulting from the increase in the capital stock of the manufacturing industry of Rio Grande do Sul, which varies in intensity. However, the effects of the increase in the deflator and of the reduction in real GDP are influenced by the resulting growth of investments in the chemical and petrochemical sector of Rio Grande do Sul. In the absence of a shock in this sector, the results would be influenced by the activity effect and there would be a positive impact on real GDP, at least in Rio Grande do Sul.[18]

In Rio Grande do Sul, the chemical and petrochemical sector is the one with the largest demand for investment goods among other sectors (26.1%) and with strong domestic sectoral and interregional relationships. The growth of current capital stock in this sector exerts a strong pressure on the prices of investment goods, and increases the cost of capital in the sector and also the cost of production. Since the goods pro-

GRAPH 1. Decomposition of Long-Run Percentage Effects on GDP by Sectoral Shocks

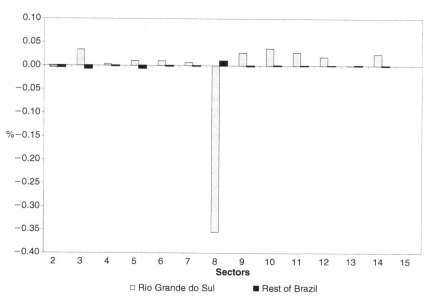

GRAPH 2. Decomposition of Long-Run Percentage Effects on GDP Deflator by Sectoral Shocks

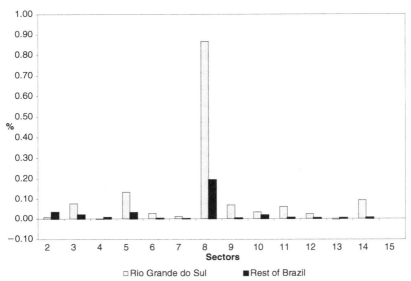

duced by the chemical and petrochemical sector feed the chain of intermediate inputs in several economic sectors of Rio Grande do Sul and also in the Rest of Brazil, price increases are passed along. The final result is a more noticeable price increase in Rio Grande do Sul compared to the Rest of Brazil. In such a way, the interregional substitution effects prevail over the activity effect, causing a decrease in real GDP for Rio Grande do Sul and an increase in GDP for the Rest of Brazil (see Graph 2).

FINAL REMARKS

This paper has used a general equilibrium approach to evaluate the effects of a regional tax incentive program for attracting investments. The analysis focused mainly on the financing of new private investments through tax revenue relief and public investment expenditures by regional and federal governments. The interregional general equilibrium model used to run the simulations captures the effects of regional interdependence and of vertical relationships between the governments.

The results showed that the effects on employment and the household welfare of consumers are positive for the region implementing such an incentive policy. However, the effect on real GDP may not follow the same path and this would occur mainly because of the specialized pattern of production in the region. As shown, the specificity of the productive structure of Rio Grande do Sul plays an important role. The absence of a solidified investment goods sector and the demand for these goods concentrated in sectors that produce basic inputs caused a sharp increase in the production factor prices. The increase in the input prices extended to goods produced by other sectors and in the regional production chains due to forward linkages. This sector specific effect dominates the positive impacts on the real GDP of Rio Grande do Sul when the shocks are implemented in the other manufacturing sectors. At the aggregate level, the advantages of this incentive policy tend to benefit investors and consumers, while costs are absorbed by export agents. Surprisingly, although the effects of interregional competition prevail over the Rest of Brazil due to the re-location of production factors, the intensity is relatively smaller and does not seem to affect consumers' utility level. In this region, the effects wind up absorbed by foreign investors and exporters.

Another interesting result concerns the effects on the public finances of regional and federal governments. The net result on the indirect taxes revenue is positive due to the increase in the tax base, even considering the tax revenue relief offered by the regional government to thoroughly finance the increase in private investments. A key role may be ascribed to the federal government's tax policy. If the federal government increases the income tax rates in order to meet the demand for federal public investments, regional governments are benefited through income transfer mechanisms. The transfers received by the Rest of Brazil government exceed the loss that arises from relocation of the tax base. Additionally, the impact of an increase in the federal income tax rate on disposable income is not negative due to the relatively higher gains produced on the primary factors income and other earnings.

These results show that the general equilibrium approach is a useful framework for investigating the economic effects produced by tax incentive programs that seek to attract business investments. This methodology enables analyzing the welfare effects of such policies using a consistent model that captures important second order effects. The focus of the present study has been on a situation in which only one region uses a tax incentive program to attract new investments and the federal government adjusts its tax policy according to the high demands for public investments. Since regional asymmetries and the pattern of inter-regional linkages may play a crucial role in the welfare effects, we may think of an alternative environment where both regions adopt tax incentive programs to attract new investments. Investigation of the sensitivity of the results to different closures for the federal government tax policy also appears to be relevant. Finally, this approach can also be used to assess issues related to interregional tax competition.

NOTES

1. The available literature on interjurisdictional competition has not yet reached a common agreement on implications related to the efficiency of the allocation of public goods. Some studies suggest that this type of competition results in the suboptimal allocation of public goods, whereas others consider allocation to be efficient when the federal government keeps tabs on competition. For a literature review see Kenyon (1997) and Wilson and Wildasin (2004).

2. In this case, the region that grants tax benefits may have an increase in its revenues due to the transfers of revenues since undertaken investments tend to produce a positive effect on the collection of federal taxes.

3. Within a context of capital and labor mobility, we cannot rule out the possibility of indirect effects of tax incentives on the spatial distribution of investments.

4. Following this tradition, the models use the Johansen approach, where the mathematical framework is represented by a set of linearized equations and the solutions are obtained as growth rates. In the Brazilian economy, the PAPA (Guilhoto, 1995), EFES (Haddad and Domingues, 2001) and EFES-IT (Haddad et al., 2001; 2002) models, among others, use this approach.

5. The full description of the model is available in Porsse (2005). A miniature version for tests and evaluation is available from the authors upon request. This miniature model can be implemented in the demo version of the GEMPACK program (*www. monash.edu.au/policy/gpdemo.htm*).

6. For product differentiation in the world market and CGE models, see De Melo and Robinson (1989). The behavior of several classes of CES functions is analyzed in Perroni and Rutherford (1995).

7. For the parameters necessary for calibrating this specification, see Dixon et al. (1982). The LES specification is non-homothetic, such that an increase in the household expenditure (income) causes changes in the share of goods in overall expenditures, *ceteris paribus*.

8. See next section.

9. For closures in CGE models, see Dixon and Parmenter (1996), and Dixon et al. (1982).

10. Prado and Cavalcanti (2000) conducted an excellent review of state incentive programs implemented during this period.

11. The ICMS is an excise tax and is collected like a value added tax by Brazilian state governments. Considering the revenues from all indirect taxes collected by Rio Grande do Sul's governments (state and municipalities), the ICMS accounts for 91.7% of the total, according to the database calibrated for the B-MARIA-RS model.

12. The Rio Grande do Sul state government actually has a tax incentive program to attract business investments that covers up to 100% of the fixed capital augmenting by the firms through ICMS exemption. This program is denominated FUNDOPEM and applies the following rules: a 4% annual nominal interest rate, up to six years to start the loan payments and up to eight years to amortize each monthly debt quote. Taking into account the depreciation rate and the real interest rate, in some cases the tax exemptions fully cover private investments; thus, our hypothesis is not unrealistic.

13. This value is deflated by the GDP deflator.

14. The federal government collects income tax and indirect taxes on industrialized products and approximately one quarter of this revenue is transferred from the federal government to regional governments.

15. In the implemented simulation, the income tax rate had a 4.86% endogenous increase.

16. The Kandir Law came into force in 1997 and the base year for the B-MARIA-RS model is 1998.

17. In the B-MARIA-RS model, the manufacturing industry is stratified into 14 sectors: metallurgy (2), machinery and tractors (3), electrical and electronic equipment (4), transportation material (5), wood products and furniture (6), paper and printing (7), chemical and petrochemical products (8), leather and footwear (9), processed vegetables (10), meat products (11), dairy products (12), vegetable oils (13), other food industries (14), and other industries (15).

18. The simulation was implemented in the same context, only leaving out the chemical and petrochemical sector, and the results showed a variation of 0.125% and −0.014%, respectively, for the real GDP of Rio Grande do Sul and of the Rest of Brazil.

REFERENCES

Armington, P. S. (1969). "A Theory of Demand for Products Distinguished by Place of Production." *International Monetary Fund Staff Papers*, Vol. 16, No. 1, pp. 159-178.

De Melo, J., and Robinson, S. (1989). "Product Differentiation and Foreign Trade in CGE Models of Small Economies." *Policy, Planning and Research Working Papers*, WPS 144. Washington DC, World Bank.

Dixon, P. D., and Parmenter, B. R. (1996). "Computable General Equilibrium Modeling for Policy Analysis and Forecasting." In H. M. Amman, D. A. Kendrick and J. Rust (Eds.), *Handbook of Computational Economics*, Vol. 1, pp. 3-85, Amsterdam, Elsevier.

Dixon, P. D., Parmenter, B. R., Sutton, J., and Vincent, D. P. (1982). "ORANI: A Multisectoral Model of the Australian Economy." Amsterdam: North-Holland.

Guilhoto, J. J. M. (1995). "Um Modelo Computável de Equilíbrio Geral para Planejamento e Análise de Políticas Públicas (PAPA) na Economia Brasileira." *Tese de Livre Docência*. Piracicaba: ESALQ. June.

Haddad, E. A. (1999). "Regional Inequality and Structural Changes: Lessons from the Brazilian Experience." Aldershot: Ashgate.

Haddad, E. A., and Domingues, E. P. (2001). "EFES: Um Modelo de Aplicado de Equilíbrio Geral para a Economia Brasileira: Projeções Setoriais para 1999-2004." *Estudos Econômicos*, Vol. 31, No. 1, pp. 89-125.

Haddad, E. A., Domingues, E. P., and Perobelli, F. S. (2002). "Regional Effects of Economic Integration: The Case of Brazil." *Journal of Policy Modeling*, Vol. 24, No. 5, pp. 453-482.

Haddad, E. A., and Hewings, G. J. D. (1999). "The Short-Run Regional Effects of New Investments and Technological Upgrade in the Brazilian Automobile Industry: An Interregional Computable General Equilibrium Analysis." *Oxford Development Studies*, Vol. 27, No. 3, pp. 359-383.

Kenyon, D. A. (1997). "Theories of Interjurisdictional Competition." *New England Economic Review*, March-April, pp. 13-28.

Perroni, C., and Rutherford, T. F. (1995). "Regular Flexibility of Nested CES Functions." *European Economic Review*, Vol. 39, No. 2, pp. 335-343.

Peter, M. W. et al. (1996). The Theoretical Structure of MONASH-MRF." *Preliminary Working Paper no. OP-85*, IMPACT Project, Monash University, Clayton, April.

Porsse, A. A. (2005). "Competição Tributária e Efeitos Econômicos Regionais: Uma Análise de Equilíbrio Geral Computável." *Doctoral Dissertation.* Porto Alegre: Universidade Federal do Rio Grande do Sul.

Prado, S., and Cavalcanti, C. E. G. (2000). "A Guerra Fiscal no Brasil." São Paulo: Fundap/ Fapesp.

Wilson, J. D., and Wildasin, D. E. (2004). "Capital Tax Competition: Bane or Boon?" *Journal of Public Economics*, Vol. 88, No. 6, pp. 1065-1091.

doi:10.1300/J140v07n03_09

Index

Page numbers in *italics* designate figures; page numbers followed by "t" designate tables.

Printed in the United States
by Baker & Taylor Publisher Services